FREE
WITHIN
OURSELVES

ALSO BY JEWELL PARKER RHODES

Voodoo Dreams

Magic City

FREE
WITHIN
OURSELVES

FICTION LESSONS
FOR BLACK AUTHORS

Jewell Parker Rhodes

MAIN STREET BOOKS / DOUBLEDAY
NEW YORK   LONDON   TORONTO   SYDNEY   AUCKLAND

A MAIN STREET BOOK
PUBLISHED BY DOUBLEDAY
a division of Random House, Inc.
1540 Broadway, New York, New York 10036

MAIN STREET BOOKS, DOUBLEDAY, and the portrayal of a building
with a tree are trademarks of Doubleday, a division of Random
House, Inc.

Designed by Richard Oriolo

LIBRARY OF CONGRESS CATALOGING-IN-PUBLICATION DATA

Rhodes, Jewell Parker.
Free within ourselves: fiction lessons for Black authors /
by Jewell Parker Rhodes. — 1st ed.
p. cm.
1. Blacks—Authorship. 2. Afro-Americans in literature.
3. Afro-Americans—Authorship. 4. Blacks in literature.
5. Fiction—Authorship. 6. Fiction—Technique. I. Title.
PN3423.R49 1999
808′.02′08996073—dc21 99-21963
CIP

We build our temples for tomorrow, as strong as we know how, and we stand on top of the mountain, free within ourselves.

—LANGSTON HUGHES, "The Negro Artist and the Racial Mountain," *The Nation* (1926)

ACKNOWLEDGMENTS

I am deeply appreciative of all the wonderful people who helped with this project. Heartfelt thanks to Jane Dystel, my wonderful agent; to Miriam Goderich, a superb reader; and to Janet Hill, a most gifted and visionary editor. Sincere thanks to my research assistants—Papatya Bucak, Sanderia Smith, and Tayari Jones. A special thank-you to Lenard Moore for his most supportive and encouraging words. And, finally, much love to my daughter, Kelly, who inspired me with her own love of words and dedication to writing stories.

CONTENTS

PART IV:

WISDOM AND ADVICE
FROM BLACK AUTHORS

PART V:

TOOLS YOU MAY NEED

PART I

CELEBRATING

OURSELVES

PREFACE

CELEBRATING SELF AND

COMMUNITY

You might think all writers do is write. It's not that simple. Good writing demands your whole self—writing freely, without limits, from your unique connections to your world.

As an African American, you have incredible riches to draw upon, including a bittersweet history which created a new ethnic group capable of transforming heartache into art.

African Americans have not only survived but *thrived* creatively and spiritually despite hardships and challenges. This book is meant to celebrate us—our connections to ourselves and our community. Words are powerful. Artists create the mirrors which reflect and critique the blessings and complexity of being African American people. We are spirited, powerful people; at times, rough-edged, but always real, authentic, always striving to unearth and transmit what W. E. B. Du Bois called the "souls of black folk."

African American writers share pieces of themselves and their heritage through the power of words. Listen to the spirit, rhythm, and unique quality of self in the following examples:

> "What you mean, 'What's this?' " She looked as
> perplexed as if someone had asked her why the sun burned
> in the sky. "It's collards, with some mustard greens mixed
> in. A little bit of fatback, rice, and cornbread. What you
> been eating all your life. What you think it is?"
> —Randall Kenan, "The Origin of Whales"

> allegra found ambrosia. her hair grew pomegranates &
> soil, rich as round the aswan. allegra woke in her bed to
> bananas/avocados/collard greens/the Tramp's latest disco hit/
> fresh croissant/pouilly-fuisse/ishmael reed's essays/charlotte
> carter's stories/streamed from each strand of her hair.
> everything in the universe that allegra needed
> fell from her hair.
> —Ntozake Shange, "Oh She Got a Head Full of Hair"

> Then they all gathered around Sonny and Sonny
> played. Every now and again, one of them seemed to say,
> amen. Sonny's fingers filled the air with life, his life. But his
> life contained so many others.
> —James Baldwin, "Sonny's Blues"

> "I think," say Sugar pushing me off her feet like she
> never done before, cause I whip her ass in a minute, "that
> this is not much of a democracy if you ask me. Equal
> chance to pursue happiness means an equal crack
> at the dough, don't it?"
> —Toni Cade Bambara, "The Lesson"

Each of these examples conveys our heritage in different ways. But they all begin with the writer's sense of self as African American and a commitment to sharing African American culture.

Because black people are infinitely varied, heritage can be drawn from very personal meanings about yourself and how you experience your culture and the world around you. Culture includes remembering slavery, witnessing present-day events, celebrating ancestral and familial connections. For some, Harlem may be the epitome of the black experience; for others, it may be a pastoral setting in the South. The concrete world encourages the sensual—the taste, sight, smell, and sound of our beautifully dark spirit.

Our heritage is in the leftover scraps slaves transformed into "soul food." It is in the images of undaunted, rock-steady people captured by Gordon Parks. It is in the smell of a mother's hands cradling a child. In the silken sweat of hard work and passion. Our people are celebrated in Monk's syncopated piano, in the rolling cadences of the preacher, and the high-pitched shrills of children playing jacks and singing about Miss Mary Mack who never came back. Our stories celebrate our deeply rooted cultural ties.

Self—Family—Community—this is the stuff of life. You cannot be a great writer if you're afraid to live. And living a life colored by a unique heritage is truly glorious! *Celebrate your body, soul, and culture.* Even when you're experiencing and writing about hardships and horrors, there is grace in your spirit and among our people. *Feel it. Believe it.*

As a writer you have the opportunity to explore what it means to be human, to conjure through words those passions, those spirits which are important to you and which echo the legacy of our people.

Good writers probe themselves and their world; good writers laugh and cry; good writers observe; good writers don't just talk about writing, they write.

1

GETTING READY TO WORK:

CLAIMING A JOURNAL,

THE WRITER WITHIN

Select a three-ring binder, a glamorous notebook, a diary with lock and key, whatever's most comfortable for you. This journal is where you'll begin your initial explorations of self and community. First, you can use it as a place to do the exercises in this book. Later it'll become a workbook for recording dreams, story ideas, characterizations, and comments about stories you've read. Your journal is your passport to thinking like, acting like, and becoming a writer!

Don't try to do the following exercises all at once. Take time between exercises to experience, observe, reflect, and revise.

Writing is a process.

The exercises should be done sequentially. No more than one a day. Each exercise is designed to increase your confidence in your writing, step by step, and to teach you specific fiction skills. If you're struggling with an exercise, repeat it. Move on when you feel your writing is improving. Remember: exercises are an easier beginning than starting a story from scratch. By doing the exercises in this book, you'll be allowed to make mistakes, to explore thoughts and feelings, to learn as you go. After practicing these exercises, when you *do* sit down to write a story, you'll be much better prepared to succeed.

MY BEST ADVICE
Treasure your journal. It is your first, best learning tool.

For those of you who are new to writing, this chapter will help limber your skills of observing, listening, imagining, and assembling portraits of your world. For those of you who have been writing for a while, these opening exercises will give you the opportunity to sharpen your skills and reflect again how heritage can influence and deepen your writing. In either case, your journey to becoming a better writer has begun. When you're anxious or filled with self-doubt, remember: the collective spirit of our people is with you. You are walking a path that all writers have walked. This path is, at times, both crooked and demanding, but always infinitely rewarding.

Open your journal. Take a deep breath. Begin.

EXERCISE 1
EXPERIENCING A COMMUNITY EVENT

Describe an event you'd like to celebrate—it can be as large as a Kwanzaa celebration or as intimate as a picnic. Write quickly for twenty minutes; don't edit.

When you've finished, reread your description—and ask yourself: Is it specific? Are there sounds in your description? Are there colors, textures, smells, tastes? What did you fail to observe? What did you leave out? What did you write just right?

For twenty minutes, rewrite the description, adding more details.

. . .

Compare the two versions and decide which one you like best. Which version conveys the more complete picture?

EXERCISE 2

EXPERIENCING THE FOLK

Look for a person to describe, someone worth celebrating. It can be someone you know, a bus driver, a street-corner musician, or a child playing double Dutch in the street. Write quickly for twenty minutes; don't edit.

When you've finished, reread your description. How well did you describe the person? Would I recognize them if I saw them on the street? How does your person dress, talk, move? What do they feel? Joy? Wistfulness? How can you tell? What outward signs best express their personality? How do they react to touch, sight, taste, and sound? What makes this person special to you? What about them are you celebrating? Revise your description for twenty minutes, adding new details.

Compare the two versions and decide which one you like best. Which version is more accurate? The more vibrant and "lifelike"?

EXERCISE 3

TALKING THAT TALK: COMMUNITY STORYTELLERS

Listen for stories! "I remember . . . ," "Girl, let me tell you . . . ," "Back home, we used to . . . ," "Listen up! It's like this . . ."

Storytelling is a fundamental human activity—some stories are short (leaving you breathless for more), some are long and twisting, some teach, some give praise, some slander, some help you imagine a time and place where you've never lived. In Africa, the griot was honored as master storyteller, responsible for maintaining the stories and legends of the tribe. The griot tradition did not die with the advent of American slavery. Indeed, cultural storytelling kept alive a past and sustained a newly born people. Slaves were not "blank slates" but a community who mirrored, shaped, celebrated, informed, and inspired themselves through stories.

Go out and find a storyteller—a preacher telling biblical stories to a Sunday school class, a teenager bragging about a birthday party to her two friends, a grandmother on the front porch spinning stories about her Alabama childhood.

Listen to the voice of this storyteller, the rhythms in his or her speech. Is the talk slow and meandering or fast and focused? Is the voice loud or soft, rough or smooth? Is the voice conversational or formal? Write a page in the voice of the storyteller you've studied. Try to recapture their story—feel free to elaborate, improve upon your memory—the important thing is to keep writing the voice of the storyteller you heard. To keep imitating the rhythm, sounds, and speech.

Reread your writing. Can you hear the storyteller's voice? Rewrite any sentences that don't sound like your storyteller.

Repeat this exercise with two other people. If you wrote a teenager's rap in the first exercise, try capturing the nostalgic voice of an elderly deacon. Stretch yourself—look for a variety of voices to challenge you. If you haven't heard enough good storytellers, don't underestimate the power of simply asking: "Please, tell me a story." You'll be surprised at what you might hear.

Once you've captured three storytellers, list the differences among the three voices. Which voice did you capture best? Who told the best story? Why was it the best? How did the voice make the story more interesting?

. . .

Over time you'll train yourself to hear nuances of speech, differences of grammar, word choice, rhythm, and sound.

For now, listen up! Just as a musician daily practices scales fast and slow, high and low, loud and soft; as a writer you need daily practice in listening to people talk—becoming more in tune with the full range of human sounds.

EXERCISE 4

TALKING THAT TALK: FAMILY TALES

Our ancestors shape our family's stories. Talk to an aunt, a grandparent, a second cousin about your family's heritage. Ask to see pictures, mementos, genealogy charts, family Bibles which have special significance. What stories are attached to these objects? What do these stories reveal about the African American spirit in your family? What makes these stories dramatic and intriguing?

Certain stories are easily passed down through the generations within families. Other stories are told in whispers, with long silences between incidents. Listen for the "gaps" in one of your family's stories. Listen for the silences, for what might be left unsaid, the secrets, then—*imagine.*

For an hour, write the family tale you found; write the story just as your family tells it.

Next, put a star by all the points in the story where you *don't* know what happened. These starred points represent opportunities for imagining, for writing fiction.

For example, here's a bare-bones tale from my family history:

. . .

One spring, Cousin James packed his bags and left Carolina for California. As a kid, James could outrun, outclimb any kid. He was smart beyond belief, sweet; he dreamed of flying airplanes. When his father remarried, there was a family fight. The next morning, just shy of eighteen, James left and nobody has ever heard from him again.

What was said during the fight between father and son? Were they really arguing about the stepmother? Or some hurt done to the dead mother? Or were they arguing about money? James's career? What happened to James in California? Is he a truck driver—bitter with drink? Or a homeless person dreaming of his mother? Or a counselor for troubled kids? Did he ever learn to fly?

When I begin to imagine what happened, what I don't know, I begin creating stories. Stories which draw upon both my family and community heritages.

Remember: imagination soars from what is most real in the world around you, what is most real about yourself, your family, and your community.

Now revise your family story, filling in the gaps with imagination.

Compare your two tales—the one told to you and your revision. How has your imagination changed the story? Was it harder or easier to imagine because you started with family history? Which version is more compelling? Which story is more satisfying to you as a reader?

Celebrate! You've finished Chapter One.

Reread all the writing in your journal! You've written description, created characters with actions and dialogue, imagined plots, and conveyed your own unique sense of what is special about your family and community—all the things a good writer does!

You're on your way!

2

LITERARY ANCESTORS

Telling tales is telling culture, communing with your literary ancestors. Alice Walker dedicates *The Color Purple:*

> *To the Spirit:*
>
> *Without whose assistance*
> *Neither this book*
> *Nor I*
> *Would have been*
> *Written.*

I, too, have felt the spirit's presence, heard the voices of an ancient tradition of "talking stories" from Africa to the Americas. While writing *Voodoo Dreams,* I was absolutely convinced Marie Laveau was beside me, whispering in my ear, *"Tell it. Tell it all."*

Words have power. If we don't tell our own stories, then the historical "gaps," the "silences" become ripe for someone else's lies, distortions, half-truths.

For African Americans, literacy began as a subversive act. Since slaves were forbidden to read or write, stories had to be passed orally, down through the generations. Yet, ever since the eighteenth century, black people have contrived to create a written record, to create literature. In 1789, *The Interesting Narrative of the Life of Olaudah Equiano* was published, beginning a tradition of autobiography/memoir which would include, among others, Frederick Douglass, Harriet Jacobs, W. E. B. Du Bois, Richard Wright, Maya Angelou, Veronica Chambers, and Nathan McCall.

Charles Chesnutt at the age of twenty-two on May 29, 1880, wrote in his journal:

> I think I must write a book. I am almost afraid to under-
> take a book so early and with so little experience in com-
> position. But it has been my cherished dream, and I feel
> an influence that I cannot resist calling me to the task.

Chesnutt wrote poems, plays, fiction, and nonfiction. He especially excelled in short fiction; his story collection *The Conjure Woman* (1899) explores the "folk magic" of roots and spells and celebrates our cultural link to an African-inspired spiritual tradition. Chesnutt, true to his vision, explored the diversity of African American life; and, remarkably for his era, was a best-selling author.

In 1859, Harriet Wilson wrote *Our Nig,* the first novel by an African American published in the United States. Six years earlier, in 1853, William Wells Brown published in London *Clotel; or, The President's Daughter.* Both books were important examinations of black women's lives. *Clotel* described southern slavery and, following the pattern of more familiar slave narratives, told of Thomas Jefferson's daughter's flight to freedom. On the other hand, *Our Nig* tackled northern racial hypocrisy and gender hypocrisy, and tried to invent a new fictional form by blending women's fiction, memoir, and the slave narrative. Significantly, *Our Nig,* not *Clotel,* was lost. In 1982, Henry Louis Gates, Jr., discovered Wilson's important work while browsing in a used bookstore.

Our Nig tells the tragic life of Frado, a biracial indentured servant who, abandoned by her mother, suffers physical and psychological abuse in a corrupt Christian household. Frado is later deserted by her husband and turns to writing fiction as a way to earn money for herself and her dying son. By blending autobiography, slave narratives, the seduction tale, and the sentimental novel, Wilson became the literary grandmother of black women's fiction. Her work is a harsh critique of northern racism and debunks the notion that white women, by virtue of their sex, were naturally kind. Wilson, who self-published the manuscript, wrote specifically to a black audience. Unlike Brown, she was not supported by (nor outwardly seemed to support) white abolitionists. Her novel clearly would not have fit the political contours of the nineteenth-century abolitionist movement. Her gender, harsh critique, and use of the hated word "nigger" would probably have put her "beyond the pale." Given Wilson's attack upon racial, gender, and northern hypocrisies and her trailblazing literary form, is it any wonder that Wilson's novel was "lost"? After 1863, no other historical trace of Harriet Wilson exists. She conveniently "disappears," yet her novel, unearthed over one hundred years later, still reminds us of the inspirational and creative power of black women artists.

Like the "new" people they were, African Americans created a "new" literature influenced by Western traditions but dynamically inspired by the pain-filled *and* pleasure-filled experience of being black in America.

MY BEST ADVICE
Read our literary ancestors.
It is the quintessential path to becoming a better writer!

To be a good writer, read, then read some more. There are twelve months in a year. In your journal, commit to reading three new books a month—more if you can. (The Reading List on pages 315–318 is a good starting point.) Most important, *expand your horizons.* If you read only contemporary authors, try your nineteenth-century sisters! If you favor women authors, read the brothers as well. If you like realism, read science fiction. Memoir, mystery, romance, folktales, children's tales, fantasy, adventure, social realism, humor, horror, and much, much more have been written and written well by black authors.

Read *first* for sheer enjoyment. Read *second* for craft and technique.

A writer *always* learns from reading. Even if you think a story isn't well done, reading refines your own sense of literature, what you value, how you approach writing.

Look at this selection from *Cane,* Jean Toomer's Harlem Renaissance masterpiece:

> Men had always wanted her, this Karintha, even as a
> child, Karintha carrying beauty, perfect as dusk when the
> sun goes down. Old men rode her hobby-horse upon
> their knees. Young men danced with her at frolics when
> they should have been dancing with grown-up girls. God
> grant us youth, secretly prayed the old men. The young
> fellows counted the time to pass before she would be old
> enough to mate with them. This interest of the male,
> who wishes to ripen a growing thing too soon, could
> mean no good to her.

When you first read "Karintha," the rhythmic language lulls you with its beauty. The poison of early sexuality is veiled, almost overlooked. A second reading makes it clearer that the paragraph isn't directly about Karintha at all, but about the men's distorted perceptions. Toomer uses strong, active verbs to show the men's desires:

> Men . . . always wanted her . . . rode her hobby-horse
> . . . danced with her . . . secretly prayed . . . counted
> the time . . . before she would be old enough to
> mate . . .

By making men the subject, Toomer conveys how Karintha *is acted upon*. Instead of saying "everyone" wanted her, he repeats: *old men, young men, old men, young fellows*. The repetition and the age range (old to young) lets the reader feel more dramatically how males of every age desired Karintha.

A writer's job is to make prose seem effortless. As a reader/artist, your job is to read for technique: *Why does the dialogue sound so real? How do actions shape character? Why does description make the story seem more sinister?*

Like magicians, writers create marvelous effects. Your reading task is to figure out why a writer used abrupt sentences rather than flowing dialogue for a furious man—why the writer chose first person ("I") rather than third person ("he") to tell a story. Why did the writer select Florida's mosquito-infested marshlands for the murder scene instead of the red rock and jutting cacti of the Arizona desert? What was gained or lost by the choice of setting? How did the writer convince you the setting was authentic?

Don't worry if you don't know all the fictional terms. Jargon is less important than building your own personal understanding for "how and why" a good story works. You'll be amazed by the multitude of choices a writer has to make.

In your journal, commit to writing a page about each book or story you read. Don't simply write: "I liked it." Narrow your focus, be specific. Select an excerpt—an intriguing opening, a climactic scene, a three-person dialogue—and study it. What makes it marvelous? Incredible detail? A strong, comforting voice? A plot surprise? Conflict? A fascinating character?

Studying other writers will help you become a better editor of your own stories. Writing is never just inspiration; it is also skill; it is about extending a literary tradition that has survived, sustained, educated, and entertained us.

Literary ancestors are your foundation: their texts will whisper, shout, preach the glory of our people and teach you about fine writing. Like the finest continuum, contemporary authors are becoming our future ancestors. Once you've read the past, you'll better understand how writers today are "talking back" to our literary forefathers and foremothers, how they're reshaping and replacing older visions, extending the funk.

You are part of a wonderful legacy. Read and remember—you do not write alone.

Read all you can.

EXERCISE 1

READING IMMERSION

Immerse yourself in reading. This is particularly important if you haven't been in the habit of reading. I often teach students who proclaim: "I write a lot but don't read." You must marry the two! Just as you can't breathe without inhaling *and* exhaling, you can't develop as a writer without being a devoted reader.

Even if you have a stack of books by your bedside, go to the bookstore or library and select three new and varied books reflecting our culture. You'll have great fun browsing, uncovering new authors. In your journal, begin a "What to Read Next" List to remind you of authors and titles to try in the future. (Clearly, books by all authors are potentially valuable to you as a writer. But, for now, focus on the African American heritage. Once you've become well acquainted with your own literary tradition, proceed to any and all books you're interested in. Beyond the wide diversity of American authors, there are also terrific international authors to explore: Jorge Luis Borges, Yukio Mishima, Bharati Mukherjee, Elena Poniatowska, Isabel Allende, Chinua Achebe, Margaret Atwood, and far more.)

You might not read three books in a month, but try. Substitute reading time for television, housecleaning, or laundry time. Carry a book everywhere—on the train, to the hairdresser's or doctor's office. Order take-out and curl up with a book instead of a hot stove and dirty dishes. Read a young adult novel in the evenings with your children. If your days and nights are especially fragmented, short story anthologies might be a better choice.

Once you've jump-started your reading, strive for the reachable goal of *four* books a month. In the meantime, have fun! Browse, buy, or borrow terrific books from your local bookstore, a used bookstore, or the library. If you're truly strapped for time, listen to audiotapes. Listen closely for how the story unfolds, how characters are described and interact. Still, be vigilant in setting aside time to study written texts. Audiotapes are wonderful but an experienced reader can "hide" textual flaws.

When selecting books, focus on variety. Mix male and female authors. Mix genres. Mix time periods. A historical novel has a different promise and fulfillment than a contemporary tale. Try, too, to reflect the sensibilities of living authors versus those dead. Ann Petry writing in the twenties reflects vastly different social concerns than Diane McKinney-Whetstone writing in the nineties. Walter Mosely's private investigator, Easy Rawlins, contrasts interestingly with Chester Himes's detective duo, Grave Digger Jones and Coffin Ed Johnson.

If you buy or borrow more than three books, bravo! Be inspired by the books available—and remember, each time you read a book, you are pursuing your goal of becoming and being a better writer.

Select your first book and read for pleasure, both intellectual and emotional! When you've finished, move on to Exercise 2.

EXERCISE 2

READING AS A WRITER

You've finished the first book of your monthlong readathon! Good for you! Now grab your journal and write a one-page response to it. Be specific.

Was the book interesting? Exciting? Suspenseful? Intellectually challenging? What made it so?

What ideas, feelings, was the writer trying to communicate? Was she effective?

What did you like best? The author's message? Description? Narrative voice? Dialogue? Plot? Characters? Historical elements? Contemporary focus?

What didn't you like?

Don't hesitate to write any response you think is relevant. The key is to focus on *your thoughts* about the book.

Reread the book. You can skim passages, but plan on spending an hour or two studying the book. As you're moving from page to page, mark with a highlighter passages you thought were particularly good, particularly well written. You might highlight a lovely descriptive paragraph. Or a dialogue scene between the main characters. You might highlight a mother-daughter scene, a courtroom scene, the introduction of a new character, the concluding paragraph, or an especially eloquent sentence.

As when using a magnifying glass, you're isolating elements that make the book a success. All fine books are greater than the sum of their parts. But learning to write well is an incremental process—learning, bit by bit, what elements contribute to good writing and learning how to execute those aspects well.

When you thoughtfully reread a book and contemplate why you think a passage, a scene, or a sentence is well done, you are training yourself to read for technique—the "how" of good writing.

With each element you highlight, ask: "Why do I like it?" "What makes this good writing?" "What did the writer choose to do or not to do?"

Encouraging the habit of more thoughtful reading encourages the habit of more thoughtful and skilled writing!

EXERCISE 3

READING AS A WRITER, STAGE TWO

For further study, select one of the passages you marked in the preceding exercise. Read it both silently and aloud. Study the passage, asking again: "Why do I like it? What makes this good writing? What did the author do to make it effective?"

Finally, ask: "What is the author teaching me about good writing?" In your journal, write at least three specific answers.

For example, one of my favorite stories is John Edgar Wideman's "Fever." It is a tale about yellow fever, about how the "dead and dying wrested control of the city from the living" in 1893 Philadelphia. In documenting the start of the epidemic, Wideman imagines a newly captured slave who is infected with the disease by a mosquito:

> Curled in the black hold of the ship he wonders why his life on solid green earth had to end, why the gods had chosen this new habitation for him, floating, chained to other captives, no air, no light, the wooden walls shuddering, battered, as if some madman is determined to destroy even this last pitiful refuge where he skids in foul puddles of waste, bumping other bodies, skinning himself on splintery beams and planks, always moving, shaken and spilled like palm nuts in the diviner's fist, and Esu cast his fate, constant motion, tethered to an iron ring.
>
> In the darkness, he can't see her, barely feels her light touch on his fevered skin. Sweat thick as oil but she doesn't mind, straddles him, settles down to do her work. She enters him and draws his blood up into her belly. When she's full, she pauses, dreamy, heavy. He could kill her then; she wouldn't care. But he doesn't. Listens to the whine of her wings lifting till the whimper is lost in the roar and crash of waves, creaking wood, prisoners groaning. If she returns tomorrow and carries away another drop of him, and the next day and the next, a drop each day, enough days, he'll be gone. Shrink to nothing, slip out of this iron noose and disappear.

I could easily study these two superb paragraphs for an hour. Wideman brilliantly captures the cruel irony of the slave being exposed to yellow fever and how this exposure results in widespread fever and suffering in his captors' city.

In particular, I admire how Wideman's single-sentence first paragraph makes me experience the boat's motion. Like the ocean journey, the sentence seems to go on and on and on. The short sentences in the second paragraph further heighten drama by making each action discrete and significant. Sentence fragments beginning with strong verbs ("Listens . . ." "Shrink . . .") also emphasize actions, the horror of what's happening to the captive.

It's interesting, too, how Wideman makes the mosquito a "she," almost making her infectious bite seem like a sexual act. Wideman also repeats consonants like: "whine . . . wings . . . whimper" and "skinning . . . splintery . . . shaken . . . spilled." This sound repetition makes the story more "oral," more lush to me.

I admire how in *two* paragraphs Wideman renders and suggests the African's entire slave life. Paragraph One gives the stark brutality of the Middle Passage. Paragraph Two sets up the notion of the slave's lifeblood draining away. He *will* die, "shrink to nothing" as much from the yellow fever as from his unjust enslavement. His freedom, his "slip out of this iron noose" will sadly come at a great cost. Wideman doesn't preach, doesn't tell us what to think: rather, his details *show* us actions that allow us to imagine.

In my journal, I might write:

"What is Wideman teaching me about good writing?"

ANSWER: "Good writing needs strong, descriptive language. Strong verbs and strong verb combinations like 'shuddering, battered,' 'bumping . . . skinning,' 'shaken and spilled,' help to make stories seem more active, alive.

"Good writing means paying attention to sentence length. Sentences can mirror content. Violation, biting stings from an animal might be better told by quick, sharp, fragmented sentences. Longer, winding sentences might be used for more rhythmic events—like a sea journey (a train or car ride?).

"Good writing can mean giving human qualities to animals or things. A mosquito full with its victim's blood/body fluid can subtly hint at sexual/human satisfaction: '. . . she pauses, dreamy, heavy.' "

In my journal, I might translate all of the above as writing reminders to:

§ Try more interesting verb choices;

§ Try varying sentence lengths to suit content;

§ Try ascribing human qualities to animals or things.

Remember, even if you don't have a degree in literature, you *can*, through thoughtful reading and analyzing, become a better writer. For the most part, I've avoided using literary jargon. I could have said that Wideman uses alliteration (repeating consonants), personification (ascribing human qualities to inhuman beings or things), imagery (descriptive pictures), metaphor (figurative language), and symbol (yellow fever also represents the disease of slavery).

Whether you use literary jargon or not, it's essential never to doubt your ability to better understand fine writing. In the meantime, don't be intimidated. Just keep reading!

For each of the three books you read during your monthlong immersion, repeat Exercises 1–3. During this month, you'll better train yourself to read like a working writer—you'll become more conscious of *what* you're reading, *how* the author constructed it, and you'll become more articulate at expressing what kinds of writing you like and why.

Each book you read has the potential to be a twofold pleasure: (1) the joy of reading and experiencing the author's creative world and (2) the joy of studying more intently what makes good writing so good.

At the end of your monthlong readathon, review your comments about what you've learned about writing from the books you've read.

You should have at least fifteen key points about good writing. Don't worry if some points are repetitive. It is helpful for even the best writers to remind themselves to be precise, to write with more descriptive clarity, to suit style to content, etc.

Next, reread the writing exercises you did for Chapter One. Would you change anything about your writing? I bet you would. You're probably reading your own prose with a more critical, observant, and self-conscious eye. That's good! Pop open a bottle of champagne or celebrate in another way. Learning to read like a writer means becoming a better editor of your own work—becoming what you desire, the best writer you can be!

Keep to your commitment to read three books a month, to highlight and study specific passages, and to record in your journal what the authors are teaching you about writing.

Immersion in literature should be a lifelong passion for a writer.

PART II

SPIRITUAL

PREPARATIONS

3

UNEARTHING TALES

W here do you get your ideas?"
        Lurking behind that question is the need to know what makes fiction compelling, interesting, and workable. How do you know when you've got a good story? Where do story ideas come from? Sometimes lurking, too, is the very real anxiety of *not* knowing what to write about—of being fearful that you're not really a writer, but a pretender. Of being fearful that you don't have anything significant to say. This insidious fear can undermine the very courage you need to write.

        First, accept that every writer at one time or another gets stuck, feels at a loss for ideas. Occasionally, sometimes often, you may flounder. If you've been sitting at your desk for hours and words simply will not come, then get up, get out, and remind yourself that stories flourish everywhere. Pack your journal and write what you see, hear, smell, and feel in Golden Gate Park, on Staten Island, or strolling down New Orleans' Riverwalk. Take a bus ride and observe people. Collect snippets of dialogue from a restaurant, a train station, a hospital lobby. Study a cloud and dream. Imagine actions—a fight scene, a love scene, or a lost child searching for her father—tailored to fit your favorite music. Visit a museum, an arboretum and meditate; imagine what stories might take place in a landscape of flowers or cacti or in a painted landscape of surreal color. Or begin an oral history of your family. Study old photographs.

Berating yourself for not writing is counterproductive; rather, you need to encourage yourself to explore both your inner self and the world for stories.

John Edgar Wideman reminded me of the Ibo proverb "All stories are true." This proverb is truly liberating because it encourages you to draw from real-life experiences as well as imaginary dreams. All stories have value; all of life is potentially a good story waiting to be told.

Chapter One demonstrated that family and personal history, neighborhood characters and rituals, are all great foundations for shaping stories. So, too, anything you dream, live, or read is potentially a good story. Succeeding chapters will help you practice the mechanics of getting a story to work. In the meantime, you need to generate story ideas and believe in your right to write about them.

MY BEST ADVICE

Search for ideas that involve your passions, your need to know, and seek to understand yourself and your world.

Good ideas are those with which you most deeply connect. In deciding which story to write about, follow your intuitive feelings. Emotions unearth tales, liberate your imagination. The only emotions worth ignoring are those which make you tentative and hamper your ability to write; otherwise dig deep into your emotions.

· · ·

Open your journal and write five story ideas. Consider only those ideas you feel passionate about. What story made you first desire to be a writer? What stories do you feel compelled to tell? If you're uninspired, the following exercises should stimulate your imagination, encourage a host of new ideas, new possibilities.

Always reserve a space in your journal for story ideas. Faithfully keep a list. On those days when inspiration fails, an idea on your list may very well nudge, inspire, or itself become a splendid tale.

EXERCISE 1

EMOTION LOG

In any given day, there are intense emotional moments. For three days, keep a log of your emotional ups and downs—what makes you angry, happy, sad, insecure. Be specific, as descriptive as possible. What types of incidents trigger strong emotional responses in you? Is there a connection between events? Do you rail against unfairness, get overwhelmed by parenting, find joy in volunteering? Are you sensitive to gossip, betrayal by friends? Has your fiftieth birthday depressed you because you're still uncertain about the meaning of your life? Do you feel guilty because you survived a tragedy and your best friend didn't?

At the end of each day, note the most emotional moment of the day. For example:

- Reading E-mail, you discover you've been passed over for promotion; you feel both furious and worthless.

- As you're racing to work, photo radar snaps your picture. It's a bad start to the day; you worry how you'll pay the fine. Your car note is already past due.

- Making love, you feel gloriously alive and at peace with the world. Afterward, it bothers you that your partner didn't whisper, "Love you."

Study your "emotional peaks" of each day. Any similarities, differences between the emotional triggers as well as the emotions themselves? How many of your emotions were involved? One or several? Wait a week, and then see which emotional peaks are still the most vivid, the most memorable?

When you reread your emotion log, how many potential stories can you find?

Write two pages about the most powerful emotional trigger, beginning with the incident, the words, the setting which set off your most passionate response.

Repeat this exercise over another three days, preferably during a critical period which involves personal, familial, and social rituals. For example, write about your emotions preceding your birthday, the night of your tenth high school reunion, or the sorrowful preparations for moving a favorite relative to a nursing home. Holidays, too, are especially fruitful for writing material—Juneteenth, Fourth of July, Thanksgiving, Kwanzaa, New Year's Day, etc. Celebrations often intensify emotions and stimulate interesting tensions; occasionally, holidays inspire reconciliations of personal and family conflicts.

Which incident, which day generated the strongest emotion from you? Write another two pages about this incident.

Another approach is to try to re-create an emotion log based upon a still-strong, concrete memory. Remember, too, not all stories have to be bleak, some can be downright funny. For example, I can remember a particularly stormy, yet appallingly hilarious Thanksgiving holiday.

My emotion log for this memory might look like this:

Joy as I helped Grandmother get ready for Thanksgiving;
Excitement as guests began arriving;
Shy about meeting my cousin's new boyfriend;

Surprise by the boyfriend asking only for salad;
Astonishment as a free-for-all argument began;

⧨ **Wonder** as I found out secrets/complaints I'd never
had an inkling about;
Laughing at my cousin's startled face when a
comment struck home;

⧨ **Anger** at my cousin's boyfriend's arrogance;

⧨ **Contentment** after the family feast had been
defended.

I've emphasized the emotional peaks. Note how these moments include conflict and it's this conflict which creates story energy and excitement. The holiday setting, with its expectations of a pleasant, uneventful Thanksgiving, adds more drama and helps to focus the most intense moments which intertwine with the family drama.

A writer's next step is to sketch the incident, flesh out the details and action behind the emotional peaks. A "sketch" is much like an outline. In two to three pages, you write the story's essential elements—the main characters, the basic plot—to discover whether your idea holds your interest and has potential for a longer story.
Here's my example of a sketch based upon my emotion log:

> *One Thanksgiving, my grandmother sweated over a stove for three days to make a delicious feast but one laden with enough butter, fatback, and turkey drippings to make arteries weep and enough sugar, syrup, and molasses to glue a mouth shut!*
>
> *With the feast overflowing the table and two sideboards, my cousin's latest boyfriend, hair slicked, wearing a wool plaid vest, suddenly declared he wouldn't eat anything except dry green salad. The family was astonished. Grandmother paused in slicing the turkey. My cousin began cursing: "What do you mean you won't eat? You too good for my grandma's food? What's Thanksgiving, if it ain't food?"*
>
> *Peas cooling, gravy hardening, butter pooling on potatoes, the two heatedly argued. Uncles, aunts, cousins, even the tired-out toddlers were all mesmerized. The argument was amazing in its*

scope, drifting from diet ("You wouldn't know good food if you saw it." "We need to stop cooking like slaves." "You need to eat something other than lettuce") to personal attacks ("I hate your hair." "Your clothes." "Your shoes." "Your brain is no bigger than a bug." "You stink up the bathroom." "Your breath smells"). Then on to money ("You spend too much." "You need to make more." "Your friends are leeches." "At least they've got jobs"). Then on to who was sleeping around on whom.

It was better than watching a soap opera. We were awe-struck, mesmerized by the passions, the huffing chests. We specu-lated: Would they turn violent? Would she hit him? He, hit her? Finally, my cousin pointed at the door. "Leave," she screeched, then burst into tears and flew up the stairs.

Gleefully, I escorted the sullen boy to the door. "Serves you right," I said.

Grandmother murmured, "Well!" Then hollered, "Bernice, Gladys, help me reheat this food." She was smiling. She had a holiday to remember. We had a great time—seeming to be more loving, more joyful, eating all day, all night. We watched the Steelers beat the Redskins, comforted our cousin ("He was no good anyhow") and started diets the next day.

In this sketch, I tried to be "concrete"—using specific sensory details of sight, sound, taste, smell, and touch. With this kind of sketch, you should have plenty of material to construct a more complete story.

Think back to an incident that still holds powerful emotions for you—one that still makes you angry or embarrassed, or makes you wish you could go back in time and do something different. Log what you feel.

From the emotion log, write another concrete sketch.

EXERCISE 2

DREAMS

Dreams come from a special place inside you. Night dreams are often about what you fear. Daydreams are most often about what you intensely desire. Either way, dreams engage your whole self—which is the best place for a writer to begin. Dreams offer vivid, evocative pictures, too; these images will evoke emotions within your readers; these images will be crucial to organizing the action of your story.

For three nights, record your dreams in your journal. Don't censor them; instead, as soon as you wake, try to capture your experience in words as quickly as possible.

Review your dream log and star any items that intrigue you. Consider their potential as stories. Is there conflict? A mystery you want to explore? What are the key emotions in the dreams? Next, underline any images which are dominant—a train, water, a child playing hopscotch. How are these pictures critical to your dreaming?

Write a sketch based upon one of your dreams. Retain as much detail from the dream as possible.

If you don't remember your dreams or have trouble dreaming, you might want to try the exercise in reverse. Namely, take a story idea which you haven't been able to write or have been afraid to write and schedule daydreaming time. Find a quiet park, a library, or immerse yourself in a bath, surrounded by lighted candles and incense, if need be. As in night dreaming, you want to encourage your unconscious mind, the soil for your imagination. For at least an hour, don't write, just daydream—visualize your characters. Where are they? What are they doing? Dream in color. Dream details. Are there sounds and smells? What are the characters doing first, second, third, et cetera? Linger on those moments when you're not certain of your characters' actions. As much as possible, play and replay the dreaming sequences and scenes in your mind.

Later, writing quickly for twenty minutes, create a sketch based on your daydreaming. More than likely this will help jump-start your story.

For me, writing is often my dreams made visible. Dream worlds, dream characters reflect sometimes my deepest desires, my happiest musings.

Encourage your own dreaming.

EXERCISE 3

CURRENT EVENTS

Local and national newspapers and magazines can inspire stories. For at least a week, cut out articles which interest you and have dramatic appeal.

For example, here's a *USA Today* (October 23, 1997) editorial by Ellis Cose which intrigued me:

⚡

HOW MUCH IS ENOUGH WHEN TELLING PEOPLE WHAT THEY WANT TO KNOW?

ONE OF MY most discomforting memories about journalism is also one of my earliest. I was in Chicago, in my first real job, and was sent out on a fairly typical big-city assignment. The body of a teenager had been found in a park on the South Side. The city desk had identified the mother. And it fell to me to appear on her doorstep to conduct the requisite interview.

As events would have it, a staff reporter for the competing morning newspaper came on the scene within seconds of my arrival. Normally, I might have resented her being there, but that day, I was rather grateful; for I had no idea of how to approach a parent at such a time and no stomach for the task. My competitor apparently had no such compunctions.

She knocked on the door without hesitation. When the mother came out, she greeted her with something along the lines of, "I understand your son's body has been found. I'm very sorry about that. What can you tell me about him?" The ice having been broken, we proceeded to ask our respective questions.

As I recall—and a part of me has always wanted to bury the memory—the woman took our intrusion rather well. She was naturally desperate for information on her son, a bit of which we were able to supply. She was also, as it turned out, eager to talk about him—even with a couple of unfamiliar reporters. At the time, I felt intensely conflicted—caught between my desire to respect the privacy of a mother in pain and the demands of my newspaper, and presumably my readers, for information that only she could provide. Virtually every reporter experiences at one time or another a similar sense of conflict. For reporting, by its very nature, often means seeking information from people who are hurt in the process of providing or confirming it.

Indeed, in a larger sense, many of the very things we consider news—personal tragedies, scandals, deaths—are intrinsically hurtful to somebody. So, this complex balancing act goes on constantly in many news organizations as they attempt to determine where the bounds of decency begin and the public's so-called right to know ends.

Should Marv Albert, the disgraced sports broadcaster who will be sentenced this Friday, have to endure the spectacle of seeing his sexual peccadilloes broadcast into millions of households and bannered across the front pages of America's tabloid newspapers? Should celebrities, royal or otherwise, be driven to distraction by photographers attempting to chronicle their private moments for a public eager for any glimpse of their lives? Should there, in other words, be lines that the press simply doesn't cross? The short answer is yes. The problem, of course, is determining where those lines should be.

It's difficult to conceive of legislation that could define such limits in any meaningful way without crossing into the terrain of censorship. But it's also difficult to imagine any real consensus within the media—a designation that takes in everything from *The New York Times* to *Hard Copy* to the Playboy Channel.

This is not to say that journalism is a field entirely without ethical rules. Most individuals engaged in so-called mainstream journalism have a very clear idea of what is strictly forbidden—at least within their particular institution. But there are many gray areas, and it is within those areas that public sensibilities are often offended as media types push the bounds of decency in pursuit of a story or a picture. Finding a way through such gray patches can be perplexing even for insiders.

In his book *Journalism Ethics,* John Merrill, an emeritus journalism professor at the University of Missouri, asked how journalists know "if we are doing the right thing." The answer is that "quite often we don't know," Merrill acknowledged. "We consider our moral rules, our alternative possibilities for action, our general values, our personal commitments and loyalties—and then we do the best we can."

Just how much deference are news subjects owed? Exactly how much information will satisfy the public demand? Both seem to change with time, and both are interrelated. As such, neither question can have an absolute answer.

That may be a maddening thought. The fact that the conflict is not totally and neatly resolvable, however, does not mean that issues of appropriateness of coverage should not be raised, or strongly debated. They should be. For the very discussion—whether touched off by the death of Princess Diana, revelations about John Kennedy, or by an incident involving a relative unknown—illuminates what kinds of trade-offs society is willing to make, at a given moment, to balance two intrinsically incompatible demands: for privacy on one hand and for information on the other.

§

In this wonderful editorial, Cose makes us think about the moral dimensions of serving a newspaper and how readers' desire to know may contribute to many of the ethical dilemmas facing journalists.

". . . body of a teenager found in a park . . ."

Cose "felt intensely conflicted—caught between [my] desire to respect the privacy of a mother in pain and the demands of [my] newspaper . . ." This might be a good theme for a story. But, most important, as with the highlighted points of an emotion log, I'd narrow my focus to the dramatic elements of the editorial, the phrases which convey the most conflict, the most highly charged emotions. For example, there are: (1) the external conflict of the murder itself; (2) the internal conflict the reporter feels asking questions of the grieving mother; and (3) depending upon the mother's reactions, there may be verbal and/or physical conflict between her and the reporter.

While these tensions give the current event *story potential,* what is fundamentally needed is your emotional investment. Are you drawn to a possible story involving murder, grief, ethical questioning? If the answer is no, then find a different story. Emotional investment is absolutely necessary to spur your imagination.

File the articles you collect in your journal. Gradually, narrow your focus and decide which clippings inspire the most provocative questions, the most passion in you. It is that story idea you should write about.

Once you've found a dramatic idea that excites you, then imagine it, begin weaving fine story lies. You can do this by listing questions about character, plot, and point of view.

". . . body of a teenager found in a park . . ."; reporter "intensely conflicted—caught between . . . privacy of a mother in pain . . . the demands of my newspaper . . ."

CHARACTER QUESTIONS

Who was the teenager? Was it a girl or boy? What were the teen's likes/dislikes? What was he or she doing in the park? Was he or she killed? If so, how? Was he or she beaten, robbed, raped? Or did the teen have a severe asthma attack and nobody helped?

Who is the reporter? A male or female? What are his vulnerabilities? Secret pleasures? Guilt? Is he naive and innocent? Or worn-out from too many assignments which involve death? Is the reporter a parent? A child-hater?

Are there any significant racial/cultural differences between the teenager and the reporter?

Who is the mother? How old is she? Had she dreamt her child's death? Did she consider her child to be a "good child"? Or a troubled, sometimes threatening adolescent? Did she mourn him sincerely? Or with a guilty relief? Does she have any other children?

Who and where is the child's father?

PLOT/ACTION QUESTIONS

What happens next? Does the reporter finish his story? Does he quit the paper, go home to rock his infant, or does he later accept a similar assignment? What happens to the mother once she closes the door on the reporter? What does she do to survive?

POINT OF VIEW

Who tells the story? The reporter? The mother? Or both? Or some third person who knew the teenager's family? Or are the mother and reporter incidental? Do you decide to tell the story from the teenager's view, leading up to the death in the park?

With your current event try to generate questions similar to the questions I've listed above for reporter Ellis Cose's example.

Review your questions. Are they intriguing? Interesting? Do you think you could create a story by answering your questions?

If you find it difficult to think of questions, you might not have discovered a good story idea yet. Search for another current event. If the questions come easily, then you're probably on to something!

Like leaping off a diving board, an article, a newspaper headline can stimulate imaginative stories. African American newspapers, in particular, can offer unique perspectives and cultural stories. A good metropolitan or university library will have back issues of magazines and newspapers. You may also find interesting texts and journals on-line or, if you prefer, listen to radio and television. Jot down ideas in your journal or on four-by-five note cards.

Spend a quiet hour writing at least one concrete sketch based upon one of the articles you collected.

If your sketch is promising, be encouraged. You have the beginnings of a short story, perhaps even a novel.

EXERCISE 4

HISTORY SPEAKS

Take a weekend and visit local historical societies, African American museums, your family attic, and look for old photographs, newspaper and magazine articles, artifacts that interest you. Don't hesitate to speak with the curator, local volunteers, your grandparents—they'll have invaluable gems to share about your local community and the world. Speak to your elders—they have stories to stir your creativity.

What was life like in 1910? 1920? 1930? 1940? Or step back to the nineteenth, eighteenth, seventeenth, or sixteenth century—as far as you believe your research and imagination can carry you.

Narrow your focus to one decade in particular. In your journal, write about the national and global events of the era. What were the social and economic concerns and problems? The cultural trends in music, dance, painting? Narrow your focus still more—search for a particular event or person on a particular day in a particular year in a particular community that interests you.

For example: February 17, 1919, the heroic all-black 369th Infantry of World War I paraded through Harlem; October 28, 1954, the movie-opera *Carmen Jones,* starring Dorothy Dandridge, premiered in Los Angeles; July 5, 1975, Arthur Ashe defeated Jimmy Connors, 6–1, 6–1, 5–7, 6–4, to win the Wimbledon tennis championship.

What don't you know about the incident or the people that you'd like to know? Unlike a nonfiction writer, a fiction writer can use history to "imagine" and, in some instances, "reimagine" history from a different perspective. Just like the intentional gaps relatives leave in family tales, history has gaps about African American culture.

Review what you learned in your history weekend. Did you find any possible stories? As in prior exercises, you'll want to write about the historical events and people which fascinate you and which have the most conflict. Try using the "questions exercise" from the prior section to expand the historical details which interest you. *Who are these people? What happens next? Who tells the story?* You can research "facts" pertinent to all your questions—but "facts" can be slippery, skewered by biases too. A fiction writer's obligation is always to tell a good story. So don't hesitate to daydream, to imagine characters and events to make your historical explorations more vital, alive.

For an hour, write at least one sketch based upon your historical investigations.

Story ideas have come to me through all different types of avenues—photographs, tales told by loved ones, newspapers, overhearing a passing conversation. Being curious and engaged in life rewards you with more stories.

I adore history—the national and global, as well as the personal. One afternoon, stuck in Logan Airport, waiting for a flight to Los Angeles, I began daydreaming about my childhood, my grandmother, and the summer block parties we used to have. Opening my journal, I began to write:

Block Party

We lived in the dark green hills of Pittsburgh, where the smoke from J. L. Steel dusted our clothes gray and blanketed the sky, causing sunsets to streak bright pink and orange. Streetcar wires crisscrossed overhead, making perches for the hungry crows, who flew high when the lumbering cars came, spewing electric sparks. Sometimes we'd put pennies in the metal tracks and wait for them to be squashed flat as the streetcars rumbled over them, carrying passengers down the hills into the heart of the city that rested by the three rivers: Monongahela, Allegheny, and Ohio.

But what I remember most about growing up in Pittsburgh was living in a neighborhood where everyone acted like a relative—an aunt, an uncle, a brother, or a sister. Lots of women acted like my mother, bossing me, feeding me. Many would hold me on their laps and tell me folktales about "High John the Conqueror" or "John Henry." Some felt no shame about whipping out a comb and fixing my hair when they thought I looked too raggedy. And days when I was lucky, one of my neighborhood mothers would jump in the circle and join me in a waist-twisting, hip-rolling Hula-Hoop. Sometimes it drove me crazy to have so many mothers, but it also made me feel safe. My real mother was gone—divorced from us—living in another city. But I lived with my dad, my grandparents, an aunt, a sister, and a cousin who was like another sister.

Dad, Aunt, and Grandpa went off to work while Grandma took care of us. On Tuesdays, she did laundry in the basement and she let us stir the Argo starch and turn the roller drums to wring out all the wet in the clothes. She'd let us help hang the clothes on the line and, when the sheets were dry, she turned a blind eye when we played hide-and-seek among them. In the house we'd hike to the third floor and slide down the two banisters, smooth and fast, convinced it was better than any roller coaster ride at Kennywood Park.

We had a red tricycle with a bell. My sister Tonie had outgrown it. I was just the right size, while cousin Aleta was too small. But when Grandma made chitlins, we would share the bike and make a game of driving through the stinking kitchen while Grandma cleaned out the pig's guts (yuck!) and boiled them. We'd ride our bike through dangerous territory, ringing our bell once we hit the kitchen's linoleum, hollering and hooting like "wild ones."

Or, as Grandma would say, "Silly children without no sense!" If
you held your nose you couldn't ring the bell and steer at the same
time. So we'd count how many bells to figure out who won, who
braved the skunky odor and didn't hold their nose the most.

The best part of growing up was the world we saw from our
front stoop. Widow Chalmers mothered all the children, watching
over us from her porch, waving her fan from the Methodist church
to cool herself in the summer heat. Mr. Berry, who had a splotch
of pink roses on his cheek, liked checkers and, carrying his own
lawn chair, would roam the street looking for a partner. He even
played with Aleta, who was five and had to be told every move.
There was Jim, who played ball, spinning, ducking and diving
and throwing hoops into a basketball net, and would only stop if
someone was in trouble. "Jim, my car stalled." "Jim, can you
drive me to the grocery?" "Jim, my sink is clogged." Jim later
joined the Army and came home and dunked three baskets in his
black clodhoppers and khaki uniform. My sister Tonie, at eleven,
swore she'd marry him.

Stuck-up Rachel liked to cheat at jacks and had to be black-
mailed into playing double Dutch. "I'll give you some of
Grandma's chicken from Sunday dinner," I'd offer. I promised a
drumstick for each twenty minutes she turned the ropes while I
sang and dreamed of winning the double Dutch championship at
the Y. Truth be told, Grandma would have given anyone who
asked a piece of her chicken. Rachel knew it, I knew it. Everyone
knew it. But Rachel was two years older than I and, like another
"big sister," she was nice enough to let me think I was putting one
over on her.

Sitting on the steps, looking up and down the block, I saw
and felt a world where I was safe, where I knew everybody and
everybody knew me. Everybody was brown and black, and when
babies were born, we'd all wait for them to grow into their skin.
Their shades would sometimes grow lighter, sometimes darker.
Even the color of their eyes would change—blue became brown,
hazel changed to deep green, and brown irises could mellow to a

luminous black. Hair textures all varied: soft, bouncy waves, strands curled in tight, fuzzy spirals, or even hair thick and straight because of a throwback to a Cherokee relative. I knew we all were beautiful.

Summer block parties were the best. We'd close off traffic and sometimes the fire department would open the hydrants and we'd dance and sing while water gushed at us. A spray of wet beneath the moon and stars. Tonie, Aleta, and I pushed boxes together to make a stage and lip-synched to the record player, pretending we were the Supremes, singing "Stop! In the Name of Love!" And we'd giggle as the grown-ups clapped and the other children squealed, and everyone danced, even fat Charlie, who could boogie so well you'd swear there was magic in his shoes.

The best block parties happened for no reason. Anyone—even a child—could wake up one day and call for "Block Party Day." And we'd share ribs, corn, chicken, sweet potato pie, and collard greens, and Miss Sarah, who had never married, always made punch with vanilla ice cream, and it would melt into a swishy mess. Finally, when legs wouldn't move another dance step, the record player was taken away, and the street was swept. There were cries and whispers of "Good night." My real family and I, we'd go into the house. Grandma, Grandpa, Aunt, and Daddy would tuck us in bed and kiss me, Tonie, and Aleta good night. And I would wait until Tonie and Aleta were asleep in the small twin beds (I didn't want them to think I was off my head) and I'd go to the window. Then, peeking over the ledge, I'd whisper my own private "G'night" to the rest of my family tucked in their beds inside the tall houses all along my street, there in the city where the three rivers meet.

This memory was later published in *All Together*, a Health Middle Level Literature Anthology. I think of this brief memoir as a gift. Wasted time in an airport became prime writing time because I had paper and pen and encouraged my own memories of a specific time and place.

When history speaks, you open a treasure trove of ready-made details to create setting and atmosphere. A story is always waiting to be born.

A Sunday afternoon in 1983, drinking coffee, eating a toasted bagel, I read the following article by Irving Wallace, David Wallechinsky, and Amy Wallace in *Parade* magazine:

§

FIRST U.S. CITY TO BE
BOMBED FROM THE AIR

IN 1921, DURING one of the worst race riots in American history, Tulsa, Okla., became the first U.S. city to be bombed from the air. More than 75 persons—mostly blacks—were killed.

Before the riot, Tulsa blacks were so successful that their business district was called "The Negro's Wall Street." Envy bred hatred of the blacks, who accounted for a tenth of the segregated city's population of 100,000.

Then on May 30, 1921, a white female elevator operator accused Dick Rowland, a 19-year-old black who worked at a shoeshine stand, of attacking her. Though he denied the charge, Rowland was jailed. The Tulsa *Tribune* ran a sensational account of the incident the next day, and a white lynch mob soon gathered at the jail. Armed blacks, seeking to protect Rowland, also showed up. Someone fired a gun, and the riot was on.

Whites invaded the black district, burning, looting and killing. To break up the riot, the police commandeered private planes and dropped dynamite. Eventually, the National Guard was called in and martial law declared.

The police arrested more than 4000 blacks and interned them in three camps. All blacks were forced to carry green ID cards. And when

Tulsa was zoned for a new railroad station, the tracks were routed through the black business district, thus destroying it.

"First U.S. City to Be Bombed from the Air" from *Parade* magazine. Reprinted with permission of the authors. Reprinted with permission from *Parade,* copyright ©1983.

My novel *Magic City* was born. For over a decade, the subject haunted me emotionally and intellectually. *How was it that I'd never heard of the Tulsa riot? How and why did blacks migrate to Oklahoma? Given racism, why was the black community allowed to thrive? What else was occurring in America? Prohibition? The dawn of the Roaring Twenties? The rise of the Klan?*

I kept the original newspaper clipping in my journal and periodically, while still working on *Voodoo Dreams,* I'd reread it and spend a few hours collecting research. I always knew my main characters were going to be called Joe and Mary. I spent years dreaming about how they looked, what they did, how they spoke. I did my best to imagine their yearnings, desires, and needs before I even wrote a single line. Becoming a mother to a son, watching Rodney King's beating on TV, the fiftieth anniversary of D-Day with its attendant articles about black soldiers whose courage went unheralded due to discrimination, all profoundly influenced *Magic City.*

My novel *Voodoo Dreams* was inspired by a Time-Life cookbook on Creole and Acadian cooking. In college, I needed to write a story for a fiction workshop class; I wanted to imagine something grand, different from my experiences. I stumbled upon a paragraph containing Marie Laveau, Bayou Teché ("bayou of snakes"), and the Creole lullaby *"Fais dodo. Mon píti bebe."* Spiritually moved, I wrote from midnight to dawn. The story, "Bayou Teché," which is now part of Chapter Two in the novel, became my literary beacon. For the next fifteen years, I spent my time researching, dreaming, writing sketches about Marie, Creole culture, and drawing snakes. *Voodoo Dreams* was my first fictional passion.

You may have already found your fictional passion. If you haven't, nonetheless believe that one day you will find it. Keep collecting material in your journal. Be attuned to your dreams and emotions.

Set free the stories stirring inside you. Creativity is nurtured by your optimism, your passion for both reading and writing words.

4

HOW TO KEEP GOING

I hope you've begun feeling and believing you're a working writer. Good for you! Writing can be sheer pleasure. But if you're like most writers I know, you'll also experience sheer terror. Overwhelmed, you might even moan and curse because writing is so difficult. You might have days when you're tempted to drink, break a vase, or tear out great clumps of your hair. Literally. You might feel your self-esteem shift beneath you and lie awake debating whether your prose is signaling you to go to law school or become an accountant.

Who dreamed this job up anyway?

WANTED: Writer. Poor pay. Poor benefits. Must be capable of working in isolation, alienated from society. Requirements: Ability to peck a typewriter, computer, or hold a pen; spell; know grammar. Willingness to tell the emotional truth even if it hurts; comfortable with self-doubt and revising lines a thousand times.

Why do most writers write? Why do we breathe?

Truth: I write to know myself and to celebrate my culture and heritage. I write to stave off death, hoping words will lend me immortality. I write to shape a better world—less racism and sexism, more love and forgiveness—for my children and all children to thrive in. But bottom line: I can't help myself.

Writers write because they must. The process, unfortunately, sometimes locks you in misery and can undermine the creativity you need to excel. By accepting painful aspects of the process as a natural extension of life, you can find some ease and comfort. I hope the preceding chapters have shown you that writing, at its core, is a liberating exploration of self and community.

MY BEST ADVICE

Believe in yourself—always.

Accept your imperfections but don't accept the possibility of failing.

As a beginning writer, I often berated myself when I didn't have ideas to write about or when I was trapped rewriting the same paragraph. Worried that I couldn't write well enough, fearful of pursuing my innermost self, I cringed in front of the computer screen. Pages written became equated with my self-esteem. Obviously, I had some bad days . . . then one bad day became another, then another, and I became locked in a cycle of not writing and feeling worthless. I defeated the cycle when I made a simple bargain with myself:

1. Write only what I feel compelled to write.
2. Be disciplined. Write for at least two hours each morning and evening.
3. If, after two hours, my writing is going poorly, I get up, get out, and do something else.

Step 3 sometimes included going to bookstores, listening to Wynton Marsalis or Nina Simone, or feeding ducks on a pond. Sometimes I'd "free write." For ten minutes, I'd write in my journal without censoring or editing, just letting the pen flow and shape words. "Free writing" released stress, allowed me to relax into my day's writing, and, occasionally, gave me new ideas. Playing with my children always soothed, since it engaged me completely; and, invariably, I received warm smiles and laughter, and a spirited sense that all was right with me and the world.

Step 3 *always* included reminding myself that unproductive writing meant I hadn't found the right tale to imagine, nothing more or less. A bad day writing didn't mean I was a bad person. A bad day didn't necessarily mean I was an untalented writer.

Writing is like falling in love—sometimes you pick the wrong lover and it's time to pack up and move on; sometimes you pick the right lover but it's still hard work nurturing the relationship to its full potential.

Just as you can't just *think* yourself in love—you either are or are not—you need to *be* a writer who writes. When the writing doesn't go well, have the courage to come back either later that day or the next, with a full commitment to try again to write well and strong.

Relish the hard parts of writing because that's when you're learning the most—you're learning discipline, you're learning new skills. If writing were always easy, you wouldn't feel such wonderful satisfaction when you've done it right.

Strike a bargain with yourself—you *will* write, no matter what.

But what about my day job? Child care? Grocery shopping? Spending time with my husband?

Once I felt my goal to become a writer was a pipe dream. I used to read author interviews in which time after time, men (many Anglo) spoke about spending as much as six to eight hours a day writing. Envious, I insisted upon the same standard for myself and made myself absolutely miserable.

Fact: I had to raise my kids.

Fact: I needed my teaching to pay the bills.

Fact: I needed to sleep.

But what inspired me was reading about other women who wrote, had day jobs, and raised kids. Toni Morrison. Terry McMillan. Alice Walker. Dozens of women, less famous, are still carrying a double or triple load. Clearly, writing can be done.

I survived by learning to appreciate the time I had, rather than regretting the time I lost. I survived by laughing and reminding myself that interruptions, too, were a part of life.

I wrote bedridden during pregnancies. I wrote after the 2 A.M. feeding, racing the dawn and my son's early rising. I learned to write while the children were doing homework, and when they had a question, I always found my best ideas could withstand interruption. I learned to trust that my best work was waiting patiently for me to mine it like ore—and, bit by bit, I finished one novel, then another. Could I have written faster if I had fewer obligations? Undoubtedly. On the other hand, how can I say family and teaching are obligations? I love my family. I love teaching. And I can't help but believe that these "loves" inspire and sustain my writing.

Male writers have their travails too, carrying multiple loads of family and work responsibilities. Some teach like Charles Johnson, Clarence Major, and Arthur Flowers. Others work as journalists, cab-drivers, carpenters, short-order cooks. All of them have relationships and responsibilities which need tending. Most of us aren't rich and probably won't ever be rich, but that doesn't preclude financial sacrifice. E. Lynn Harris quit work and relied upon the kindness of friends and family while he finished his first novel. In the past, I've chosen to teach less (and earn less) so I can plow through a rough spot in my writing.

Artist colonies can be helpful as well—Chapter One of *Voodoo Dreams* was written at Yaddo, an artists' retreat in upstate New York. I remember quite clearly not only the four weeks of uninterrupted writing time, freedom from household chores, but the enormous boost to my writer's self-esteem. There are fellowships, too, such as the Zora Neale Hurston/Richard Wright Scholarship and the Nilon Minority Fellowship. The Mary Roberts Rinehart Foundation awards monies to help authors finish projects. Writing Resources in Part V is a good place to start searching for artists' colonies and fellowships which may be helpful to you. However, if you aren't awarded a fellowship or space in a cottage to write, continue to write nonetheless. You may want to seek out a writers' group—such as the Carolina African American Writer's Collective, the Harlem Writers' Guild, or the Frederick Douglass Creative Arts Center, all of which have been supporting writers for years. The National Writer's Voice Project, through its affiliation with the YMCA, sponsors beginning as well as advanced community-based workshops. Or if you're in a reading group, ask some of your friends if they want to create a writers' group. An essential key for restraining fear and self-doubt is to have a supportive network. This network may be composed of other writers, it may include friends or family members, or it may be one "trusted reader" who will seriously (and honestly) respond to your writing. It is far more valuable to have a reader be critical of your writing than it is to have a friend spare your feelings by responding dishonestly. Fellowships, scholarships, writers' retreats make life easier, but they don't change a basic fact of life: *"To be a writer, write!"*

All writers—male and female—manage the complex demands of family (extended and/or nuclear) and the struggle to pay room and board. All writers manage anxiety and self-doubt. All writers must make peace with what they can do as artists and not berate themselves for what they're unable to do.

If you must slow down and write only two hours a day or one hour a day, okay. Do the best you can. Children will grow. Dirty dishes don't alter the meaning of life. Be positive. Write on your lunch hour. Use your vacation time for a personal writer's retreat. When commuting, listen to books on tape. Carry your journal everywhere.

Remember: Slowing down doesn't mean stopping.

Consistently writing for small amounts of time will reward you far more than inconsistent binges.

EXERCISE 1

GOAL SETTING

If you've come this far, you know you can go further in your development as a writer. Take ten minutes and write down your goals.

LONG-TERM GOALS

What do you want to accomplish as a writer? How many books do you dream of writing? What kind of books? Do you have a particular audience you want to reach? Children? Young men? A general fiction audience? What do you want to communicate to your audience? What ideas? What themes? What do you want to be remembered for as a writer? Your social consciousness? Your drama and complex characterizations? Your ability to write affecting romances? What skills do you want to improve?

Over a lifetime, what accomplishments as a writer would make *you* most proud?

SHORT-TERM GOALS

What are you going to do on a daily basis to help you achieve your long-term goals as a writer? Be specific. "Write," yes, of course. But how much? When? Days when the air conditioning shuts off, your dog gets lost then found, your children are ill, do you have a backup plan for accomplishing your daily writing goals? Do you stay up late? Add an extra hour of writing to each day for a week?

Be sure to create a realistic schedule for yourself. Writing seven days a week doesn't work for everyone. Even when I'm not teaching, I schedule one day a week for miscellaneous chores. It's also important, of course, to reserve time for rest and relaxation.

Finally, is there any additional reading, research, or exercises you need to do to succeed at any or all of your short- and long-term goals?

· · ·

Once you've written down your long- and short-term goals, type them and paste them on a wall above your desk.

EXERCISE 2
CONFRONTING FEARS

What are you afraid of?

Take some time to think hard about this question. What scares you most about becoming and being a writer?

Write your fears on paper. Any common themes? Or maybe you have one huge fear? Ask yourself why you fear it.

Fears are deeply personal and particular. However, the following are the fears I've heard expressed most often:

I'm afraid I won't be a good writer. You won't become a better writer if you don't try.

I'm afraid I won't get published. You won't know until you complete a book and try.

I'm afraid readers won't like my work. You won't revise and improve your work until you invite readers to respond to your work.

"Try." A powerful word. You *will* fail as a writer if you don't try.

You might not dispel all your writing fears, but try. Think positively. Try to keep fears at bay by focusing on your goals. Write. Always. Even when you remain fearful, try to write consistently. Don't let fear paralyze you. If one book doesn't get published, write another. If respected readers don't like your work, listen to their opinions and consider revisions. Try harder to capture and convey your vision in words. Writing is communication—a powerful social act between you and an audience waiting to read your thoughts, your story.

Review the fears you've written—are any of them truly crippling? Use your fears to motivate—say "I can" instead of "I can't." Take your list of fears and scratch them out with a nice thick marker. Then crumple the sheet, tear it into bits, and toss it in the trash. Believe me, these small actions will make you feel wonderful. (If you need to repeat this exercise every month until you turn ninety, then do so! Fears can be recurring but so, too, is your strength for overcoming them!)

Remember: This is your one and only life. Don't cheat yourself on your goals.

EXERCISE 3

SEARCHING FOR INSPIRATION

Select an author you admire and spend an afternoon researching her career. There is often the perception that writers never stumble in their ascent to become "overnight sensations." When we see a finished book, we forget or are unaware of the author's years of effort and anxiety, her discarded pages and struggle to get published. Writers, like anyone else, experience child-care problems, racism, sexism, professional jealousy, writer's block, and insecurities. No special glow protects a writer from unfairness, pain, depression, or hostility. The brutal fact remains that despite hardships, successful writers hold fast to their dreams and create. This is worth remembering and celebrating! Encourage your own stubbornness and steadfastly pursue your career goals!

Magazines and journals such as *Callaloo, Poets & Writers,* and the *African American Review* regularly provide author interviews. Local libraries often carry video interviews and/or documentaries of celebrated authors such as Gloria Naylor, Alice Walker, James Baldwin, Rita Dove, Dorothy West, and Langston Hughes. On-line bookstores

(Amazon.com, BarnesandNoble.com, Borders.com) promote contemporary authors' interviews and interactive question-and-answer sessions; also, many of these sites will refer you to an author's home page and E-mail tie-in.

Memoirs provide insightful glimpses into authors' lives. *Black Boy* is a heart-wrenching look into Richard Wright's development as both a man and a writer. Jamaica Kincaid, nominated for a National Book Award for her memoir *My Brother,* provides a potent picture of the childhood she escaped to become a writer.

Alice Walker's *In Search of Our Mother's Gardens* inspired me to honor and celebrate Zora Neale Hurston. Life was never easy for Hurston yet she did field research in African American folklore and wrote splendid books, both nonfiction and fiction. Hurston always struggled to support herself and, when necessary, she buoyed the ego of her untalented patron, Mrs. Mason, and requested funds so she could get on with her work. She was reduced, at times, to itemizing money for car fare and medicine. In a letter dated, April 27, 1932, she pleaded:

> Godmother darling . . . I really need a pair of shoes
> . . . My big toe is about to burst out of my right
> shoe . . .

Though she'd later die poverty-stricken, Hurston, when she was able, nonetheless sought out the financial and emotional support she needed to achieve her goals. Throughout her career, she collected folklore for the WPA (Works Progress Administration), won a Guggenheim Fellowship and a Rosenwald Fellowship in Anthropology, and worked at various times as a domestic servant.

Some writers of the Harlem Renaissance accused her of "playing darky," of creating characters which pandered to white stereotypes. This is ludicrous, in view of the content of her work and character. However, Hurston's estrangement from and misunderstanding by other notable black writers affected her deeply. Still, she kept writing and pursuing her goals.

Given Hurston's trailblazing (and often misunderstood) literature, which focused on the glory of self-contained black communities rather than protesting interracial conflicts, given her financial need to mollify a less talented (and often pinchpenny) white patron, what excuse do you or I have for not working?

"Complaining" has never once authored a book.

Hurston wrote four novels, a memoir, two collections of folk research, and over fifty stories, essays, and plays. Though unlucky at love, falsely accused of molesting a child, maligned because she worried about the damage desegregation might wreak on thriving black schools, Hurston kept writing. Though fame was achieved posthumously, Hurston wouldn't have been "rediscovered" as a courageous, brilliant author had she not consistently and continually filled blank pages with words capturing the beauty, the spirit, and the foibles of black people.

Hurston remains the foremost literary godmother of black women's fiction.

Hurston's life reminds me: All roads are hard. But that's not an excuse for not writing.

After researching the career of an admired author, contemplate how her struggles to be a successful writer may help you to put your fears and self-doubts in perspective. In your journal, write three positive steps you can take to improve your attitude about writing.

Above all, remember you're already successful because you're devoting time to becoming a better writer. *Success doesn't necessarily mean easy.* Success is devotion and hard work.

Since you started this book, you've been reading, writing, thinking, observing, and motivating yourself to become a better writer. Bravo! If your journal is more than half full, consider purchasing another. I have boxfuls of old journals. These journals are a great resource for ideas as well as a visible comfort and reminder that I am a working writer.

The next eight chapters are devoted to writing fiction. You'll plunge deeper into imaginative worlds, exploring more challenging fictional skills. Don't hurry your learning. Don't berate yourself if your execution as a writer is less advanced than your understanding. Repeat any exercises you choose. Focusing on process and practice will undoubtedly make you a better writer. Think of each successive chapter as another opportunity to celebrate and enhance your unique creativity.

PART III

LEARNING THE

CRAFT

CREATING CHARACTER

Love all your characters.
There is no "story" if readers don't care about your characters. Before a reader will care, you need to feel passionately loyal to each and every one of your characters. Even a character who abuses and hurts others needs to be loved enough to be understood.

In Toni Morrison's *The Bluest Eye,* Cholly Breedlove is the perfect example of a despicable character who is rendered compassionately. Drunk, alienated, overwhelmed by his own self-loathing, Cholly rapes his daughter. Confusing the image of his daughter's foot with a happier memory of loving his wife, the horrible, incestuous touch occurs. But his *motive* was to touch her tenderly.

Even as readers hate Cholly, hate the brutality of his actions, they also feel sympathy because Morrison, in prior scenes, has *shown* Cholly, as a child, abandoned by his mother and later rejected by his father; *shown* Cholly being forced to perform sexually under the flash-light glare of racists who damage his innocent first love; *shown* how money worries, falsely romantic movies, and a punitive religion drove a wedge between the love he and his wife once shared. Cholly, a "burnt-out black man," can't "breed love" because society, over a lifetime, has poisoned his life's soil. He has no nurturing, sustaining love left to give. When Cholly rapes, we won't, don't excuse his actions, but we do mourn for him as well as for his daughter. Because Morrison cared enough about Cholly to understand him fully, she reveals him with powerful empathy.

Human behavior *is* complex; it is the writer's journey to explore the human heart and in doing so you have the pleasure of discovering more about your own heart and revealing your insights through characters. It is this fundamental sharing between writer and reader—of thought, feeling, and action—which gives fiction its power and force.

Zora Neale Hurston's Janie, in talking of her dying love for her husband, Jody, says *"she wasn't petal-open anymore with him."* Characters may love, hate, be spiteful with abandon, but a good writer always remains "petal-open." If you no longer "love" your characters or feel compelled to write about them, then stop. Without love, you are almost certain to write flat, one-dimensional characters.

MY BEST ADVICE
Approach your characters as human beings.

Black people are subject to the same human foibles as anyone else. If you're writing about a strong, wondrous black woman, be certain to shade her with vulnerabilities, weaknesses. Characters, like people, are never consistently "strong," "nice," "evil," "considerate," "beautiful"—all the time. In *Voodoo Dreams*, Marie Laveau—a gifted, spiritual leader, a woman who could walk on water—struggled with self-pity and doubted she was lovable. Because I didn't want Marie to be a "character type," a one-dimensional being, I overdid her vulnerabilities. Three hundred pages later, to my dismay, I had a novel about a pathetic, victimized young woman. I revised, working to give Marie back her glory, her affirmations of self. Ultimately, there were many Maries: the warrior Marie; the spirited, questing Marie; the battered, weeping Marie; the vengeful Marie; the shy Marie. I hope my Marie expresses, often like quicksilver, as many human emotions as she could credibly hold.

Historically, in American literature and popular culture, African Americans have been presented as variations of key stereotypes: the Brute Negro, quick to violence, desirous of white women; the Mammy, nurturing, loyal to her white family, and seemingly without emotional needs of her own; the Black Matriarch, emasculating and domineering; the Tragic Mulatto, vulnerable, victimized, and more virtuous because of her white blood; the Sambo, childish, unintelligent, interested only in singing and dancing; and the Uncle Tom, obedient, desirous of emulating whites, and disinterested in the plight of his people. Stereotypes are one-dimensional characters and are a blatant attempt by society to dehumanize and oppress.

We've all heard the golden rule: "Do unto others as you would have them do unto you." In my mind, this rule applies to literature. No person should be dehumanized. An evil character, regardless of color, created with compassion is infinitely preferable to an evil character created without understanding and without potential for change.

Unfortunately, two hundred years of racism and acculturation have had their effect. Color prejudice within the black community is a result of slavery's legacy and an early literary tradition which fostered the belief that the light-skinned, straight-haired Negro would always be more tragic than her darker cousin. Likewise, standard English versus black dialect became a code by which to judge people's intelligence both in fiction and in life.

Be conscious of your characters' appearance and speech and make sure you aren't responding to outdated, harmful images. As a writer, you choose to describe characters as you see fit. The key word is "choose." Unfortunately, it's the unconscious insidiousness of racism and American schools' historic disregard for ethnic literature that force writers to be on guard.

White American writers in the eighteenth, nineteenth, and (let's be frank) twentieth centuries would announce color as though "brown," "black," "yellow," "amber," "ebony," "coffee," "café au lait," "chocolate," "cinnamon" explained all you needed to know about a character. If a color adjective was left out, then, of course, the character was white.

When I wrote my first story for a fiction workshop, classmates chastised me: "Why didn't you tell me your characters were black?" They had wanted a page one, paragraph one clarification!

Character is much more than an announcement of skin tone, and color should never be confused with cultural identity. My cultural identity is African American, but it doesn't exclude or bar me from writing about my larger human family, which is a spectrum of myriad colors.

Like jazz artists playing with variations, African American authors took the singular dimensions of stereotypes and debunked them by re-creating and replacing those images with multifaceted characterizations.

Characters are created by situations and responses, by a writer's willingness to engage in complexity. Muhdear in Tina McElroy Ansa's *Ugly Ways* fits no simplistic pattern of motherhood; J. California Cooper's mothers in the short stories "Friends, Anyone?" and "I Told Him" are living, breathing, hurting, "trying to get by" women. Ernest Gaines has a glorious record of presenting complex women—sometimes outspoken, sometimes taciturn—surviving as best they can and often far better than racism wants to allow.

Black writers have transformed the image of singing, dancing, happy slaves into musicians whose artistic power can plumb the depths of pain, as in James Baldwin's "Sonny's Blues," or praise music as joyful liberation from Western cultural aesthetics, as in Langston Hughes's "The Blues I'm Playing."

Indeed, matriarchs and musicians have a special resonance in our literature; they can be called "stock characters." Stock characters (not to be confused with stereotypes) are characters who reappear throughout black literature, uniquely drawn and reimagined by successive generations. Drawing from our oral tradition, authors have made tricksters, preachers, and badmen/outlaws familiar stock characters. It is okay to use stock characters—all cultures have them and create them to embody cultural themes and concerns. Minor characters, in particular, can be rendered efficiently as stock characters. However, as a writer, it always pays to add complexity to as many characters as you can to avoid stereotypes.

Slaves told tales of how tricksters outwitted their masters and upset the balance of racial power. In 1899, Charles Chesnutt created Uncle Julius, a trickster, who in a series of tales subversively criticizes slavery's horrors. Ishmael Reed's *The Last Days of Louisiana Red* (1974) features PaPa LaBas as a voodoo trickster detective. Some of the earliest tricksters were animal characters—Bruh Rabbit, Anansi the spider, Lizard—who survived via oral folktales and folk literature throughout Africa and the Americas. These animals, usually small and sly, used combinations of magic, wit, and cunning to outwit larger, more powerful animals. In the African American literary tradition, these animal tricksters developed into human stock characters who defended themselves against slavery's and racism's ills. Today, almost any black character who outwits the system, trumps the "master," is, in a sense, a descendant of the trickster.

The folk hero Stackolee (also known as Staggerlee, Stagolee), sung and talked about since the 1890s, is a badman who hates and lives outside conventional norms. Because he lost his Stetson hat while gambling, Stackolee kills a man. In differing tales and songs, the sheriff refuses to capture him, or the judge refuses to convict him, or the hangman refuses to hang him for fear Stackolee will get even. The badman becomes an "antihero" because he is *"anti-," against, trying to live outside a society which typically oppressed black men.* Though their actions aren't always laudable, badmen can be envied for their audacious moments of power and control. Bigger Thomas in Richard Wright's *Native Son* is a quintessential badman. He lives outside societal norms because a racist society has made so little space for him to be a man. *The Autobiography of Malcolm X* shows the societal anger and self-hatred of a "badman" but also shows the courageous transformation of a black man re-creating himself and a space within the world for him to become the man he desires.

Preachers are often infamous stock characters, satirized for immorality, sexual promiscuity, and lack of Christian compassion. Nella

Larsen's *Quicksand,* James Baldwin's *Go Tell It on the Mountain,* Ralph Ellison's *Invisible Man,* Gloria Naylor's *The Women of Brewster Place,* all have examples of preachers who don't live Christian principles or who use Christianity to encourage passive acceptance of prejudice. These stock characters become powerful tools to remind us that faith needs to be sincerely lived.

The ancestor is another familiar character in African American literature. This moral and spiritual guide can be either a man or a woman, but quite frequently in our fiction, an elderly character, a ghost, or a spirit from an African or long-ago past gives critical advice to confused, struggling characters. Baby Suggs in *Beloved* encourages black people to love themselves. McMillan's Ma'Dear is a wise old woman with good advice about life, love, and paying the bills. The grandmother in Virginia Hamilton's classic *Roll of Thunder, Hear My Cry* always supplies comfort and nurturing support to the family struggling to maintain itself in the 1950s South.

You can't always develop all characters equally, but you should try. Inexperienced writers tend to make all their characters one-dimensional. Be bold, experiment, create characters who will live always within your story and, most important, within your readers' minds and hearts.

Sometimes a character walks in the door as a gift; most times they tantalize. You have to spend enough time to know your character. You'll need to draw upon your self, your memories, your observations. Selecting a character for a story is one of the most important choices you'll make.

Who intrigues you? Aunt Sarah, who never comes to family gatherings?

Whom do you feel passionate about? The ex-lover who disappeared without a goodbye?

Whom do you imagine? The Howard student who stumbled upon a senator's body at K Street and L?

Sometimes the best characters are composites based upon people you know. But don't try to model exactly a real person (that's how lawsuits are born). A fiction writer's job is to tell great lies which make a great story. Even a real person has thoughts and feelings which you must imagine.

Remember: The stuff of your imagination is probably more promising than reality.

EXERCISE 1

DUST INTO FLESH

In your journal, select a name for a character you'd like to write about.

For example, Anita. An Anita is different from a Barbara, a Lorraine, or an Elsa. A Jerome is unlike a Terrence, a Bobby, or a James.

A name makes a character real. So does history. Write down details about your character's past: When and where was she (or he) born? What are her parents' names? Was she a wanted child? Is she the only child, eldest child, or baby of the family? What are her parents' attitudes toward raising children? How much schooling does she have? Who was her first love? First enemy? What was her greatest fear growing up? Her best talent?

Write down details about your character's current life: Is she married? Does she practice a faith? Where does she shop? What's her profession? Her hobbies? Is she a mother? An activist? Is she inside or outside a network of friends?

What is a typical day like? Chances are you'll be writing about an untypical day, so decide what your character normally does. On Thursday, does your character eat at Jones's Deli? Work a night shift at the hospital? Or meet with a women's group to discuss books? What are her daily rituals? Rising at dawn for coffee and Frosted Flakes, then a bus ride with three transfers to work? Or does she sleep late, making the kids ready themselves for school, then awaken in time for aerobics and lunch with her friend Martha?

What does your character look like? You needn't list details as if you were writing a police report or printing a driver's license! Instead think of physical details which make your character striking and unforgettable. It may be her elegant hands, the way she moves or doesn't move through a crowded room, the slope of her neck or a rose-shaped birthmark on her shoulder.

What clothing does your character wear? What does she want it to say about her? That she's rich, stylish? What does it actually say about her? That she's a rich wannabe buying top-of-the-line Kmart instead of designer fashion? Colors and patterns can indicate moods and suggest fashion attitudes—black fabric has a different appeal than purple-striped silk or an indigo-and-gold batik.

Clothing tells a lot about your character's income group, self-esteem, and style, but it can also delightfully deceive. *Pierce Watson is affluent but prefers to wear Keds sneakers, Levi's, a Pirates baseball cap, and a torn green sweatshirt.*

Consider physical habits too—how your character smiles, laughs, tilts her head when she's angry. Does she sleep on her stomach? Eat her food item by item, starting with the vegetables?

Take thirty minutes and complete a character sketch.

Reread all the information you've written about your character so far. Would you know her if she walked into a room?

While all the details you've written are important in helping you visualize and understand your character, not all of the details will be directly used in the story. Using a highlighter, mark those details which might be critical to the plot—to what happens to your character in the story. For example, your character's love for exotic travel may not matter as much as her small (but, she believes, disfiguring) mole on her left cheek and her hatred of her daily ninety-minute commute on the D.C. subway (where she believes everybody stares at her and mocks her).

EXERCISE 2

BREATHING IN THE SPIRIT

Characterization is only half done until you've breathed spirit, soul into your character. Characters must have an interior life: desires, dreams, needs, fears.

What does your character desire? Love? Money? Friendship? Revenge? What does your character dream about? What are his fantasies and daydreams? What dreams are repressed? What nightmares wake him? What does your character truly need? Literacy? Freedom from self-doubt? A kind word?

Write at least two pages about the emotional, inner life of the character you sketched in Exercise 1. Pretending you are the character, you can begin with strong "I" statements or else begin with the character's name. This exercise will allow you to really feel, breathe, and experience the character.

Anita wants [I want]_____

I need_____

I fear_____

I dream_____

Desires/dreams/needs can and do overlap. But characters can also desire and dream about one thing only to discover they need something else. For example, in Alice Walker's story "The Wedding," a single mother is marrying, fulfilling her dream to give her children respectability and security. But what she desires is love and equality. During the wedding service, the character realizes her marriage will be repressive, patriarchal. What she needs is the courage to free herself from the relationship. But she can't.

.   .   .

Circle the overlapping desires/dreams/needs you see in your character sketch. Then underline any emotions which are at odds with each other. For example, a character dreams of being a musician but needs cocaine. Or an abused character may believe she has no desires, that she is "a speck of nothing," only to discover she needs to dream in order to survive.

Desires/dreams/needs give your characters depth and complexity. Your character's interior life will shape her motivations and how she might respond to choices and crises within your story.

Review all the information you've written about your character. What needs does she have that you're sympathetic to? Are you challenged by similar insecurities, dreams, hopes? What is your emotional stake in writing about your character? Why do you feel compelled to write about this character as opposed to any other?

In your journal, write at least a paragraph (preferably more) about how and why you connect with your character emotionally.

Name, current life and past history, appearance, feelings and desires all create the foundation for great characterization. Add in your emotional bond and you'll breathe life into your characters, making them memorable, transforming them from "dust to flesh."

EXERCISE 3

MOVING SPIRIT AND BONES

Now that you've birthed your characters by giving them a history and an appearance (flesh and bones) and a spirit (an emotional life), you need them to move, to "express themselves" in order to be fully realized and alive.

CHARACTERS
ACT—REACT—THINK—SPEAK

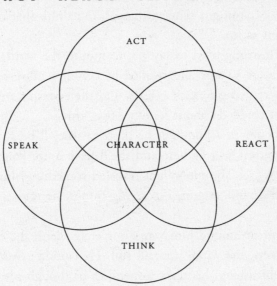

In *Your Blues Ain't Like Mine,* Bebe Moore Campbell creates a vivid portrait:

The tall younger man hit him, a heavy open-palm slap that struck against his head. Armstrong fell down in a daze. "What did I do?" he asked. He tried to get up, but his legs seemed to lock and then buckle. When he finally regained his balance and was able to stand, the man knocked him down again and began kicking him in his stomach, his chest, his head.

Nobody said anything. Armstrong repeated, "What did I do?" He began to cry, but the yelping dogs, their barking growing louder and more frenzied, drowned out his sobbing. He curled up like a baby, trying to avoid the blows. . . .

What could he do to make them stop? What did they want of him? Armstrong remembered bullies in the Chicago schoolyard where he had attended grammar school and thought of the bloodless scuffles over lunch money. And then he remembered the two ten-dollar bills in his pocket. "I have some money," he said weakly.

". . . You got money, nigger? You think that makes you good as me?" . . .

Armstrong tried to say no, to mouth the word, but his lips were so sore and swollen he couldn't move them. They were going to kick his ass, and there wasn't anything he could do about it. One, two, three . . . By the time I count to a hundred, he thought, they'll be gone and Grandma will be here and she'll fix me up. Four, five, six . . . The moonlight revealed something shiny in Floyd's hand. A gun. I'm seeing things, he told himself.

The air around him was completely silent; the dogs, the crickets, the wind, were all still. He couldn't hear himself breathing; his tears suspended, as though his sobs were dammed up in his chest, rolling around like furious ocean waves. "Please, mister," he managed to whisper. When he looked in Floyd's eyes he saw pain, rage, and loathing, but no mercy. "Mama," he cried.

Because Armstrong is a child, his actions are limited. "I have some money" is his bid to change his destiny, his act of survival. If Armstrong were an adult, if he truly was "arm strong," he would perhaps fight back. But Armstrong's bewildered actions are consistent with the survival response of a child. He begs for mercy, cries for his mother, wishes for the comfort and care of his grandmother, and he counts, believing counting might magically make his reality fade. Armstrong is not transformed by superhero powers, nor does he suddenly find the strength, mentally or physically, to outwit his captors.

Remember: well-drawn characters must always be consistent and credible within the range of who they are.

Unlike actions, which have the potential to effect change, reactions are more passive. Most of all, Armstrong *reacts:* he falls, curls up like a baby, sobs. Even his dialogue: "What did I do?" is passive and questioning, rather than a bold, assertive fact: "I didn't do anything." Armstrong's thoughts: "What could he do to make them stop? What did they want of him?" underscore his naive innocence. An adult might disclaim guilt, but a child always suspects himself to be guilty of something.

Reread Campbell's excerpt again. With a pencil, cross out Armstrong's thoughts. How significant is the loss? Does Armstrong seem less vulnerable? Less real? Next, delete Armstrong's dialogue. How vivid is Armstrong when you can't hear his voice? Next, cross out Armstrong's actions, his reactions. The scene no longer makes any sense. Armstrong has disappeared, his spirit and bones have fallen apart; the character we care about no longer lives.

Using a character created in the previous exercises, imagine a scene in which your character is responding to a specific event or person. Because you already know your character's history, appearance, and emotional life, you are much more likely to "breathe life" into your character in a credible, consistent manner.

Write a two-page scene emphasizing your character's actions, re-actions, thoughts, and speech. Do these aspects have to be created in equal measure? No. Sometimes a character may *not think* but impulsively respond. Speech can be limited during a bank heist or tender love scene. A prisoner, arms and legs chained, may only be capable of limited actions/reactions to a sentencing. However, characters will be more vivid if you use as many character-building techniques as you can.

Remember: characters **act, react, think, and speak.**

Reread your scene. Revise it, imagining how a reader first meeting your character might respond. What other actions/reactions would make your character more vital and distinct? Can you add any thoughts/words which would reveal desires, secrets, needs? Which would encourage empathy? Which would make the character seem so real a reader could recognize her walking down the street or in a crowded lobby?

• • •

Invite your characters into your life. If you let them, they'll guide you to shape better stories.

Character is the essence and foundation of fiction.

CHARACTERIZATION STUDY

EDWIDGE DANTICAT'S "NEW YORK DAY WOMEN"

Read the following story. Take out your journal and record your reactions to the characters. Try to express what you think Danticat did as a writer which made the characters alive and three-dimensional.

TODAY, WALKING DOWN the street, I see my mother. She is strolling with a happy gait, her body thrust toward the DON'T WALK sign and the yellow taxicabs that make forty-five-degree turns on the corner of Madison and Fifty-seventh Street.

I have never seen her in this kind of neighborhood, peering into Chanel and Tiffany's and gawking at the jewels glowing in the Bulgari windows. My mother never shops outside of Brooklyn. She has never seen the advertising office where I work. She is afraid to take the subway, where you may meet those young black militant street preachers who curse black women for straightening their hair.

Yet, here she is, my mother, whom I left at home that morning in her bathrobe, with pieces of newspapers twisted like rollers in her hair. My mother, who accuses me of random offenses as I dash out of the house.

Would you get up and give an old lady like me your subway seat? In this state of mind, I bet you don't even give up your seat to a pregnant lady.

My mother, who is often right about that. Sometimes I get up and give my seat. Other times, I don't. It all depends on how pregnant the woman is and whether or not she is with her boyfriend or husband and whether or not *he* is sitting down.

As my mother stands in front of Carnegie Hall, one taxi driver yells to another, "What do you think this is, a dance floor?"

My mother waits patiently for this dispute to be settled before crossing the street.

In Haiti when you get hit by a car, the owner of the car gets out and kicks you for getting blood on his bumper.

My mother, who laughs when she says this and shows a large gap in her mouth where she lost three more molars to the dentist last week. My mother, who at fifty-nine says dentures are okay.

You can take them out when they bother you. I'll like them. I'll like them fine.

Will it feel empty when Papa kisses you?

Oh no, he doesn't kiss me that way anymore.

My mother, who watches the lottery drawing every night on Channel 11 without ever having played the numbers.

A third of that money is all I would need. We would pay the mortgage, and your father could stop driving that taxicab all over Brooklyn.

I follow my mother, mesmerized by the many possibilities of her journey. Even in a flowered dress, she is lost in a sea of pinstripes and gray suits, high heels and elegant short skirts. Reebok sneakers, dashing from building to building.

My mother, who won't go out to dinner with anyone.

If they want to eat with me, let them come to my house, even if I boil water and give it to them.

My mother, who talks to herself when she peels the skin off poultry.

Fat, you know, and cholesterol. Fat and cholesterol killed your aunt Hermine.

My mother, who makes jam with dried grapefruit peel and then puts in cinnamon bark that I always think is cockroaches in the jam. My mother, whom I have always bought household appliances for, on her birthday. A nice rice cooker, a blender.

I trail the red orchids in her dress and the heavy faux leather bag on her shoulders. Realizing the ferocious pace of my pursuit, I stop against a wall to rest. My mother keeps on walking as though she owns the sidewalk under her feet.

As she heads toward the Plaza Hotel, a bicycle messenger swings so close to her that I want to dash forward and rescue her, but she stands dead in her tracks and lets him ride around her and then goes on.

My mother stops at a corner hot-dog stand and asks for something. The vendor hands her a can of soda that she slips into her bag. She stops by another vendor selling sundresses for seven dollars each. I can tell that she is looking at an African print dress, contemplating my size. I think to myself, Please, Ma, don't buy it. It would be just another thing I would bury in the garage or give to Goodwill.

Why should we give to Goodwill when there are so many people back home who need clothes? We save our clothes for the relatives in Haiti.

Twenty years we have been saving all kinds of things for the relatives in Haiti. I need the place in the garage for an exercise bike.

You are pretty enough to be a stewardess. Only dogs like bones.

This mother of mine, she stops at another hot-dog vendor's and buys a frankfurter that she eats on the street. I never knew that she ate frankfurters. With her blood pressure, she shouldn't eat anything with sodium. She has to be careful with her heart, this day woman.

I cannot just swallow salt. Salt is heavier than a hundred bags of shame.

She is slowing her pace, and now I am too close. If she turns around, she might see me. I let her walk into the park before I start to follow again.

My mother walks toward the sandbox in the middle of the park. There a woman is waiting with a child. The woman is wearing a leotard with biker's shorts and has small weights in her hands. The woman kisses the child good-bye and surrenders him to my mother, then she bolts off, running on the cemented stretches in the park.

The child given to my mother has frizzy blond hair. His hand slips into hers easily, like he's known her for a long time. When he raises his face to look at my mother, it is as though he is looking at the sky.

My mother gives this child the soda that she bought from the vendor on the street corner. The child's face lights up as she puts a straw in the can for him. This seems to be a conspiracy just between the two of them.

My mother and the child sit and watch the other children play in the sandbox. The child pulls out a comic book from a knapsack with Big Bird on the back. My mother peers into his comic book. My mother, who taught herself to read as a little girl in Haiti from the books that her brothers brought home from school.

My mother, who has now lost six of her seven sisters in Ville Rose and has never had the strength to return for their funerals.

Many graves to kiss when I go back. Many graves to kiss.

She throws away the empty soda can when the child is done with it. I wait and watch from a corner until the woman in the leotard and biker's shorts returns, sweaty and breathless, an hour later. My mother gives the woman back her child and strolls farther into the park.

I turn around and start to walk out of the park before my mother can see me. My lunch hour is long since gone. I have to hurry back to work. I walk through a cluster of joggers, then race to a *Sweden Tours* bus. I stand behind the bus and take a peek at my mother in the park. She is standing in a circle, chatting with a group of women who are taking other people's children on an afternoon outing. They look like a Third World Parent-Teacher Association meeting.

I quickly jump into a cab heading back to the office. Would Ma have said hello had she been the one to see me first?

As the cab races away from the park, it occurs to me that perhaps one day I would chase an old woman down a street by mistake and that old woman would be somebody else's mother, who I would have mistaken for mine.

Day women come out when nobody expects them.

Tonight on the subway, I will get up and give my seat to a pregnant woman or a lady about Ma's age.

My mother, who stuffs thimbles in her mouth and then blows up her cheeks like Dizzy Gillespie while sewing yet another Raggedy Ann doll that she names Suzette after me.

I will have all these little Suzettes in case you never have any babies, which looks more and more like it is going to happen.

My mother, who had me when she was thirty-three—*l'âge du Christ*—at the age that Christ died on the cross.

That's a blessing, believe you me, even if American doctors say by that time you can make retarded babies.

My mother, who sews lace collars on my company softball T-shirts when she does my laundry.

Why, you can't you look like a lady playing softball?

My mother, who never went to any of my Parent-Teacher Association meetings when I was in school.

You're so good anyway. What are they going to tell me? I don't want to make you ashamed of this day woman. Shame is heavier than a hundred bags of salt.

ξ

Clearly Danticat loves both her characters: the mother and the daughter.

Like a fine writer, the daughter in "New York Day Women" is an excellent observer. Through her observations, we come to "see" and "know" her mother.

In your journal, answer the following questions:

§ What does the mother look like? Why doesn't Danticat give us all the physical details at once? What is gained by giving these details gradually?

§ What do we know about the mother's history? Her memories? Her habits?

§ Buying hot dogs, sewing lace collars on a softball uniform, watching the lottery drawing but never playing, never visiting her daughter's work, all mean something. What do these actions say about the mother's character? What do her reactions to the bicycle messenger, the white child, the taxi drivers say about her?

§ Though the mother doesn't speak directly in the story, Danticat nonetheless lets us hear her voice. *"Oh, no, he doesn't kiss me that way anymore." "Many graves to kiss when I go back."* Examine the mother's dialogue. How do her comments deepen her character? Tell us more about her?

The daughter is an interesting character. Her main action is following her mother on her lunch hour and near the story's end she decides to give up her seat on the subway to a pregnant lady or someone about her mother's age. What does this decision mean? How is this decision based upon the daughter's reactions to her mother? Reread the story, paying careful attention to the daughter's reactions, thoughts about, and speech with her mother. What do you learn about the daughter?

Danticat's story *shows* us a great deal about the mother and daughter in a brief amount of time. What is the history between the two women? How far apart is the Haitian immigrant mother and her Americanized daughter? How close are they?

The more typical mother/daughter actions/reactions are absent. The daughter doesn't walk up and say "Hi, Mom." Instead, the daughter is, literally, spying on her mother and the two women never once meet.

Danticat's characters are neither typical nor stereotypical; they are complex, multidimensional people with actions, reactions, thoughts, and speech captured on the page.

In your journal, write a paragraph about what you have learned about characterization reading Danticat's story.

Revise the characterization you wrote in Exercise 2, adding and developing other qualities of your character.

Readers *want* to become involved in characters' lives. Readers *want* thoughts and feelings. Readers *want* you to create successful stories about what it means to be human.

Celebrate your new understanding of characterization!

6

CREATING PLOT

Character drives plot.

Plot happens; it is the action, the sequence of events in your story. Action disconnected from character is bound to fail. An erupting volcano, while interesting, becomes terrifying when readers fear for the young boy trapped by it. A moonlit romantic evening is insignificant without star-crossed lovers. High school rituals lack comedy if we don't care about the too tall girl anxious about college, her latest outbreak of acne, and finding a date for the senior prom. Once readers care about characters, they'll want to know what happens to them next.

The best plots never run smoothly. As a writer, loving your characters also means, paradoxically, putting them at risk. Risk is generated by plot conflict—specific obstacles, trials, challenges to your characters' emotional, spiritual, psychological, and/or physical well-being.

Sexual conflicts, family conflicts, cultural conflicts, money conflicts, all can present obstacles and challenges to your characters. Sometimes the unexpected—a brutal slaying, an accident, a mugging—can create conflict. Even good news—inheriting a great deal of money, being asked to perform as the star's understudy—can create tension and stress. The fundamental difference between comedy and drama is how lightly a writer manages risk. Inheriting money can lead to murder or giddy excitement. An accident which kills a family member is infinitely more tragic than a broken leg on the slopes. Ultimately, it will be the sequence of plot choices you make which will determine whether your story has a happy or unhappy ending.

The Cinderella story *always* has a happy ending. A lost glass slipper, a wicked stepmother and stepsisters provide modest obstacles for the lovers to overcome. The newest televised version of Cinderella, starring Brandy and Whitney Houston, follows the same basic plot, providing the typical feel-good wedding conclusion. However, more conflict, more risk to the characters' well-being could lead to a bittersweet or possibly downright unhappy ending. What if the royal subjects objected to the Prince's interracial marriage? What if Cinderella was an antimonarchist? What if another woman—possibly a stepsister?—also fit that incredibly small shoe and forced the Prince to marry her? What if there wasn't a fairy godmother? Like ordinary people, the Prince and Cinderella would have had to stumble their way to true love, and like ordinary people, they would have risked missing their opportunity to live happily ever after.

Most plots will involve a key *protagonist* and *antagonist*—in other words, a good person (flawed but modestly or outrageously heroic) and a bad person (a tormentor, with possibly redeemable qualities). Protagonist Thelma wants/needs/desires something while antagonist Damien tries to undermine/terrorize/stop her.

MY BEST ADVICE
Good plotting means forcing the "unthinkable,"
risking your characters until they surrender or else
rise to the challenge.

Most plots are familiar—boy meets girl, loses girl, finds girl; a hero's/heroine's adventurous journey to self-identity; an innocent pitted against a corrupt political society, etc.—but every culture contributes a new lens, a refreshing take on familiar stories.

One plot, however, that is truly cultural-specific to the African American tradition is the slave narrative. Slave narratives, originally autobiographical memoirs and abolitionist tracts, have become fictionalized cores of our literary tradition. William Wells Brown's *Clotel; or, The President's Daughter,* Gayle Jones's *Corregidora,* Alex Haley's *Roots,* Margaret Walker's *Jubilee,* Sherley Anne Williams' *Dessa Rose,* Toni Morrison's *Beloved,* Charles Johnson's *Middle Passage,* Jewelle Gomez's *The Gilda Stories,* Octavia Butler's *Kindred,* and many other novels and stories evoke slavery and its legacy.

The basic plot of a slave narrative is always intensely character-based. Readers follow the travails of a slave who escapes to freedom. Add a compelling historical and emotional pull, and you have a superb conflict-based plot. Even the newly popular *Amistad* story is a variant on the traditional slave narrative.

Oral slave narratives were recorded as early as 1720. Frederick Douglass' 1845 narrative, *"written by himself,"* begins with *"I was born . . ."* Douglass systematically establishes sympathy for the child, Douglass, who as the bastard son of his master doesn't know his birthday, rarely sees his mother, and witnesses the horrific whipping of his Aunt Hester. Douglass' tale of escape is character-driven. Once readers care about Douglass, how can we not care about what happens to him?

Plot is sometimes explained as "Beginning," "Climactic Middle," and "End."

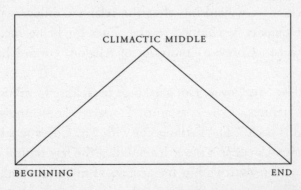

Unfortunately, this graph is misleading because it oversimplifies conflict. Except for the climactic middle, readers are bound to be bored because the story line is too smooth and structured.

Good story conflict is much more like a strong, intensifying heartbeat—with tension rising and falling, rising and falling until a climactic pitch is reached. After each pulse, the reader is pulled forward by the question "Then what happens?"

For example, Douglass, in his narrative, experiences many conflicts which put him at risk psychologically, physically, and emotionally.

On Colonel Lloyd's plantation in Maryland, the child Douglass experiences the "savage barbarity" of overseer Gore. He is traumatized when Gore shoots a slave through the head and he learns it was worth "a half-cent to kill a 'nigger,' and a half-cent to bury one."

Then what happens?

Douglass is shipped to Baltimore to serve as personal slave for the child Thomas Auld. He discovers the power of reading. Risking punishment, he "tricks," like a trickster figure, the white boys into teaching him to read.

Then what happens?

Learning makes Douglass more aware of slavery's subtler cruelties. At twelve, he despairs about being a slave for life and contemplates suicide. Hearing about abolitionists gives him hope. He forms a new desire—to learn how to write so he might one day write a pass which would allow him to escape.

And then?

Douglass is sent back to Colonel Lloyd's plantation and the barbarity is even more a hardship after the relative "milder slavery" of Baltimore. Douglass is whipped several times for being incorrigible. He's given to Mr. Covey, a "professor of religion," to be "broken."

Then?

Abused by Mr. Covey, Douglass begs for release from his Master. His Master refuses. Covey assaults Douglass and, unexpectedly, Douglass fights back! "The battle point with Mr. Covey was the turning-point in my career as a slave. It rekindled the few expiring embers of freedom, and revived within me a sense of my own manhood."

Then?

Douglass resolves to plot an escape and plans to take his friends along with him. They are betrayed and taken to jail. Douglass is accused of being the ringleader and is shipped back to Baltimore. Having vowed to strike back when attacked, he is battered by white carpenters. He resolves to escape again.

Then?

He takes flight to New York and succeeds in escaping slavery's cruelty. Homeless, without funds, subject to "legalized kidnappers," bounty hunters, distrustful of everyone, he nonetheless rejoices, sends for his intended wife, and after marrying, the two travel on to New Bedford, Massachusetts, and a new, the reader hopes, far happier life.

If you chart the conflict in Douglass' *Narrative,* it might look like this:

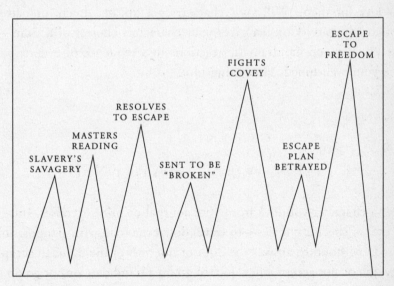

Passionate, spiking heartbeats. Continual conflicts thwart Douglass' desires until he achieves his goal of freedom, the resolution to his conflicts.

The plot—what happens, the sequence of events—is always a point/counterpoint, attack/counterattack to the protagonist's desires and needs. Conflicts actually help Douglass change and grow into his manhood. This transformation of Douglass from an enslaved boy into a free man is what makes the conclusion so satisfying! The risks he took for freedom were well worth it.

Plots can have many variations. Gender, in particular, can potently alter tales. In 1861, Harriet Jacobs published *Incidents in the Life of a Slave Girl.* The plot is essentially a heroine's escape from slavery into freedom. But rather than Douglass' physical battles against oppressive males, the protagonist, Linda Brent (who is Harriet Jacobs' stand-in), battles psychologically the sexual harassment of her Master and the humiliating disdain of her Mistress. Also, unlike the childless Douglass, Jacobs escapes for seven years to a stuffy coffin-sized garret so she can watch over her growing children and still evade her Master's sexual advances. Her freedom, in large measure, is psychological and spiritual until, eventually, she physically escapes to the North.

By exploring the struggles of your characters, you demonstrate your love for them. Will your character get up, get down, or barrel through adversity? Conflict gives your characters choices of actions—these choices, specific dramatic reactions to a sequence of events, become your well-tuned, fascinating plot!

EXERCISE 1

"THEN WHAT HAPPENS?"

Select a character you love from your journal or prior exercises. Imagine a set of specific choices—to travel down the road with signposts or the road without, to answer the door or not answer the door, to accept a new job or not accept a new job, to go on a blind date or not go on a blind date.

After your character makes the first choice, ask yourself, "Then what happens? What goes wrong? What conflict does my character have to face?" Write a summary paragraph detailing your character's reactions to the conflict.

Then what happens? Introduce another set of choices. Something else goes wrong. What choices does your character have to face now?

Then what happens? Something else goes awry. What does your character choose to do?

Then what happens?

Continue this exercise for at least six paragraphs and include six choices your character has to make in response to obstacles.

Reread your paragraphs. Did you introduce an antagonist? Chances are you did. It's natural and dramatic to have another person serve as adversary. Sometimes adversaries can be inanimate. Nature offers a wide range of elements which can threaten your character's survival—desert heat, arctic cold, a storm-tossed sea, the vacuum of outer space, etc. Malfunctioning computers are antagonists in many science fiction dramas; a magic elixir may threaten a fantasy's hero's soul. Most realistic fiction, however, will be about communities and social relationships.

Of the six conflicts your character had to face, did they get increasingly riskier, harsher? If not, revise, making the conflicts increasingly more significant, more threatening to your character's well-being.

Were the six conflicts you imagined only external or internal? Can you revise and do both? Can your character be threatened physically and physiologically?

Review your sequence of events. How much more would have to happen before your character could have either a happy or an unhappy ending? Do you like your plot sketch? Are there elements which can be used to craft a story? What conflicts would you keep? Which would you discard? Why?

EXERCISE 2

PLOT'S PASSIONATE EKG

Select a short story and a novel you admire. These should be tales you couldn't put down—stories that held your interest and refused to let you sleep, eat, do anything besides live in its fictional world!

Graph the conflict for the story and then for the novel. For every significant obstacle to the character's needs and desires, draw a line sloping upward; whenever the tension is resolved (even momentarily), draw a line sloping downward. As the risks to the protagonist's well-being increase, pitch the upward slope more steeply. Continue until the story's conclusion. (See the Douglass example on page 85.)

How erratic is the heartbeat? In a well-plotted story, the tension will rise and fall, rise and fall, then rise until the intensity, as in sex, demands a passionate and heartfelt climax. Is the story's resolution still relatively intense or does the plot unwind to a moment's peace?

Compare the electrocardiogram, the EKG, of the short story versus that of the novel. What are the differences? The novel's plot should be a complicated, extended, pulsing heartbeat; the story is distilled, a more focused EKG—still complicated but to a lesser degree than the novel form.

Just as I graphed Douglass' plot, try graphing one of your own stories or stories-in-progress. Remember to spike upward (/) for each conflict, then downward (\) as the conflict is temporarily or permanently resolved.

Is your plot's heartbeat an interesting, passionate array of spikes and deep declines (ascents and descents)? If not, why not? Is the plot character-driven? Are there enough challenges to your characters to make an interesting sequence of events?

For further study, an excellent example of a novel plot is Wright's *Native Son.* The pulse of this story is never still. Broadly, the conflict rises during the rat killing in Chapter One . . . then it spikes dramatically when Bigger unintentionally murders the white girl . . . then it spikes even higher when Bigger intentionally kills his girlfriend . . . then higher still as Bigger is chased and captured by the police . . . the resolution is Bigger's trial and impending death. Graphing *Native Son,* you'll find dozens of smaller, midsized conflicts in the story. Visually, the graph demonstrates why the character-driven plot is so incredibly gripping.

. . .

Novels with multiple main characters will require a graph for each character. Girlfriend stories, in particular, alternate plots of the girlfriends overcoming obstacles to achieve varying levels of happiness. In Lorene Cary's *Pride,* for example, four women overcome different love conflicts. Roz discovers that one of her best friends has been sleeping with her husband. Tam, in love with her sister's boyfriend, has to decide whether she wants to be vulnerable to romance and marriage. Arneatha, a widow, has to decide whether to nurture an abandoned African child. Audrey needs to overcome alcoholism to win her son's love and respect. Each individual's conflict affects the group; when the friends' travails are resolved, the girlfriends heal and strengthen their emotional bonds.

Someday you may be encouraged to write about multiple protagonists—their lives might be unified by friendship or family relations, by setting, adversity, or ideology. Remember, the key is to create conflict individually as well as within the web of relationships. Whether you have one, two, or three protagonists, tensions within and between characters will fuel your story and keep readers interested.

EXERCISE 3

SIFTING, DIGGING THROUGH PLOTS

Studying plots, you begin to understand how stories work from the inside out.

Toni Cade Bambara's "My Man Bovanne" is a favorite story of mine. The plot is simple: a middle-aged woman asks an old blind man to dance:

> . . . I press up close to dance with Bovanne who blind
> and I'm hummin and he hummin, chest to chest like
> talkin. Not jammin my breasts into the man. Wasn't bout
> tits. Was bout vibrations. And he dug it and asked what
> color dress I had on and how my hair was fixed and how

I was doin without a man, not nosy but nice-like, and
who was at this affair . . .

Everyone at the party objects, spiking moments of conflict with
snide remarks and glares. Eventually, the woman's three children draw
her into the kitchen to chastise her: "You were making a spectacle of
yourself out there dancin like that" . . . "Like a bitch in heat" . . .
"How do you think that look for a woman your age?" The conflict
intensifies.

Then what happens?

After trying to defend herself against her children, whom she
thinks ought to understand her better, the mother declares, climacti-
cally, "You know what you can all kiss."

The resolution, the ending.

The mother decides to take the blind man home, where she
imagines she'll feed him, bathe him, massage him, and love him—
"just like the hussy my daughter always say I was."

The above plot is character-driven. Passionate. Risks to the
mother's image of herself as a still attractive, sensual woman spur the
story's events.

Go to your bookshelf and spend an evening sifting through
old stories you've enjoyed. When you find one you especially like,
write down the basic plot. Then add a new conflict for the protagonist. You've added a plot twist! Next, have the protagonist be
thwarted in his/her resolution. If the story you're modeling had a
happy ending, then create conflicts and choices which make for a
sad ending (or vice versa). Lastly, redo the plot so the ending is
mixed, bittersweet.

Examine the original basic plot and the plot changes you've
made. Is the story still interesting? How many new events did you add
make the new endings work plausibly? What did you learn by
ulating someone else's basic plot? Will you approach your own
differently in the future?

· · ·

In your journal, explain what you have learned about plot.

PLOT STUDY

ZORA NEALE HURSTON'S "SWEAT"

Hurston's Delia Jones is a woman with the desire for a little less "sweat," or hard work, in her life and the need to be respected and well loved. When her husband thwarts her needs and desires, she chooses to take action. The plot is simple, but it illuminates well how one character's quest for deliverance—one decision to take direct action—can transform self-identity, a marriage, an entire fictional world.

IT WAS ELEVEN o'clock of a Spring night in Florida. It was Sunday. Any other night, Delia Jones would have been in bed for two hours by this time. But she was a washwoman, and Monday morning meant a great deal to her. So she collected the soiled clothes on Saturday when she returned the clean things. Sunday night after church, she sorted them and put the white things to soak. It saved her almost a half day's start. A great hamper in the bedroom held the clothes that she brought home. It was so much neater than a number of bundles lying around.

She squatted in the kitchen floor beside the great pile of clothes, sorting them into small heaps according to color, and humming a song in a mournful key, but wondering through it all where Sykes, her husband, had gone with her horse and buckboard.

Just then something long, round, limp and black fell upon her shoulders and slithered to the floor beside her. A great terror took hold of her. It softened her knees and dried her mouth so that it was a full minute before she could cry out or move. Then she saw that it was the big bull whip her husband liked to carry when he drove.

She lifted her eyes to the door and saw him standing there bent over with laughter at her fright. She screamed at him.

"Sykes, what you throw dat whip on me like dat? You know it would skeer me—looks just like a snake, an' you knows how skeered Ah is of snakes."

"Course Ah knowed it! That's how come Ah done it." He slapped his leg with his hand and almost rolled on the ground in his mirth. "If you such a big fool dat you got to have a fit over a earth worm or a string, Ah don't keer how bad Ah skeer you."

"You aint got no business doing it. Gawd knows it's a sin. Some day Ah'm gointuh drop dead from some of yo' foolishness. 'Nother thing, where you been wid mah rig? Ah feeds dat pony. He aint fuh you to be drivin' wid no bull whip."

"Yo sho is one aggravatin' nigger woman!" he declared and stepped into the room. She resumed her work and did not answer him at once. "Ah done tole you time and again to keep them white folks' clothes outa dis house."

He picked up the whip and glared down at her. Delia went on with her work. She went out into the yard and returned with a galvanized tub and set it on the washbench. She saw that Sykes had kicked all of the clothes together again, and now stood in her way truculently, his whole manner hoping, *praying,* for an argument. But she walked calmly around him and commenced to re-sort the things.

"Next time, Ah'm gointer to kick 'em outdoors," he threatened as he struck a match along the leg of his corduroy breeches.

Delia never looked up from her work, and her thin, stooped shoulders sagged further.

"Ah aint for no fuss t'night Sykes. Ah just come from taking sacrament at the church house."

He snorted scornfully. "Yeah, you just come from de church house on a Sunday night, but heah you is gone to work on them clothes. You ain't nothing but a hypocrite. One of them amen-corner Christians—sing, whoop, shout, then come home and wash white folks clothes on the Sabbath."

He stepped roughly upon the whitest pile of things, kicking them helter-skelter as he crossed the room. His wife gave a little scream of dismay, and quickly gathered them together again.

"Sykes, you quit grindin' dirt into these clothes! How can Ah git through by Sat'day if Ah don't start on Sunday?"

"Ah don't keer if you never git through. Anyhow, Ah done promised Gawd and a couple of other men, Ah aint gointer have it in mah house. Don't gimme no lip neither, else Ah'll throw 'em out and put mah fist up side yo' head to boot."

Delia's habitual meekness seemed to slip from her shoulders like a blown scarf. She was on her feet; her poor little body, her bare knuckly hands bravely defying the strapping hulk before her.

"Looka heah, Sykes, you done gone too far. Ah been married to you fur fifteen years, and Ah been takin' in washin' for fifteen years. Sweat, sweat, sweat! Work and sweat, cry and sweat, pray and sweat!"

"What's that got to do with me?" he asked brutally.

"What's it got to do with you, Sykes? Mah tub of suds is filled yo' belly with vittles more times than yo' hands is filled it. Mah sweat is done paid for this house and Ah reckon Ah kin keep on sweatin' in it."

She seized the iron skillet from the stove and struck a defensive pose, which act surprised him greatly, coming from her. It cowed him and he did not strike her as he usually did.

"Naw you won't," she panted, "that ole snaggle-toothed black woman you runnin' with aint comin' heah to pile up on *mah* sweat and blood. You aint paid for nothin' on this place, and Ah'm gointer stay right heah till Ah'm toted out foot foremost."

"Well, you better quit gittin' me filed up, else they'll be totin' you out sooner than you expect. Ah'm so tired of you Ah don't know whut to do. Gawd! how Ah hates skinny wimmen!"

A little awed by this new Delia, he sidled out of the door and slammed the back gate after him. He did not say where he had gone, but she knew too well. She knew very well that he would not return until nearly daybreak also. Her work over, she went on to bed but not to sleep at once. Things had come to a pretty pass!

She lay awake, gazing upon the debris that cluttered their matrimonial trail. Not an image left standing along the way. Anything like flowers had long ago been drowned in the salty stream that had been pressed from her heart. Her tears, her sweat, her blood. She had brought love to the union and he had brought a longing for the flesh. Two months after the wedding, he had given her the first brutal beating. She had the memory of numerous trips to Orlando with all of his wages when he had returned to her penniless, even before the first year had passed. She was young and soft then, but now she thought of her knotty, muscled limbs, her harsh knuckly hands, and drew herself up into an unhappy little ball in the middle of the big feather bed. Too late now to hope for love, even if it were not Bertha it would be someone else. This case differed from the others only in that she was bolder than the others. Too late for everything except her little home. She had built it for her old days, and planted one by one the trees and flowers there. It was lovely to her, lovely.

Somehow before sleep came, she found herself saying aloud: "Oh well, whatever goes over the Devil's back, is got to come under his belly. Sometime or ruther, Sykes, like everybody else, is gointer reap his sowing." After that she was able to build a spiritual earthworks against her husband. His shells could no longer reach her. *Amen.* She went to sleep and slept until he announced his presence in bed by kicking her feet and rudely snatching the cover away.

"Gimme some kivah heah, an' git yo' damn foots over on yo' own side! Ah oughter mash you in yo' mouf fuh drawing dat skillet on me."

Delia went clear to the rail without answering him. A triumphant indifference to all that he was or did.

The week was as full of work for Delia as all other weeks, and Saturday found her behind her little pony, collecting and delivering clothes.

It was a hot, hot day near the end of July. The village men on Joe Clarke's porch even chewed cane listlessly. They did not hurl the caneknots as usual. They let them dribble over the edge of the porch. Even conversation had collapsed under the heat.

"Heah comes Delia Jones," Jim Merchant said, as the shaggy

pony came 'round the bend of the road toward them. The rusty buckboard was heaped with baskets of crisp, clean laundry.

"Yep," Joe Lindsay agreed. "Hot or col', rain or shine, jes ez
reg'lar ez de weeks roll roun' Delia carries 'em an' fetches 'em on
Sat'day."

"She better if she wanter eat," said Moss. "Syke Jones aint wuth
de shot an' powder hit would tek tuh kill 'em. Not to *huh* he aint."

"He sho' aint," Walter Thomas chimed in. "It's too bad, too,
cause she wuz a right pritty lil trick when he got huh. Ah'd uh mah'ied
huh mahseff if he hadnter beat me to it."

Delia nodded briefly at the men as she drove past.

"Too much knockin' will ruin *any* 'oman. He done beat huh
'nough tuh kill three women, let 'lone change they looks," said Elijah
Mosely. "How Syke kin stommuck dat big black greasy Mogul he's
layin' roun' wid, gets me. Ah swear dat eight-rock couldn't kiss a
sardine can Ah done thowed out de back do' 'way las' yeah."

"Aw, she's fat, thass how come. He's allus been crazy 'bout fat
women," put in Merchant. "He'd a'been tied up wid one long time
ago if he could a' found one tuh have him. Did Ah tell yuh 'bout him
come sidlin' round *mah* wife—bringin' her a basket uh pee-cans outa
his yard fuh a present? Yes-sir, mah wife! She tol' him tuh take 'em
right straight back home, cause Delia works so hard ovah dat washtub
she reckon everything on de place taste lak sweat an' soapsuds. Ah jus'
wisht Ah'd a' caught 'im 'roun' dere! Ah'd a' made his hips ketch on
fiah down dat shell road."

"Ah know he done it, too. Ah sees 'im grinnin' at every 'oman
dat passes," Walter Thomas said. "But even so, he useter eat some
mighty big hunks uh humble pie tuh git dat lil' 'oman he got. She wuz
ez pritty ez a speckled pup! Dat wuz fifteen years ago. He useter be so
skeered uh losin' huh, she could make him do some parts of a husband's duty. Dey never wuz de same in de mind."

"There oughter be a law about him," said Lindsay. "He aint fit
tuh carry guts tuh a bear."

Clarke spoke for the first time. "Taint no law on earth dat kin
make a man be decent if it aint in 'im. There's plenty men dat takes

a wife lak dey do a joint uh sugar-cane. It's round, juicy an' sweet when dey gits it. But dey squeeze an' grind, squeeze an' grind an' wring tell dey wring every drop uh pleasure dat's in 'em out. When dey's satisfied dat dey is wrung dry, dey treats 'em jes lak dey do a cane-chew. Dey throws 'em away. Dey knows whut dey is doin' while dey is at it, an' hates theirselves fuh it but they keeps on hangin' after huh tell she's empty. Den dey hates huh fuh bein' a cane-chew an' in de way."

"We oughter take Syke an' dat stray 'oman uh his'n down in Lake Howell swamp an' lay on de rawhide till they cain't say 'Lawd a' mussy.' He allus wuz uh ovahbearin' niggah, but since dat white 'oman from up north done teached 'im how to run a automobile, he done got too biggety to live—an' we oughter kill 'im," Old Man Anderson advised.

A grunt of approval went around the porch. But the heat was melting their civic virtue and Elijah Moseley began to bait Joe Clarke.

"Come on, Joe, git a melon outa dere an' slice it up for yo' customers. We'se all sufferin' wid de heat. De bear's done got *me!*"

"Thass right, Joe, a watermelon is jes' whut Ah needs tuh cure de eppizudicks," Walter Thomas joined forces with Moseley. "Come on dere, Joe. We all is steady customers an' you aint set us up in a long time. Ah chooses dat long, bowlegged Floridy favorite."

"A god, an' be dough. You all gimme twenty cents and slice away," Clarke retorted. "Ah needs a col' slice m'self. Heah, everybody chip in. Ah'll lend y'll mah meat knife."

The money was quickly subscribed and the huge melon brought forth. At that moment, Sykes and Bertha arrived. A determined silence fell on the porch and the melon was put away again.

Merchant snapped down the blade of his jackknife and moved toward the store door.

"Come on in, Joe, an' gimme a slab uh sow belly an' uh pound uh coffee—almost fuhgot 'twas Sat'day. Got to git on home." Most of the men left also.

Just then Delia drove past on her way home, as Sykes was ordering magnificently for Bertha. It pleased him for Delia to see.

"Git whutsoever yo' heart desires, Honey. Wait a minute, Joe.

Give huh two botles uh strawberry soda-water, uh quart uh parched ground-peas, an' a block uh chewin' gum."

With all this they left the store, with Sykes reminding Bertha that this was his town and she could have it if she wanted it.

The men returned soon after they left, and held their watermelon feast. "Where did Syke Jones git dat 'oman from nohow?" Lindsay asked.

"Ova Apopka. Guess dey musta been cleanin' out de town when she lef'. She don't look lak a thing but a hunk uh liver wid hair on it."

"Well, she sho' kin squall," Dave Carter contributed. "When she gits ready tuh laff, she jes' opens huh mouf an' latches it back tuh de las' notch. No ole grandpa alligator down in Lake Bell ain't got nothin' on huh."

Bertha had been in town three months now. Sykes was still paying her room rent at Della Lewis'—the only house in town that would have taken her in. Sykes took her frequently to Winter Park to "stomps." He still assured her that he was the swellest man in the state.

"Sho' you kin have dat lil' ole house soon's Ah kin git dat 'oman outa dere. Everything b'longs tuh me an' you sho' kin have it. Ah sho' 'bominates uh skinny 'oman. Lawdy, you sho' is got one portly shape on you! You kin git *anything* you wants. Dis is *mah* town an' you sho' kin have it."

Delia's work-worn knees crawled over the earth in Gethsemane and up the rocks of Calvary many, many times during these months. She avoided the villagers and meeting places in her efforts to be blind and deaf. But Bertha nullified this to a degree, by coming to Delia's house to call Sykes out to her at the gate.

Delia and Sykes fought all the time now with no peaceful interludes. They slept and ate in silence. Two or three times Delia had attempted a timid friendliness, but she was repulsed each time. It was plain that the breaches must remain agape.

The sun had burned July to August. The heat streamed down like a million hot arrows, smiting all things living upon the earth.

Grass withered, leaves browned, snakes went blind in shedding and men and dogs went mad. Dog days!

Delia came home one day and found Sykes there before her. She wondered, but started to go on into the house without speaking, even though he was standing in the kitchen door and she must either stoop under his arm or ask him to move. He made no room for her. She noticed a soap box beside the steps, but paid no particular attention to it, knowing that he must have brought it there. As she was stooping to pass under his outstretched arm, he suddenly pushed her backward, laughingly.

"Look in de box dere Delia, Ah done brung yuh somethin'!"

She nearly fell upon the box in her stumbling, and when she saw what it held, she all but fainted outright.

"Syke! Syke, mah Gawd! You take dat rattlesnake 'way from heah! You *gottuh*. Oh, Jesus, have mussy!"

"Ah aint gut tuh do nothin' uh de kin'—fact is Ah aint got tuh do nothin' but die. Taint no use uh you puttin' on airs makin' out lak you skeered uh dat snake—he's gointer stay right heah tell he die. He wouldn't bite me cause Ah knows how tuh handle 'im. Nohow he wouldn't risk breakin' out his fangs 'gin *yo'* skinny laigs."

"Naw, now Syke, don't keep dat thing 'roun' heah tuh skeer me tuh death. You knows Ah'm even feared uh earth worms. Thass de biggest snake Ah evah did see. Kill 'im Syke, please."

"Doan ast me tuh do nothin' fuh yuh. Goin' 'roun' tryin' to be so damn asterperious. Naw, Ah aint gonna kill it. Ah think uh damn sight mo' uh him dan you! Dat's a nice snake an' anybody doan lak 'im kin jes' hit de grit."

The village soon heard that Sykes had the snake, and came to see and ask questions.

"How de hen-fire did you ketch dat six-root rattler, Syke?" Thomas asked.

"He's full uh frogs so he caint hardly move, thass how Ah eased up on 'm. But Ah'm a snake charmer an' knows how tuh handle 'em. Shux, dat aint nothin'. Ah could ketch on eve'y day if Ah so wanted tuh."

"Whut he needs is a heavy hick'ry club leaned real heavy on his head. Dat's de bes 'way tuh charm a rattlesnake."

"Naw, Walt, y'll jes' don't understand dese diamon' backs lak Ah do," said Syke in a superior tone of voice.

The village agreed with Walter, but the snake stayed on. His box remained by the kitchen door with its screen wire covering. Two or three days later it had digested its meal of frogs and literally came to life. It rattled at every movement in the kitchen or the yard. One day as Delia came down the kitchen steps she saw his chalky-white fangs curved like scimitars hung in the wire meshes. This time she did not run away with averted eyes as usual. She stood for a long time in the doorway in a red fury that grew bloodier for every second that she regarded the creature that was her torment.

That night she broached the subject as soon as Sykes sat down to the table.

"Syke, Ah wants you tuh take dat snake 'way fum heah. You done starved me an' Ah put up widcher, you done beat me an Ah took dat, but you done kilt all mah insides bringin' dat varmint heah."

Sykes poured out a saucer full of coffee and drank it deliberately before he answered her.

"A whole lot Ah keer 'bout how you feels inside uh out. Dat snake aint goin' no damn wheah till Ah gits ready fuh 'im tuh go. So fur as beatin' is concerned, yuh aint took near all dat you gointer take ef yuh stay 'roun' *me.*"

Delia pushed back her plate and got up from the table. "Ah hates you, Sykes," she said calmly. "Ah hates you tuh de same degree dat Ah useter love yuh. Ah done took an' took till mah belly is full up tuh mah neck. Dat's de reason Ah got mah letter fum de church an' moved mah membership tuh Woodbridge—so Ah don't haftuh take no sacrament wid yuh. Ah don't wantuh see yuh 'round' me atall. Lay 'round' wid dat 'oman all yuh wants tuh, but gwan 'way fum me an' mah house. Ah hates yuh lak uh suck-egg dog."

Sykes almost let the huge wad of corn bread and collard greens he was chewing fall out of his mouth in amazement. He had a hard time whipping himself to the proper fury to try to answer Delia.

"Well, Ah'm glad you does hate me. Ah'm sho' tiahed uh you hangin' ontuh me. Ah don't want yuh. Look at yuh stringey ole neck! Yo' raw-bony laigs an' arms is enough tuh cut uh man tuh death. You looks jes' lak de devvul's doll-baby tuh *me*. You caint hate me no worse dan Ah hates you. Ah been hatin' *you* fuh years."

"Yo' ole black hide don't look lak nothin' tuh me, but uh passle uh wrinkled up rubber, wid yo' big ole yeahs flappin' on each side lak up paih uh buzzard wings. Don't think Ah'm gointuh be run 'way fum mah house neither. Ah'm goin' tuh de white folks about *you*, mah young man, de very nex' time yo lay yo' hand's on me. Mah cup is done run ovah." Delia said this with no signs of fear and Sykes departed from the house, threatening her, but made not the slightest move to carry out any of them.

That night he did not return at all, and the next day being Sunday, Delia was glad that she did not have to quarrel before she hitched up her pony and drove the four miles to Woodbridge.

She stayed to the night service—"love feast"—which was very warm and full of spirit. In the emotional winds her domestic trials were borne far and wide so that she sang as she drove homeward,

"Jurden water, black an' col'
Chills de body, not de soul
An' Ah wantah cross Jurden in uh calm time."

She came from the barn to the kitchen door and stopped.

"Whut's de mattah, ol' satan, you aint kickin' up yo' racket?" She addressed the snake's box. Complete silence. She went on into the house with a new hope in its birth struggles. Perhaps her threat to go to the white folks had frightened Sykes! Perhaps he was sorry! Fifteen years of misery and suppression had brought Delia to the place where she would hope *anything* that looked towards a way over or through her wall of inhibitions.

She felt in the match safe behind the stove at once for a match. There was only one there.

"Dat niggah wouldn't fetch nothin' heah tuh save his rotten

neck, but he kin run thew whut Ah brings quick enough. Now he done toted off nigh on tuh haff uh box uh matches. He done had dat 'oman heah in mah house, too."

Nobody but a woman could tell how she knew this even before she struck the match. But she did and it put her into a new fury.

Presently she brought in the tubs to put the white things to soak. This time she decided she need not bring the hamper out of the bedroom; she would go in there and do the sorting. She picked up the pot-bellied lamp and went in. The room was small and the hamper stood hard by the foot of the white iron bed. She could sit and reach through the bedposts—resting as she worked.

"Ah wantah cross Jurden in uh calm time." She was singing again. The mood of the "love feast" had returned. She threw back the lid of the basket almost gaily. Then, moved by both horror and terror, she sprang back toward the door. *There lay the snake in the basket!* He moved sluggishly at first, but even as she turned round and round, jumped up and down in an insanity of fear, he began to stir vigorously. She saw him pouring his awful beauty from the basket upon the bed, then she seized the lamp and ran as fast as she could to the kitchen. The wind from the open door blew out the light and the darkness added to her terror. She sped to the darkness of the yard, slamming the door after her before she thought to set down the lamp. She did not feel safe even on the ground, so she climbed up in the hay barn.

There for an hour or more she lay sprawled upon the hay a gibbering wreck.

Finally she grew quiet, and after that, coherent thought. With this, stalked through her a cold, blood rage. Hours of this. A period of introspection, a space of retrospection, then a mixture of both. Out of this an awful calm.

"Well, Ah done de bes' Ah could. If things aint right, Gawd knows taint mah fault."

She went to sleep—a twitchy sleep—and woke up to a faint gray sky. There was a loud hollow sound below. She peered out. Sykes was at the wood-pile, demolishing a wire-covered box.

He hurried to the kitchen door, but hung outside there some minutes before he entered, and stood some minutes more inside before he closed it after him.

The gray in the sky was spreading. Delia descended without fear now, and crouched beneath the low bedroom window. The drawn shade shut out the dawn, shut in the night. But the thin walls held back no sound.

"Dat ol' scratch is woke up now!" She mused at the tremendous whirr inside, which every woodsman knows, is one of the sound illusions. The rattler is a ventriloquist. His whirr sounds to the right, to the left, straight ahead, behind, close under foot—everywhere but where it is. Woe to him who guesses wrong unless he is prepared to hold up his end of the argument! Sometimes he strikes without rattling at all.

Inside, Sykes heard nothing until he knocked a pot lid off the stove while trying to reach the match safe in the dark. He had emptied his pockets at Bertha's.

The snake seemed to wake up under the stove and Sykes made a quick leap into the bedroom. In spite of the gin he had had, his head was clearing now.

"Mah Gawd!" he chattered, "ef Ah could on'y strack uh light!"

The rattling ceased for a moment as he stood paralyzed. He waited. It seemed that the snake waited also.

"Oh, fuh de light! Ah thought he'd be too sick"—Sykes was muttering to himself when the whirr began again, closer, right underfoot this time. Long before this, Sykes' ability to think had been flattened down to primitive instinct and he leaped—onto the bed.

Outside Delia heard a cry that might have come from a maddened chimpanzee, a stricken gorilla. All the terror, all the horror, all the rage that man possibly could express, without a recognizable human sound.

A tremendous stir inside there, another series of animal screams, the intermittent whirr of the reptile. The shade torn violently down from the window, letting in the red dawn, a huge brown hand seizing the window stick, great dull blows upon the wooden floor punctuating the gibberish of sound long after the rattle of the snake had abruptly subsided. All this Delia could see and hear from her place beneath the window, and it made her ill. She crept over to the four-o'clocks and stretched herself on the cool earth to recover.

She lay there. "Delia, Delia!" She could hear Sykes calling in a most despairing tone as one who expected no answer. The sun crept on up, and he called. Delia could not move—her legs were gone flabby. She never moved, he called, and the sun kept rising.

"Mah Gawd!" She heard him moan, "Mah Gawd fum Heben!" She heard him stumbling about and got up from her flower-bed. The sun was growing warm. As she approached the door she heard him call out hopefully, "Delia, is dat you Ah heah?"

She saw him on his hands and knees as soon as she reached the door. He crept an inch or two toward her—all that he was able, and she saw his horribly swollen neck and his one open eye shining with hope. A surge of pity too strong to support bore her away from that eye that must, could not, fail to see the tubs. He would see the lamp. Orlando with its doctors was too far. She could scarcely reach the Chinaberry tree, where she waited in the growing heat while inside she knew the cold river was creeping up and up to extinguish that eye which must know by now that she knew.

‰

In your journal, answer the following questions:

‰ Describe the "old" Delia versus the "new" Delia. Why is the husband, Sykes, awed by the "new" Delia? What is the essential change in Delia's actions and reactions?

‰ In the paragraph beginning: "She lay awake, gazing upon the debris that cluttered their matrimonial trail," Hurston allows Delia to reflect on her fifteen years of marriage to Sykes. Why is this necessary? What does it add to the story?

≷ Do the villagers' comments about the marriage make you more sympathetic to Delia? Why?

≷ Caught as she is in an abusive marriage, why does the house remain one thing Delia is determined to keep? How does her desire to keep the house fuel the rage she feels when she discovers Sykes has had sex with Bertha in her bed?

≷ *Foreshadowing* is a direct or implied promise that some detail or event will recur significantly within the plot. In the beginning of the story, how does Sykes's bullwhip and Delia's response to it foreshadow Sykes's death by snakebite?

≷ When does Delia actively decide to allow Sykes to be killed?

≷ Scene by scene, graph the conflict in Hurston's "Sweat." You should have a series of rising tensions with releases until, ultimately, the tension keeps rising and building through Sykes's death. What does the last line of the story mean? How does it add a final twist of tension?

In your journal, write a paragraph about what Hurston has taught you about creating an effective plot.

PLOT STUDY

ALICE WALKER'S "NINETEEN FIFTY-FIVE"

All good plots are character-driven. But all plots aren't told in exactly the same way. Time—how much of it passes, how much is condensed—can alter a story's structure. Hurston's "Sweat" takes place during a highly condensed two-month period. Walker's story skips over twenty-two years; yet she marks only the significant years with dates, giving the tale a personal, diarylike, yet also social history effect.

§

1955

THE CAR IS a brandnew red Thunderbird convertible, and it's passed the house more than once. It slows down real slow now, and stops at the curb. An older gentleman dressed like a Baptist deacon gets out on the side near the house, and a young fellow who looks about sixteen gets out on the driver's side. They are white, and I wonder what in the world they doing in this neighborhood.

Well, I say to J. T., put your shirt on, anyway, and let me clean these glasses offa the table.

We had been watching the ballgame on TV. I wasn't actually watching, I was sort of daydreaming, with my foots up in J. T.'s lap.

I seen 'em coming on up the walk, brisk, like they coming to sell something, and then they rung the bell, and J. T. declined to put on a shirt but instead disappeared into the bedroom where the other television is. I turned down the one in the living room; I figured I'd be rid of these two double quick and J. T. could come back out again.

Are you Gracie Mae Still? asked the old guy, when I opened the door and put my hand on the lock inside the screen.

And I don't need to buy a thing, said I.

What makes you think we're sellin'? he asks, in that hearty Southern way that makes my eyeballs ache.

Well, one way or another and they're inside the house and the first thing the young fellow does is raise the TV a couple of decibels. He's about five feet nine, sort of womanish looking, with real dark white skin and a red pouting mouth. His hair is black and curly and he looks like a Loosianna creole.

About one of your songs, says the deacon. He is maybe sixty, with white hair and beard, white silk shirt, black linen suit, black tie and black shoes. His cold gray eyes look like they're sweating.

One of my songs?

Traynor here just *loves* your songs. Don't you Traynor? He nudges Traynor with his elbow. Traynor blinks, says something I can't catch in a pitch I don't register.

The boy learned to sing and dance livin' round you people out in the country. Practically cut his teeth on you.

Traynor looks up at me and bites his thumbnail.

I laugh.

Well, one way or another they leave with my agreement that they can record one of my songs. The deacon writes me a check for five hundred dollars, the boy grunts his awareness of the transaction, and I am laughing all over myself by the time I rejoin J. T.

Just as I am snuggling down beside him though I hear the front door bell going off again.

Forgit his hat? asks J. T.

I hope not, I say.

The deacon stands there leaning on the door frame and once again I'm thinking of those sweaty-looking eyeballs of his. I wonder if sweat makes your eyeballs pink because his are sure pink. Pink and gray and it strikes me that nobody I'd care to know is behind them.

I forgot one little thing, he says pleasantly. I forgot to tell you Traynor and I would like to buy up all of those records you made of the song. I tell you we sure do love it.

Well, love it or not, I'm not so stupid as to let them do that without making 'em pay. So I says, Well, that's gonna cost you. Because, really, that song never did sell all that good, so I was glad they was going to buy it up. But on the other hand, them two listening to my song by themselves, and nobody else getting to hear me sing it, give me a pause.

Well, one way or another the deacon showed me where I would come out ahead on any deal he had proposed so far. Didn't I give you five hundred dollars? he asked. What white man—and don't even need to mention colored—would give you more? We buy up all your records of that particular song: first, you git royalties. Let me ask you, how much you sell that song for in the first place? Fifty dollars? A hundred, I say. And no royalties from it yet, right? Right. Well, when we buy up all of them records you gonna git royalties. And that's gonna make all them race record shops sit up and take notice of Gracie Mae Still. And they gonna push all them other records of yourn they got. And you no doubt will become one of the big name colored recording artists. And then we can offer you another five hundred dollars for letting us do all this for you. And by God you'll be sittin' pretty! You can go out and buy you the kind of outfit a star should have. Plenty sequins and yards of red satin.

I had done unlocked the screen when I saw I could get some more money out of him. Now I held it wide open while he squeezed through the opening between me and the door. He whipped out another piece of paper and I signed it.

He sort of trotted out to the car and slid in beside Traynor, whose head was back against the seat. They swung around in a u-turn in front of the house and then they was gone.

J. T. was putting his shirt on when I got back to the bedroom. Yankees beat the Orioles 10–6, he said. I believe I'll drive out to Paschal's pond and go fishing. Wanta go?

While I was putting on my pants J. T. was holding the two checks.

I'm real proud of a woman that can make cash money without leavin' home, he said. And I said *Umph*. Because we met on the road with me singing in first one little low-life jook after another, making ten dollars a night for myself if I was lucky, and sometimes bringin' home nothing but my life. And J. T. just loved them times. The way I was fast and flashy and always on the go from one town to another. He loved the way my singin' made the dirt farmers cry like babies and the womens shout Honey, hush! But that's mens. They loves any style to which you can get 'em accustomed.

1956

My little grandbaby called me one night on the phone: Little Mama, Little Mama, there's a white man on the television singing one of your songs! Turn on channel 5.

Lord, if it wasn't Traynor. Still looking half asleep from the neck up, but kind of awake in a nasty way from the waist down. He wasn't doing too bad with my song either, but it wasn't just the song the people in the audience was screeching and screaming over, it was that nasty little jerk he was doing from the waist down.

Well, Lord have mercy, I said, listening to him. If I'da closed my eyes, it could have been me. He had followed every turning of my voice, side streets, avenues, red lights, train crossings and all. It give me a chill.

Everywhere I went I heard Traynor singing my song, and all the little white girls just eating it up. I never had so many ponytails switched across my line of vision in my life. They was so *proud*. He was a *genius*.

Well, all that year I was trying to lose weight anyway and that and high blood pressure and sugar kept me pretty well occupied. Traynor had made a smash from a song of mine, I still had seven hundred dollars of the original one thousand dollars in the bank, and I felt if I could just bring my weight down, life would be sweet.

1957

I lost ten pounds in 1956. That's what I give myself for Christmas. And J. T. and me and the children and their friends and grandkids of all description had just finished dinner—over which I had put on nine and a half of my lost ten—when who should appear at the front door but Traynor. Little Mama, Little Mama! It's that white man who sings – – –. The children didn't call it my song anymore. Nobody did. It was funny how that happened. Traynor and the deacon had bought up all my records, true, but on his record he had put "written by Gracie Mae Still." But that was just another name on the label, like "produced by Apex Records."

On the TV he was inclined to dress like the deacon told him. But now he looked presentable.

Merry Christmas, said he.

And same to you, Son.

I don't know why I called him Son. Well, one way or another

they're all our sons. The only requirement is that they be younger than us. But then again, Traynor seemed to be aging by the minute.

You looks tired, I said. Come on in and have a glass of Christmas cheer.

J. T. ain't never in his life been able to act decent to a white man he wasn't working for, but he poured Traynor a glass of bourbon and water, then he took all the children and grandkids and friends and whatnot out to the den. After while I heard Traynor's voice singing the song, coming from the stereo console. It was just the kind of Christmas present my kids would consider cute.

I looked at Traynor, complicit. But he looked like it was the last thing in the world he wanted to hear. His head was pitched forward over his lap, his hands holding his glass and his elbows on his knees.

I done sung that song seem like a million times this year, he said. I sung it on the Grand Ole Opry, I sung it on the Ed Sullivan show. I sung it on Mike Douglas, I sung it at the Cotton Bowl, the Orange Bowl. I sung it at Festivals. I sung it at Fairs. I sung it overseas in Rome, Italy, and once in a submarine *underseas.* I've sung it and sung it, and I'm making forty thousand dollars a day offa it, and you know what, I don't have the faintest notion what that song means.

Whatchumean, what do it mean? It mean what it says. All I could think was: These suckers is making forty thousand a *day* offa my song and now they gonna come back and try to swindle me out of the original thousand.

It's just a song, I said. Cagey. When you fool around with a lot of no count mens you sing a bunch of 'em. I shrugged.

Oh, he said. Well. He started brightening up. I just come by to tell you I think you are a great singer.

He didn't blush, saying that. Just said it straight out.

And I brought you a little Christmas present too. Now you take this little box and you hold it until I drive off. Then you take it outside under that first streetlight back up the street aways in front of that green house. Then you open the box and see . . . Well, just *see.* What had come over this boy, I wondered, holding the box. I looked out the window in time to see another white man come up and get in the car with him and then two more cars full of white mens start out behind him. They was all in long black cars that looked like a funeral procession.

Little Mama, Little Mama, what it is? One of my grandkids come running up and started pulling at the box. It was wrapped in gay Christmas paper—the thick, rich kind that it's hard to picture folks making just to throw away.

J. T. and the rest of the crowd followed me out the house, up the street to the streetlight and in front of the green house. Nothing was there but somebody's gold-grilled white Cadillac. Brandnew and most distracting. We got to looking at it so till I almost forgot the little box in my hand. While the others were busy making 'miration I carefully took off the paper and ribbon and folded them up and put them in my pants pocket. What should I see but a pair of genuine solid gold caddy keys.

Dangling the keys in front of everybody's nose, I unlocked the caddy, motioned for J. T. to git in on the other side, and us didn't come back home for two days.

1 9 6 0

Well, the boy was sure nuff famous by now. He was still a mite shy of twenty but already they was calling him the Emperor of Rock and Roll.

Then what should happen but the draft.

Well, says J. T. There goes all this Emperor of Rock and Roll business.

But even in the army the womens was on him like white on rice. We watched it on the News.

Dear Gracie Mae [he wrote from Germany],

How you? Fine I hope as this leaves me doing real well. Before I come in the army I was gaining a lot of weight and gitting jittery from making all them dumb movies. But now I exercise and eat right and get plenty of rest. I'm more awake than I been in ten years.

I wonder if you are writing any more songs?
Sincerely,
   Traynor

I wrote him back:

Dear Son,

We is all fine in the Lord's good grace and hope this finds you the same. J. T. and me be out all times of the day and night in that car you give me—which you know you didn't have to do. Oh, and I do appreciate the mink and the new self-cleaning oven. But if you send anymore stuff to eat from Germany I'm going to have to open up a store in the neighborhood just to get rid of it. Really, we have more than enough of everything. The Lord is good to us and we don't know Want.

Glad to here you is well and gitting your right rest. There ain't nothing like exercising to help that along. J. T. and me work some part of every day that we don't go fishing in the garden.

Well, so long Soldier.
Sincerely,
Gracie Mae

He wrote:

Dear Gracie Mae,

I hope you and J. T. like that automatic power tiller I had one of the stores back home send you. I went through a mountain of catalogs looking for it—I wanted something that even a woman could use.

I've been thinking about writing some songs of my own but every time I finish one it don't seem to be about nothing I've actually lived myself. My agent keeps sending me other people's songs but they just sound mooney. I can hardly git through 'em without gagging.

Everybody still loves that song of yours. They ask me all the time what do I think it means, really. I mean, they want to know just what I want to know. Where out of your life did it come from?
Sincerely,
Traynor

1968

I didn't see the boy for seven years. No. Eight. Because just about everybody was dead when I saw him again. Malcolm X, King, the president and his brother, and even J. T. J. T. died of a head cold. It just settled in his head like a block of ice, he said, and nothing we did moved it until one day he just leaned out the bed and died.

His good friend Horace helped me put him away, and then about a year later Horace and me started going together. We was sitting out on the front porch swing one summer night, dusk-dark, and I saw this great procession of lights winding to a stop.

Holy Toledo! said Horace. (He's got a real sexy voice like Ray Charles.) Look *at* it. He meant the long line of flashy cars and the white men in white summer suits jumping out on the drivers' sides and standing at attention. With wings they could pass for angels, with hoods they could be the Klan.

Traynor comes waddling up the walk.

And suddenly I know what it is he could pass for. An Arab like the ones you see in storybooks. Plump and soft and with never a care about weight. Because with so much money, who cares? Traynor is almost dressed like someone from a storybook too. He has on, I swear, about ten necklaces. Two set of bracelets on his arms, at least one ring on every finger, and some kind of shining buckles on his shoes, so that when he walks you get quite a few twinkling lights.

Gracie Mae, he says, coming up to give me a hug. J. T.

I explain that J. T. passed. That this is Horace.

Horace, he says, puzzled but polite, sort of rocking back on his heels, Horace.

That's it for Horace. He goes in the house and don't come back.

Looks like you and me is gained a few, I say.

He laughs. The first time I ever heard him laugh. It don't sound much like a laugh and I can't swear that it's better than no laugh a'tall.

He's gitting fat for sure, but he's still slim compared to me. I'll never see three hundred pounds again and I've just about said (excuse me) fuck it. I got to thinking about it one day an' I thought: aside from the fact that they say it's unhealthy, my fat ain't never been no trouble. Mens always have loved me. My kids ain't never complained. Plus they's fat. And fat like I is I looks distinguished. You see me coming and know somebody's *there*.

Gracie Mae, he says, I've come with a personal invitation to you to my house tomorrow for dinner. He laughed. What did it sound like? I couldn't place it. See them men out there? he asked me. I'm sick and tired of eating with them. They don't never have nothing to talk about. That's why I eat so much. But if you come to dinner tomorrow we can talk about the old days. You can tell me about that farm I bought you.

I sold it, I said.

You did?

Yeah, I said, I did. Just cause I said I liked to exercise by working in a garden didn't mean I wanted five hundred acres! Anyhow, I'm a city girl now. Raised in the country it's true. Dirt poor—the whole bit—but that's all behind me now.

Oh well, he said, I didn't mean to offend you.

We sat a few minutes listening to the crickets.

Then he said: You wrote that song while you was still on the farm, didn't you, or was it right after you left?

You had somebody spying on me? I asked.

You and Bessie Smith got into a fight over it once, he said.

You *is* been spying on me!

But I don't know what the fight was about, he said. Just like I don't know what happened to your second husband. Your first one died in the Texas electric chair. Did you know that? Your third one beat you up, stole your touring costumes and your car and retired with a chorine to Tuskegee. He laughed. He's still there.

I had been mad, but suddenly I calmed down. Traynor was talking very dreamily. It was dark but seems like I could tell his eyes weren't right. It was like some*thing* was sitting there talking to me but not necessarily with a person behind it.

You gave up on marrying and seem happier for it. He laughed again. I married but it never went like it was supposed to. I never could squeeze any of my own life either into it or out of it. It was like singing somebody else's record. I copied the way it was sposed to be *exactly* but I never had a clue what marriage meant.

I bought her a diamond ring big as your fist. I bought her clothes. I built her a mansion. But right away she didn't want the boys to stay there. Said they smoked up the bottom floor. Hell, there were *five* floors.

No need to grieve, I said. No need to. Plenty more where she come from.

He perked up. That's part of what that song means, ain't it? No need to grieve. Whatever it is, there's plenty more down the line.

I never really believed that way back when I wrote that song, I said. It was all bluffing then. The trick is to live long enough to put your young bluffs to use. Now if I was to sing that song today I'd tear it up. 'Cause I done lived long enough to know it's *true.* Them words could hold me up.

I ain't lived that long, he said.

Look like you on your way, I said. I don't know why, but the boy seemed to need some encouraging. And I don't know, seem like one way or another you talk to rich white folks and you end up reassuring *them.* But what the hell, by now I feel something for the boy. I wouldn't be in his bed all alone in the middle of the night for nothing. Couldn't be nothing worse than being famous the world over for something you don't even understand. That's what I tried to tell Bessie. She wanted that same song. Overheard me practicing it one day, said, with her hands on her hips: Gracie Mae, I'ma sing your song tonight. I *likes* it.

Your lips be too swole to sing, I said. She was mean and she was strong, but I trounced her.

Ain't you famous enough with your own stuff? I said. Leave mine alone. Later on, she thanked me. By then she was Miss Bessie Smith to the World, and I was still Miss Gracie Mae Nobody from Notasulga.

The next day all these limousines arrived to pick me up. Five cars and twelve bodyguards. Horace picked that morning to start painting the kitchen.

Don't paint the kitchen, fool, I said. The only reason that dumb boy of ours is going to show me his mansion is because he intends to present us with a new house.

What you gonna do with it? he asked me, standing there in his shirtsleeves stirring the paint.

Sell it. Give it to the children. Live in it on weekends. It don't matter what I do. He sure don't care.

Horace just stood there shaking his head. Mama you sure looks *good,* he says. Wake me up when you git back.

Fool, I say, and pat my wig in front of the mirror.

The boy's house is something else. First you come to this mountain, and then you commence to drive and drive up this road that's lined with magnolias. Do magnolias grow on mountains? I was wondering. And you come to lakes and you come to ponds and you come to deer and you come up on some sheep. And I figure these two is sposed to represent England and Wales. Or something out of Europe. And you just keep on coming to stuff. And it's all pretty. Only the man driving my car don't look at nothing but the road. Fool. And then *finally,* after all this time, you begin to go up the driveway. And there's more magnolias—only they're not in such good shape. It's sort of cool up this high and I don't think they're gonna make it. And then I see this building that looks like if it had a name it would be The Tara Hotel. Columns and steps and outdoor chandeliers and rocking chairs. Rocking chairs? Well, and there's the boy on the steps dressed in a dark green satin jacket like you see folks wearing on TV late at night, and he looks sort of like a fat dracula with all that house rising behind him, and standing beside him there's this little white vision of loveliness that he introduces as his wife.

He's nervous when he introduces us and he says to her: This is Gracie Mae Still, I want you to know me. I mean . . . and she gives him a look that would fry meat.

Won't you come in, Gracie Mae, she says, and that's the last I see of her.

He fishes around for something to say or do and decides to escort me to the kitchen. We go through the entry and the parlor and the breakfast room and the dining room and the servants' passage and finally get there. The first thing I notice is that, altogether, there are five stoves. He looks about to introduce me to one.

Wait a minute, I say. Kitchens don't do nothing for me. Let's go sit on the front porch.

Well, we hike back and we sit in the rocking chairs rocking until dinner.

Gracie Mae, he says down the table, taking a piece of fried chicken from the woman standing over him, I got a little surprise for you.

It's a house, ain't it? I ask, spearing a chitlin.

You're getting *spoiled,* he says. And the way he says *spoiled* sounds funny. He slurs it. It sounds like his tongue is too thick for his mouth. Just that quick he's finished the chicken and is now eating chitlins *and* a pork chop. *Me* spoiled, I'm thinking.

I already got a house. Horace is right this minute painting the kitchen. I bought that house. My kids feel comfortable in that house.

But this one I bought you is just like mine. Only a little smaller.

I still don't need no house. And anyway who would clean it?

He looks surprised.

Really, I think, some peoples advance *so* slowly.

I hadn't thought of that. But what the hell, I'll get you somebody to live in.

I don't want other folks living 'round me. Makes me nervous.

You *don't?* It *do?*

What I want to wake up and see folks I don't even know for?

He just sits there downtable staring at me. Some of that feeling is in the song, ain't it? Not the words, the *feeling.* What I want to wake up and see folks I don't even know for? But I see twenty folks a day I don't even know, including my wife.

This food wouldn't be bad to wake up to though, I said. The boy had found the genius of corn bread.

He looked at me real hard. He laughed. Short. They want what you got but they don't want you. They want what I got only it ain't mine. That's what makes 'em so hungry for me when I sing. They getting the flavor of something but they ain't getting the thing itself. They like a pack of hound dogs trying to gobble up a scent.

You talking 'bout your fans?

Right. Right. He says.

Don't worry 'bout your fans, I say. They don't know their asses from a hole in the ground. I doubt there's a honest one in the bunch.

That's the point. Dammit, that's the point! He hits the table with his fist. It's so solid it don't even quiver. You need a honest audience! You can't have folks that's just gonna lie right back to you.

Yeah, I say, it was small compared to yours, but I had one. It would have been worth my life to try to sing 'em somebody else's stuff that I didn't know nothing about.

He must have pressed a buzzer under the table. One of his flunkies zombies up.

Git Johnny Carson, he says.

On the phone? asks the zombie.

On the phone, says Traynor, what you think I mean, git him offa the front porch? Move your ass.

So two weeks later we's on the Johnny Carson show.

Traynor is all corseted down nice and looks a little bit fat but mostly good. And all the women that grew up on him and my song squeal and squeal. Traynor says: The lady who wrote my first hit record is here with us tonight, and she's agreed to sing it for all of us, just like she sung it forty-five years ago. Ladies and Gentlemen, the great Gracie Mae Still!

Well, I had tried to lose a couple of pounds my own self, but failing that I had me a very big dress made. So I sort of rolls over next to Traynor, who is dwarfted by me, so that when he puts his arm around back of me to try to hug me it looks funny to the audience and they laugh.

I can see this pisses him off. But I smile out there at 'em. Imagine squealing for twenty years and not knowing why you're squealing? No more sense of endings and beginnings than hogs.

It don't matter, Son, I say. Don't fret none over me.

I commence to sing. And I sound—wonderful. Being able to sing good ain't all about having a good singing voice a'tall. A good singing voice helps. But when you come up in the Hard Shell Baptist church like I did you understand early that the fellow that sings is the singer. Them that waits for programs and arrangements and letters from home is just good voices occupying body space.

So there I am singing my own song, my own way. And I give it all I got and enjoy every minute of it. When I finish Traynor is standing up clapping and clapping and beaming at first me and then the audience like I'm his mama for true. The audience claps politely for about two seconds.

Traynor looks disgusted.

He comes over and tries to hug me again. The audience laughs.

Johnny Carson looks at us like we both weird.

Traynor is mad as hell. He's supposed to sing something called a love ballad. But instead he takes the mike, turns to me and says: Now see if my imitation still holds up. He goes into the same song, *our* song, I think, looking out at his flaky audience. And he sings it just the way he always did. My voice, my tone, my inflection, everything. But he forgets a couple of lines. Even before he's finished the matronly squeals begin.

He sits down next to me looking whipped.

It don't matter, Son, I say, patting his hand. You don't even know those people. Try to make the people you know happy.

Is that in the song? he asks.

Maybe. I say.

1977

For a few years I hear from him, then nothing. But trying to lose weight takes all the attention I got to spare. I finally faced up to the fact that my fat is the hurt I don't admit, not even to myself, and that I been trying to bury it from the day I was born. But also when you git real old, to tell the truth, it ain't as pleasant. It gits lumpy and slack. Yuck. So one day I said to Horace, I'ma git this shit offa me.

And he fell in with the program like he always try to do and Lord such a procession of salads and cottage cheese and fruit juice!

One night I dreamed Traynor had split up with his fifteenth wife. He said: *You meet 'em for no reason. You date 'em for no reason. You marry 'em for no reason. I do it all but I swear it's just like somebody else doing it. I feel like I can't remember Life.*

The boy's in trouble, I said to Horace.

You've always said that, he said.

I have?

Yeah. You always said he looked asleep. You can't sleep through life if you wants to live it.

You not such a fool after all, I said, pushing myself up with my cane and hobbling over to where he was. Let me sit down on your lap, I said, while this salad I ate takes effect.

In the morning we heard Traynor was dead. Some said fat, some said heart, some said alcohol, some said drugs. One of the children called from Detroit. Them dumb fans of his is on a crying rampage, she said. You just ought to turn on the TV.

But I didn't want to see 'em. They was crying and crying and didn't even know what they was crying for. One day this is going to be a pitiful country, I thought.

§

In your journal, answer the following questions:

§ How does Traynor's desire to understand Gracie Mae's song and Gracie Mae's desire to lose weight drive the story's conflict?

§ Why do you think it was necessary to tell the story spanning twenty-two years?

§ In each year discussed, Walker presents conflict. Which years have the most conflict? Is the conflict mainly between characters or internal to each character?

§ Why is the Johnny Carson show performance a
significant moment for both characters? How does
the contrast between their actions and reactions serve
to suggest Traynor's later death and Gracie Mae's
inner strength?

§ What do you think of the story's resolution? Why
does Gracie Mae think "One day this is going to be
a pitiful country . . ."?

§ What has Alice Walker taught you about creating
plot?

Alice Walker and Zora Neale Hurston have created glorious stories. While the two stories are radically different from each other, they
share the hallmark of well-plotted fiction—strong characters who create tension and change through their decisions about how to approach
and live a more satisfying life.

Characters with rich, emotional lives come alive in profound
ways for readers. Close your eyes right now and conjure a mental
image of Walker's Gracie Mae. Can't you just see her newly trim,
living the life Traynor never understood and wasted? Can't you see
Hurston's Delia, happy and at peace, in her neat home, now free of
abuse?

For every story you ever write, strive to make readers "see" your
characters and "feel" their inner lives. Then, when conflict challenges,
your readers will be compelled to read on . . . *wanting to know what
happens next!*

"Tell me a story." Plot answers this basic human desire.

Celebrate as you become more skilled at weaving tales! You are a
griot for the next generation.

7

POINT OF VIEW

He says, she says. You say, I say." Point of view fundamentally reveals your story's meaning.

Whoever tells the story is powerful; the teller and their motives influence every aspect of your story. Because stories are more than just a monologue or dialogue, the person who tells the story is also a lens determining what readers see, the sequence in which they see it— memory, flashback, flash forward, linear time, and what details, thoughts, feelings are most significant. Literally, whoever tells the story, controls your story's meaning.

Selecting who tells the story is a critical decision. Many beginning writers tell stories using first person point of view, almost exclusively. Authors already comfortable with personal narratives sometimes select the "I" by default, finding it far easier to begin a story with *"I remember dancing . . ."* than with *"She danced."* Sometimes, too, the

"I" is a thinly veiled disguise for the author. For example, my unpublished first novel used an "I" narrator who was really me, and related all the anguishing trials of my adolescence. It has all the self-centered tunnel vision you'd expect. Yet while my narrator wailed, it might have been far more interesting to consider more seriously what issues my parents (also thinly veiled characters) were facing. Inadequate jobs for raising a family, divorce, jealousies, and numerous miscommunications about values, finances, and love would have made a far more interesting story than my adolescent travails. I might have gained a better perspective and more distance had I used "she," a third person point of view.

Remember, a short story or novel is not autobiography. Fiction can have autobiographical elements, but a writer is still obligated to find the best narrative voice for telling any particular story. Multiple narrators would have made my first novel more compelling. Unfortunately, like most first novelists, I was still quite young in terms of my craft and emotions. Nonetheless, my unpublished first novel was a great training ground for understanding how a poorly chosen viewpoint can undermine the potential of any good story. One day, I'll resurrect this novel and tell it with the proper characterization, the necessary "fictional lies," and the appropriate point of view it demands.

MY BEST ADVICE
Never select a point of view by default or simply because you think it's easier. Always consider who will tell your story best.

If one point of view doesn't work, don't be afraid of replacing it. After completing a first draft, it is not unusual for writers to take the opportunity to reaffirm their chosen points of view or, if necessary, transform a thousand "I" pronouns to a third person "she" (or vice versa).

What points of view are available?
What are their advantages? Disadvantages?

1. First Person Point of View

The character speaks and the focus is on the "I." Readers are immediately drawn into the "I's" account of personal experiences—how the the storyteller sees, acts, reflects, and responds within their fictional world.

The "I" is limited, however, to only what the character can reasonably be expected to know and experience. A first person character cannot, arbitrarily, become "godlike" and know "everybody else's business."

ADVANTAGES: A well-done first person protagonist puts your readers side by side, soul to soul with your main character.

DISADVANTAGES: Because the first person lens is narrow, highly focused, you need to have an interesting narrator worthy of it. A weak character with a bland voice will make your story unravel quicker than you can say "fiction."

"I overheard scuffling, then a muffled shot," presumes you'll experience the crime scene only from the "I" view. Anything different would be upsetting to a reader. *"Upstairs, Van paused, his breathing labored,"* would leave readers bewildered by the shift in point of view.

Generally, the "I" is the protagonist, the central character, and most first person narrations employ a single voice. Jervey Tervalon employs a variation on this by using multiple "I's" in his novel *Understand This*. Each chapter heading begins with the name of a character—"Michael," "Sally," "Margot," "Rika," and so forth—but each character tells their own tale in first person. Thus his novel is much like a symphony with differing voices carrying differing thematic melodies and harmonies.

First person can be very intimate, very immediate. Paulette Childress White in her short story "Getting the Facts of Life" takes us inside the heart of a young girl:

At Jefferson, we turned and there it was, halfway down
the block. The Department of Social Services. I discovered some strong feelings. That fine name meant nothing.
This was the welfare. The place for poor people. People

who couldn't or wouldn't take care of themselves. Now I
was going to face it, and suddenly I thought what I knew
the others [my brothers and sisters] had thought, *What if
I see someone I know?* I wanted to run back all those
blocks to home.

I looked at Momma for comfort, but her face was
closed and her mouth looked locked.

It is important to be aware of how beautifully the "I" storyteller
approach fits with the African American oral tradition. Arthur Flowers
in *Another Good Loving Blues* uses a first person narrator to frame his
story:

I am Flowers of the delta clan Flowers and the line of O
Killens—I am hoodoo, I am griot, I am a man of power.
My story is a true story, my words are true words, my lie
is a true lie—a fine old delta tale about a mad blues
piano player and a Arkansas conjure woman on a hoodoo
mission. Lucas Bodeen and Melvira Dupree. Plan to show
you how they found the good thing. True love. That
once-in-a-lifetime love.

While Flowers' first person griot is less directly involved in the
action, readers nonetheless feel this narrative sensibility provides
the perfect way to tell his story. The "I" narrator lends the novel the
resonance of a blues fable and morality tale; when it concludes
". . . *they lived happily ever after,*" readers are satisfied.

2. Third Person
Third person point of view employs "he" and "she" pronouns
though it is an unidentified narrator who describes the action.
There are, however, many variations and degrees of how much
this unidentified narrator intrudes or is a presence within the
story.

A. Third Person Omniscient Point of View

A "godlike" unidentified narrator manipulates and provides commentary about the story's action. This narrator knows everything about the characters and can move freely within their minds, interpreting their behavior. This narrator also knows what has happened, is happening, and what will happen.

African American fables, retellings of folktales and legends, often make good use of a godlike narrative voice. Fantasy and science fiction tales, too, will use third person omniscient to describe alien worlds and lend authority to fantastical and scientific extrapolations.

ADVANTAGES: Omniscient narrators have ultimate authority and versatility. Readers will believe whatever the godlike voice tells them and accept any shifts in time or space.

DISADVANTAGES: A too intrusive narrator tells readers what to think and feel, rather than allowing space for readers to draw their own attitudes and conclusions about the characters.

The omniscient narrator in Virginia Hamilton's *The Magical Adventures of Pretty Pearl* knows not only Pearl's thoughts but also African geography, human civilization's history, and the hierarchy of magical gods:

> One long time ago, Pretty Pearl yearned to come down
> from on high. One clear day it was, she daydreamed of
> leaving her home on Mount Kenya.
> What good it is bein' a god chile, she thought, if I
> got to hang around up here all de time? What there for
> me to do when I beat all de god chil'ren at de games,
> and I learns everthin' so fast?
> Great Mount Kenya of Africa was known as Mount
> Highness by Pretty Pearl and the other gods who lived
> there. It was a vast and glorious mountain of peaks, val-
> leys, grasslands, forests, bare rocks and glaciers. It was also
> an extinct volcano with a dome almost a hundred miles
> around. The Kikuyu, Embu and Meru human beings cul-

tivated the lower slopes of the Mount. Some of the lesser gods on high kept a watch over them.

For this award-winning young adult novel, the omniscient voice is perfect. The narrator's godlike tones and authority are well suited to a mythic tale in which a "god child" alleviates the suffering of slaves and becomes human.

B. Third Person Limited Point of View

1. The story is told using "he" or "she." As with first person, often a single character observes and/or fully participates in the story. But unlike first person, the author can, through the narrator, summarize, moralize, and provide necessary background information or information beyond the ken of the character.

2. Beyond a single third person limited point of view, a writer can also shift between multiple characters' points of view. For example, a story can juxtapose both sides of a marital argument, expressing not only what "he" feels but also what "she" grieves about within the relationship. A writer can create an entire town of characters, delving into each person's experiences, thoughts, and feelings. Third person limited with multiple characters still allows the author to summarize and moralize when desired.

ADVANTAGES: Third person has much of the immediacy of a first person narrative but more versatility. One, two, three, or more characters can be represented, widening the focus and meaning of one's story. An author can add necessary information and commentary when desired.

DISADVANTAGES: Since the narrator isn't quite a character, it may be more difficult to convey the kind of powerful voice and dialect that can be achieved in first person. Also, shifting viewpoints among characters indiscriminately and too often can confuse readers and undermine the story's focus.

Exploring the thoughts and perceptions of multiple characters is perhaps best when actions and motives within a story are suspect and open to interpretation.

In Richard Wright's "Bright and Morning Star," a mother attempting to kill her son to spare him from further Klan torture is herself shot:

> She gave up as much of her life as she could before they took it from her. But the sound of the shot and the streak of fire that tore its way through her chest forced her to live again, intensely. She had not moved, save for the slight jarring impact of the bullet. She felt the heat of her own blood warming her cold, wet back. She yearned suddenly to talk. "Yuh didnt git whut yuh wanted! N yuh ain gonna nevah git it! Yuh didnt kill me; Ah come here by mahsef . . ." She felt rain falling into her wide-open, dimming eyes and heard faint voices. Her lips moved soundlessly. *Yuh didnt git yuh didnt yuh didnt* . . . Focused and pointed she was, buried in the depths of her star, swallowed in its peace and strength, and not feeling her flesh growing cold, cold as the rain that fell from the invisible sky upon the doomed living and the dead that never dies.

If Wright had chosen only a first person narrative, then the last sentence, in particular, could not have been written. By using third, Wright gains the thoughts and feelings of his character but also reserves the right to comment and moralize. Even after death, he seems to be saying, his character still lives in a merciful universe attuned to salvation for the just.

In *Magic City,* I used third person limited with multiple characters. Chapters alternate between Joe Samuel's and Mary Keane's points of view:

> In a year of shining shoes, Joe had saved two hundred dollars. Another year, he'd have four hundred. Another year, his father might understand why he wanted to go. Might even wish him well. In another year, Joe might be able to say good-bye to his sister Hildy. To Lying Man.

His brother's grave. He might understand why, in a place he loved so much, he felt like he was dying.

Mary stopped cleaning. Children, she thought. Water drained from her hands, pooling at her feet. Bubbles floated out the window. Her mouth puckered. A fly swept by her ear and she stared out the window, studying the mound near the shed where she'd buried countless years of bloodied rags. Each month, tossing in the week's rags, shoveling dirt, she'd mourned—not just the lost babies—but all the touching, kissing she dreamed flowered between a man and woman before making life.

Dell was right. Nothing would change. There wasn't any magic in the world. His touch would sharpen another kind of loneliness. She'd cook, clean, launder, sew; when the sky filled with stars, he'd take her without asking and make her crazed, mourning for an honest loving he couldn't give.

Transitions within third person limited can be handled smoothly if the differing views are set off by new paragraphs or chapter or page breaks. Novels, too, because of their scale and scope more easily accommodate multiple viewpoints than short stories. But whether you explore one, two, or five characters, the third person point of view can, if well done, provide readers with intimacy and immediacy rivaling a first person viewpoint.

Once you've established a point of view, it is generally best not to change it within your story. Dramatic shifts can be disconcerting. However, it is also true that anything you can get to work in fiction is acceptable. Following a chapter break, Flowers in *Another Good Loving Blues* shifts from first person griot to third person limited; thus, his story is able to make use of the advantages of both points of view.

· · ·

Point of view selection is one of the most significant choices a writer can make. Readers rely on viewpoint, the narrator's perceptions, to be their guide into the best storytelling experience possible.

A poor viewpoint choice will limit what you can do in a story. You may also find that certain viewpoints are more natural to you than others. The following exercises will help you explore viewpoint choices.

EXERCISE 1

REAFFIRMING YOUR
POINT OF VIEW

You can use any point of view as long as it works and helps you tell a fine story. However, even after you've made your selection, it's worth testing it, reconsidering what you're giving up and what you're gaining. An afternoon rethinking and experimenting with point of view can enhance any story. While shifts from third to first person voice or from omniscient to third person limited can provide dramatic change, so too can narrative shifts within the same category.

Reread Edwidge Danticat's "New York Day Women" in Chapter Five. It's written in the first person voice of the daughter but italics convey the mother's voice: *"If they want to eat with me, let them come to my house, even if I boil water and give it to them." "You are pretty enough to be a stewardess. Only dogs like bones."* These italics convey a strong sense of the mother's character. Yet how would the story be changed if the mother's point of view were dominant?

The story begins: "Today, walking down the street, I see my mother." Reimagine the story opening with the mother's view: "Today, walking down the street, I see my daughter."

Even though you're still writing in first person, everything changes when you switch point of view among characters. The details, observations, reflections, and, by extension, the heart of the story are altered when the mother becomes the story's eyes and voice. Do you think the story would be as successful if the mother's viewpoint were dominant? I think not. While readers might accept a daughter "spying" on her mother and uncovering new aspects of her character, the reverse, a mother "spying" on her daughter, is less sympathetic because of the implicit power a mother has over a daughter.

Write a story or select a story you've begun in the first person point of view. Staying within first person narrative, spend twenty minutes rewriting two to three pages of it, shifting the dominant view to another character. For example, if you're writing a love story, shift the first person narrative from the boyfriend's to the girlfriend's point of view. If you're writing about a son's conflict with his father, shift the narrative to the father. (This exercise will also work for third person limited.)

The key is to remind yourself that while shifts between points of view—that is, moving from first person to third or from a limited to omniscient narrator—are powerful, so too can shifts within a particular narrative range. Question every point of view you select. If it's the right one, it'll affirm itself, or else you'll open another avenue for writing a great story!

EXERCISE 2

ANGLING FOR TRUTH, MULTIPLE VIEWS

Stories, like reality, can have multiple versions of the "truth." Like people, characters' perceptions are heavily influenced by who they are, their background and experiences, and their desires.

Imagine that a major life-changing event—the birth of a baby, the execution of a criminal, a bitter argument over a parent's will, a child's illness, etc.—has been witnessed by three separate characters.

In this exercise, you'll practice shifting among third person limited points of view. The characters' level of participation in the event can vary, but all three characters must be present at the time of the event.

First, decide the event you want to write about; second, in your journal, write three short character sketches.

For example, I might select the birth of a baby. To heighten tension, I'd imagine an emergency C-section. The mother is unconscious and, therefore, not mentally present. The newborn, likewise, would not be given a viewpoint (though it might be fascinating to imagine one).

The witnesses to the birth would be entirely medical personnel—the anesthesiologist, the obstetrician, and the nurse ready to transport the underweight infant to intensive care.

CHARACTER SKETCHES

The anesthesiologist is a young woman, two years out of medical school. Her name is Gloria. Over lunch in the hospital cafeteria, her artist husband asked for a divorce. She is distracted, bitter, suspicious that he's met another woman eager to support his career. She keeps remembering her mother's warning that men dislike successful wives.

The delivery doctor, Wallace, is still a bit hungover from a party celebrating the incorporation of his new medical practice. He suspects 300 births a month will pay the interest on his medical equipment loans. He is now delivering baby number 82, a breech birth. Though tired, his mouth dry, he is happy.

Jenny is thirty-six, good-natured, a bit plump. The last eight years she's been treated for infertility. Two weeks ago, she decided to give up her quest to have a baby. She also asked to be transferred from obstetrics. Today is her last day. She is the only one touched by the beauty of the boy's birth.

From these character sketches, I could begin writing a story which reveals the differences among the three characters, their thoughts and emotional response (or lack of one) to the baby's birth.

. . .

Once you've selected an event and sketched the history of the three characters, you're ready to practice viewpoint transitions among characters.

Remember, a paragraph break should offset each differing view. Or you can tell the story in three organized parts—I, II, and III— with each part reflecting a character's thoughts. If you prefer, the narratives needn't be equally balanced. In my story example, I might emphasize the nurse's and the anesthesiologist's emotional states and contrast their thoughts with intermittent exclamations from the doctor and with italicized explorations of his dreams of financial prosperity.

Spend an afternoon drafting a story in your journal, using three characters' voices, thoughts, and feelings. Each time you make a transition from one point of view to another, ask yourself: "Why now? What's gained by inserting this new view? How is the nature of the story changed by multiple voices? How do these characters enrich the story? How do these characters complement or contrast each other?"

As you're writing, don't worry about editing or mistakes. Let the story flow, focusing on the interactions among the narrative voices. You may finish this exercise with a story you want to develop further. At the least, you'll develop greater sensitivity for the range of a third person point of view with multiple characters.

EXERCISE 3

OMNISCIENT FOR THE THRILL OF IT

The omniscient voice isn't very popular in contemporary fiction. But an all-knowing narrator can be useful and fun, and, at times, absolutely essential for conveying information.

Samuel Delany in his fantasy short story "Tapestry" uses an unidentified voice to imagine life inside a medieval tapestry:

The Virgin is disgusted.

So is the unicorn: although he finds the smell of her
sweating flesh attractive, the medicinal pungency of alcohol and ambergris, the rancid hair oil, sweetened with
dead flowers, revolt him.

If a first person narrator talked about teeming life inside a tapestry, readers might assume the "I" was drunk or mentally unreliable.
But the omniscient voice draws not only upon the griot tradition but
also upon the Western "Once upon a time" tradition, of accepting
unquestioningly the narrator's version of reality.

Diane McKinney-Whetstone in *Tumbling* uses an omniscient
narrator to establish the social history of a community:

The black predawn air was filled with movement. Its thin
coolness rushed through the streets of South Philly, encir-
cling the tight, sturdy row houses. In 1940 the blocks
were clean and close. The people who lived here scrubbed
their steps every morning until the sand in the concrete
sparkled like diamond pins.

Alexs Pate, in his novelization of the screenplay *Amistad,* relies on
the omniscient narrator to summarize background and to explain historical context. Virginia Hamilton in *A Ring of Tricksters* uses an omniscient narrator to tell trickster legends from Africa to the Americas.
Margaret Walker's omniscient narrator in *Jubilee* weaves plot with
Civil War and slave history. Clearly, an omniscient narrator can be a
consummate storyteller, passing along traditional tales as well as in-
venting new ones.

In your journal, write at least two story ideas which you think
would benefit from an omniscient narrator. Explain why. For example,
if you're creating your own alternative-universe tale, you may need a
godlike voice to explain how the alien world functions.

From your journal, select one of your story beginnings and spend
thirty minutes rewriting the opening paragraphs using an omniscient

point of view. Read your opening aloud. Does the narrator sound authoritative? Expansive? All-knowing about your fictional world? Could you achieve the same effect using first person? Third person limited? If not, why not?

POINT OF VIEW STUDY

CHARLES JOHNSON'S "CHINA"

Johnson's short story "China" is told in third person limited with multiple characters. Johnson explores the hearts and souls of two characters reexamining their lives individually and together. China, with its sense of foreignness, unexplored geography, and distance, and the husband's growing dedication to martial arts, becomes symbolic of the conflict between them.

Evelyn, in particular, is a vulnerable, sympathetic woman afraid of change, terrified of life. Unlike a first person point of view, third person limited allows Johnson to create two complex characters with compassion. The point of view allows us to explore intimately both characters' needs and desires; it also allows Johnson to establish when necessary, through an unidentified narrator, the context and tone for understanding these two characters.

If one man conquer in battle a thousand men, and if another conquers himself, he is the greatest of conquerors.
—THE DHAMMAPADA

EVELYN'S PROBLEMS WITH her husband, Rudolph, began one evening in early March—a dreary winter evening in Seattle—when he complained after a heavy meal of pig's feet and mashed potatoes of shortness of breath, an allergy to something she put in his food perhaps, or brought on by the first signs of wild flowers around them. She suggested they get out of the house for the evening, go to a movie. He was fifty-four, a postman for thirty-three years now, with high blood pressure, emphysema, flat feet, and, as Evelyn told her friend Shelberdine Lewis, the lingering fear that he had cancer. Getting old, he was also getting hard to live with. He told her never to salt his dinners, to keep their Lincoln Continental at a crawl, and never run her fingers along his inner thigh when they sat in Reverend William Merrill's church, because anything, even sex, or laughing too loud—Rudolph was serious—might bring on heart failure.

So she chose for their Saturday night outing a peaceful movie, a mildly funny comedy a *Seattle Times* reviewer said was fit only for titters and nasal snorts, a low-key satire that made Rudolph's eyelids droop as he shoveled down unbuttered popcorn in the darkened, half-empty theater. Sticky fluids cemented Evelyn's feet to the floor. A man in the last row laughed at all the wrong places. She kept the popcorn on her lap, though she hated the unsalted stuff and wouldn't touch it, sighing as Rudolph pawed across her to shove his fingers inside the cup.

She followed the film as best she could, but occasionally her eyes frosted over, flashed white. She went blind like this now and then. The fibers of her eyes were failing; her retinas were tearing like soft tissue. At these times the world was a canvas with whiteout spilling from the far left corner toward the center; it was the sudden shock of an empty frame in a series of slides. Someday, she knew, the snow on her eyes would stay. Winter eternally: her eyes split like her walking stick. She groped along the fractured surface, waiting for her sight to thaw, listening to the film she couldn't see. Her only comfort was knowing that, despite her infirmity, her Rudolph was in even worse health.

He slid back and forth from sleep during the film (she elbowed him occasionally, or pinched his leg), then came full awake, sitting up suddenly when the movie ended and a "Coming Attractions" trailer began. It was some sort of gladiator movie, Evelyn thought, blinking, and it was pretty trashy stuff at that. The plot's revenge theme was a poor excuse for Chinese actors or Japanese (she couldn't tell those people apart) to flail the air with their hands and feet, take on fifty costumed extras at once, and leap twenty feet through the air in perfect defiance of gravity. Rudolph's mouth hung open.

"Can people really do that?" He did not take his eyes off the screen, but talked at her from the right side of his mouth. "Leap that high?"

"It's a *movie,*" sighed Evelyn. "A *bad* movie."

He nodded, then asked again, "But can they?"

"Oh, Rudolph, for God's sake!" She stood up to leave, her seat slapping back loudly. "They're on *trampolines!* You can see them in the corner—there!—if you open your eyes!"

He did see them, once Evelyn twisted his head to the lower left corner of the screen, and it seemed to her that her husband looked disappointed—looked, in fact, the way he did the afternoon Dr. Guylee told Rudolph he'd developed an extrasystolic reaction, a faint, moaning sound from his heart whenever it relaxed. He said no more and, after the trailer finished, stood—there was chewing gum stuck to his trouser seat—dragged on his heavy coat with her help and followed Evelyn up the long, carpeted aisle, through the exit of the Coronet Theater, and to their car. He said nothing as she chattered on the way home, reminding him that he could not stay up all night puttering in his basement shop because the next evening they were to attend the church's revival meeting.

Rudolph, however, did not attend the revival. He complained after lunch of a light, dancing pain in his chest, which he had conveniently whenever Mount Zion Baptist Church held revivals, and she went alone, sitting with her friend Shelberdine, a beautician. She was forty-one; Evelyn, fifty-two. That evening Evelyn wore spotless white gloves, tan therapeutic stockings for the swelling in her ankles, and a white dress that brought out nicely the brown color of her skin, the most beautiful cedar brown, Rudolph said when they were courting thirty-five years ago in South Carolina. But then Evelyn had worn a matching checkered skirt and coat to meeting. With her jet black hair pinned behind her neck by a simple wooden comb, she looked as if she might have been Andrew Wyeth's starkly beautiful model for *Day of the Fair.* Rudolph, she remembered, wore black business suits, black ties, black wing tips, but he also wore white gloves because he was a senior usher—this was how she first noticed him. He was one of four young men dressed like deacons (or blackbirds), their left hands tucked into the hollow of their backs, their right carrying silver plates for the offering as they marched in almost military fashion down each aisle: Christian soldiers, she'd thought, the cream of black manhood, and to get his attention she placed not her white envelope or coins in Rudolph's plate but instead a note that said: "You have a beautiful smile." It was, for all her innocence, a daring thing to do, according to Evelyn's mother—flirting with a randy young man like Rudolph Lee Jackson, but he did have nice, tigerish teeth. A killer smile, people called it, like all the boys in the Jackson family: a killer smile and good hair that needed no more than one stroke of his palm to bring out Quo Vadis rows pomaded sweetly with the scent of Murray's.

And, of course, Rudolph was no dummy. Not a total dummy, at least. He pretended nothing extraordinary had happened as the congregation left the little whitewashed church. He stood, the youngest son, between his father and mother, and let old Deacon Adcock remark, "Oh, how strong he's looking now," which was a lie. Rudolph was the weakest of the Jackson boys, the pale, bookish, spiritual child born when his parents were well past forty. His brothers played football, they went into the navy; Rudolph lived in Scripture, was labeled 4-F, and hoped to attend Moody Bible Institute in Chicago, if he could ever find the money. Evelyn could tell Rudolph knew exactly where she was in the crowd, that he could feel her as she and her sister, Debbie, waited for their father to bring his DeSoto—the family prize—closer to the front steps. When the crowd thinned, he shambled over in his slow, ministerial walk, introduced himself, and unfolded her note.

"You write this?" he asked. "It's not right to play with the Lord's money, you know."

"I like to play," she said.

"You do, huh?" He never looked directly at people. Women, she guessed, terrified him. Or, to be exact, the powerful emotions they caused in him terrified Rudolph. He was a pud puller, if she ever saw one. He kept his eyes on a spot left of her face. "You're Joe Montgomery's daughter, aren't you?"

"Maybe," teased Evelyn.

He trousered the note and stood marking the ground with his toe. "And just what you expect to get, Miss Playful, by fooling with people during collection time?"

She waited, let him look away, and, when the back-and-forth swing of his gaze crossed her again, said in her most melic soft-breathing voice: *"You."*

Up front, portly Reverend Merrill concluded his sermon. Evelyn tipped her head slightly, smiling into memory; her hand reached left to pat Rudolph's leg gently; then she remembered it was Shelberdine beside her, and lifted her hand to the seat in front of her. She said a prayer for Rudolph's health, but mainly it was for herself, a hedge against her fear that their childless years had slipped by like wind, that she might return home one day and find him—as she had found her father—on the floor, bellied up, one arm twisted behind him where he fell, alone, his fingers locked against his chest. Rudolph had begun to run down, Evelyn decided, the minute he was turned down by Moody Bible Institute. They moved to Seattle in 1956—his brother Eli was stationed nearby and said Boeing was hiring black men. But they didn't hire Rudolph. He had kidney trouble on and off before he landed the job at the Post Office. Whenever he bent forward, he felt dizzy. Liver, heart, and lungs—they'd worn down gradually as his belly grew, but none of this was as bad as what he called "the Problem." His pecker shrank to no bigger than a pencil eraser each time he saw her undress. Or when Evelyn, as was her habit when talking, touched his arm. Was she the cause of this? Well, she knew she wasn't much to look at anymore. She'd seen the bottom of a few too many candy wrappers. Evelyn was nothing to make a man pant and jump her bones, pulling her fully clothed onto the davenport, as Rudolph had done years before, but wasn't sex something else you surrendered with age? It never seemed all that good to her anyway. And besides, he'd wanted oral sex, which Evelyn—if she knew nothing else—thought was a nasty, unsanitary thing to do with your mouth. She glanced up from under her spring hat past the pulpit, past the choir of black and brown faces to the agonized beauty of a bearded white carpenter impaled on a rood, and in this timeless image she felt comforted that suffering was inescapable, the loss of vitality inevitable, even a good thing maybe, and that she had to steel herself—yes—for someday opening her bedroom door and finding her Rudolph face down in his breakfast oatmeal. He would die before her, she knew that in her bones.

And so, after service, Sanka, and a slice of meat pie with Shelberdine downstairs in the brightly lit church basement, Evelyn returned home to tell her husband how lovely the Griffin girls had sung that day, that their neighbor Rod Kenner had been saved, and to listen, if necessary, to Rudolph's fear that the lump on his shoulder was an early-warning sign of something evil. As it turned out, Evelyn found that except for their cat, Mr. Miller, the little A-frame house was empty. She looked in his bedroom. No Rudolph. The unnaturally still house made Evelyn uneasy, and she took the excruciatingly painful twenty stairs into the basement to peer into a workroom littered with power tools, planks of wood, and the blueprints her husband used to make bookshelves and cabinets. No Rudolph. Frightened, Evelyn called the eight hospitals in Seattle, but no one had a Rudolph Lee Jackson on his books. After her last call the starburst clock in the living room read twelve-thirty. Putting down the wall phone, she felt a familiar pain in her abdomen. Another attack of Hershey squirts, probably from the meat pie. She hurried into the bathroom, lifted her skirt, and lowered her underwear around her ankles, but kept the door wide open, something impossible to do if Rudolph was home. Actually, it felt good not to have him underfoot, a little like he was dead already. But the last thing Evelyn wanted was that or, as she lay down against her lumpy backrest, to fall asleep, though she did, nodding off and dreaming until something shifted down her weight on the side of her bed away from the wall.

"Evelyn," said Rudolph, "look at this." She blinked back sleep and squinted at the cover of a magazine called *Inside Kung-Fu,* which

Rudolph waved under her nose. On the cover a man stood bowlegged, one hand cocked under his armpit, the other corkscrewing straight at Evelyn's nose.

"Rudolph!" She batted the magazine aside, then swung her eyes toward the cluttered nightstand, focusing on the electric clock beside her water glass from McDonald's, Preparation H suppositories, and Harlequin romances. "It's morning!" Now she was mad. At least, working at it. "Where have you been?"

Her husband inhaled, a wheezing, whistlelike breath. He rolled the magazine into a cylinder and, as he spoke, struck his left palm with it. "That movie we saw advertised? You remember—it was called *The Five Fingers of Death*. I just saw that and one called *Deep Thrust.*"

"Wonderful." Evelyn screwed up her lips. "I'm calling hospitals and you're at a Hong Kong double feature."

"Listen," said Rudolph. "You don't understand." He seemed at that moment as if he did not understand either. "It was a Seattle movie premiere. The Northwest is crawling with fighters. It has something to do with all the Asians out here. Before they showed the movie, four students from a kwoon in Chinatown went onstage—"

"A what?" asked Evelyn.

"A kwoon—it's a place to study fighting, a meditation hall." He looked at her but was really watching, Evelyn realized, something exciting she had missed. "They did a demonstration to drum up their membership. They broke boards and bricks, Evelyn. They went through what's called kata and kumite and . . ." He stopped again to breathe. "I've never seen anything so beautiful. The reason I'm late is because I wanted to talk with them after the movie."

Evelyn, suspicious, took a Valium and waited.

"I signed up for lessons," he said.

She gave a glacial look at Rudolph, then at his magazine, and said in the voice she used five years ago when he wanted to take a vacation to Upper Volta or, before that, invest in a British car she knew they couldn't afford:

"You're fifty-*four* years old, Rudolph."

"I know that."

"You're no Muhammad Ali."

"I know that," he said.

"You're no Bruce Lee. Do you want to be Bruce Lee? Do you know where he is now, Rudolph? He's dead—dead here in a Seattle cemetery and buried up on Capital Hill."

His shoulders slumped a little. Silently, Rudolph began undressing, his beefy backside turned toward her, slipping his pajama bottoms on before taking off his shirt so his scrawny lower body would not be fully exposed. He picked up his magazine, said, "I'm sorry if I worried you," and huffed upstairs to his bedroom. Evelyn clicked off the mushroom-shaped lamp on her nightstand. She lay on her side, listening to his slow footsteps strike the stairs, then heard his mattress creak above her—his bedroom was directly above hers—but she did not hear him click off his own light. From time to time she heard his shifting weight squeak the mattress springs. He was reading that foolish magazine, she guessed; then she grew tired and gave this impossible man up to God. With a copy of *The Thorn Birds* open on her lap, Evelyn fell heavily to sleep again.

At breakfast the next morning any mention of the lessons gave Rudolph lockjaw. He kissed her forehead, as always, before going to work, and simply said he might be home late. Climbing the stairs to his bedroom was painful for Evelyn, but she hauled herself up, pausing at each step to huff, then sat on his bed and looked over his copy of *Inside Kung-Fu*. There were articles on empty-hand combat, soft-focus photos of ferocious-looking men in funny suits, parables about legendary Zen masters, an interview with someone named Bernie Bernheim, who began to study karate at age fifty-seven and became a black belt at age sixty-one, and page after page of advertisements for exotic Asian weapons: nunchaku, shuriken, sai swords, tonfa, bo staffs, training bags of all sorts, a wooden dummy shaped like a man and called a Mook Jong, and weights. Rudolph had circled them all. He had torn the order form from the last page of the magazine. The total cost of the things he'd circled—Evelyn added them furiously, rounding off the figures—was $800.

Two minutes later she was on the telephone to Shelberdine.

"Let him tire of it," said her friend. "Didn't you tell me Rudolph had Lower Lombard Strain?"

Evelyn's nose clogged with tears.

"Why is he doing this? Is it me, do you think?"

"It's the Problem," said Shelberdine. "He wants his manhood back. Before he died, Arthur did the same. Someone at the plant told him he could get it back if he did twenty-yard sprints. He went into convulsions while running around the lake."

Evelyn felt something turn in her chest. "You don't think he'll hurt himself, do you?"

"Of course not."

"Do you think he'll hurt *me?*"

Her friend reassured Evelyn that Mid-Life Crisis brought out these shenanigans in men. Evelyn replied that she thought Mid-Life Crisis started around age forty, to which Shelberdine said, "Honey, I don't mean no harm, but Rudolph always was a little on the slow side," and Evelyn agreed. She would wait until he worked this thing out of his system, until Nature defeated him and he surrendered, as any right-thinking person would, to the breakdown of the body, the brutal fact of decay, which could only be blunted, it seemed to her, by decaying *with* someone, the comfort every Negro couple felt when, aging, they knew enough to let things wind down.

Her patience was rewarded in the beginning. Rudolph crawled home from his first lesson, hunched over, hardly able to stand, afraid he had permanently ruptured something. He collapsed face down on the living room sofa, his feet on the floor. She helped him change into his pajamas and fingered Ben-Gay into his back muscles. Evelyn had never seen her husband so close to tears.

"I can't *do* push-ups," he moaned. "Or sit-ups. I'm so stiff—I don't know my body." He lifted his head, looking up pitifully, his eyes pleading. "Call Dr. Guylee. Make an appointment for Thursday, okay?"

"Yes, dear." Evelyn hid her smile with one hand. "You shouldn't push yourself so hard."

At that, he sat up, bare-chested, his stomach bubbling over his pajama bottoms. "That's what it means. *Gung-fu* means 'hard work' in Chinese. Evelyn"—he lowered his voice—"I don't think I've ever really done hard work in my life. Not like this, something that asks me to give *every*thing, body and soul, spirit and flesh. I've always felt . . ." He looked down, his dark hands dangling between his thighs. "I've never been able to give *every*thing to *any*thing. The world never let me. It won't let me put all of myself into play. Do you know what I'm saying? Every job I've ever had, everything I've ever done, it only demanded part of me. It was like there was so much *more* of me that went unused after the job was over. I get that feeling in church sometimes." He lay back down, talking now into the sofa cushion. "Sometimes I get that feeling with you."

Her hand stopped on his shoulder. She wasn't sure she'd heard him right, his voice was so muffled. "That I've never used all of you?"

Rudolph nodded, rubbing his right knuckle where, at the kwoon, he'd lost a stretch of skin on a speedbag. "There's still part of me left over. You never tried to touch all of me, to take everything. Maybe you can't. Maybe no one can. But sometimes I get the feeling that the unused part—the unlived life—*spoils,* that you get cancer because it sits like fruit on the ground and rots." Rudolph shook his head; he'd said too much and knew it, perhaps had not even put it the way he felt inside. Stiffly, he got to his feet. "Don't ask me to stop training." His eyebrows spread inward. "If I stop, I'll die."

Evelyn twisted the cap back onto the Ben-Gay. She held out her hand, which Rudolph took. Veins on the back of his hand burgeoned abnormally like dough. Once when she was shopping at the Public Market she'd seen monstrous plastic gloves shaped like hands in a magic store window. His hand looked like that. It belonged on Lon Chaney. Her voice shook a little, panicky, "I'll call Dr. Guylee in the morning."

Evelyn knew—or thought she knew—his trouble. He'd never come to terms with the disagreeableness of things. Rudolph had always been too serious for some people, even in South Carolina. It was the thing, strange to say, that drew her to him, this crimped-browed tendency in Rudolph to listen with every atom of his life when their minister in Hodges, quoting Marcus Aurelius to give his sermon flash, said, "Live with the gods," or later in Seattle, the habit of working himself up over Reverend Merrill's reading from Ecclesiastes 9:10: "Whatsoever thy hand findeth to do, do it with all thy might." Now, he didn't *really* mean that, Evelyn knew. Nothing in the world could be taken that seriously; that's *why* this was the world. And, as all Mount Zion knew, Reverend Merrill had a weakness for high-yellow choirgirls and gin, and was forever complaining that his salary was too small for his family. People made compromises, nodded at spiritual commonplaces—the high seriousness of biblical verses that demanded nearly superhuman duty and self-denial—and laughed off their lapses into sloth, envy, and the other deadly sins. It was what made living so enjoyably *human:* this built-in inability of man to square his performance with perfection. People were naturally soft on themselves. But not her Rudolph.

Of course, he seldom complained. It was not in his nature to complain when, looking for "gods," he found only ruin and wreckage. What did he expect? Evelyn wondered. Man was evil—she'd told him that a thousand times—or, if not evil, hopelessly flawed. Everything failed; it was some sort of law. But at least there was laughter, and lovers clinging to one another against the cliff; there were novels— wonderful tales of how things should be—and perfection promised in the afterworld. He'd sit and listen, her Rudolph, when she put things this way, nodding because he knew that in his persistent hunger for perfection in the here and now he was, at best, in the minority. He kept his dissatisfaction to himself, but occasionally Evelyn would glimpse in his eyes that look, that distant, pained expression that asked: *Is this all?* She saw it after her first miscarriage, then her second; saw it when he stopped searching the want ads and settled on the Post Office as the fulfillment of his potential in the marketplace. It was always there, that look, after he turned forty, and no new, lavishly praised novel from the Book-of-the-Month Club, no feature-length movie, prayer meeting, or meal she fixed for him wiped it from Rudolph's eyes. He was, at least, this sort of man before he saw that martial-arts B movie. It was a dark vision, Evelyn decided, a dangerous vision, and in it she whiffed something that might destroy her. What that was, she couldn't say, but she knew her Rudolph better than he knew himself. He would see the error—the waste of time—in his new hobby, and she was sure he would mend his ways.

In the weeks, then months that followed Evelyn waited, watching her husband for a flag of surrender. There was no such sign. He became worse than before. He cooked his own meals, called her heavy soul food dishes "too acidic," lived on raw vegetables, seaweed, nuts, and fruit to make his body "more alkaline," and fasted on Sundays. He ordered books on something called Shaolin fighting and meditation from a store in California, and when his equipment arrived UPS from Dolan's Sports in New Jersey, he ordered more—in consternation, Evelyn read the list—leg stretchers, makiwara boards, air shields, hand grips, bokken, focus mitts, a full-length mirror (for heaven's sake) so he could correct his form, and protective equipment. For proper use of his headgear and gloves, however, he said he needed a sparring partner—an opponent—he said, to help him instinctively understand "combat strategy," how to "flow" and "close the Gap" between himself and an adversary, how to create by his movements a negative space in which the other would be neutralized.

"Well," crabbed Evelyn, "if you need a punching bag, don't look at *me.*"

He sat across the kitchen table from her, doing dynamic-tension exercises as she read a new magazine called *Self.* "Did I ever tell you what a black belt means?" he asked.

"You told me."

"Sifu Chan doesn't use belts for ranking. They were introduced several years ago because Westerners were impatient, you know, needed signposts and all that."

"You told me," said Evelyn.

"Originally, all you got was a white belt. It symbolized innocence. Virginity." His face was immensely serious, like a preacher's. "As you worked, it got darker, dirtier, and turned brown. Then black. You were a master then. With even more work, the belt became frayed, the threads came loose, you see, and the belt showed white again."

"Rudolph, I've heard this before!" Evelyn picked up her magazine and took it into her bedroom. From there, with her legs drawn up under the blankets, she shouted: "I *won't* be your punching bag!"

So he brought friends from his kwoon, friends she wanted nothing to do with. There was something unsettling about them. Some were street fighters. Young. They wore tank-top shirts and motorcycle jackets. After drinking racks of Rainier beer on the front porch, they tossed their crumpled empties next door into Rod Kenner's yard. Together, two of Rudolph's new friends—Truck and Tuco—weighed a quarter of a ton. Evelyn kept a rolling pin under her pillow when they came, but she knew they could eat that along with her. But some of his new friends were students at the University of Washington. Truck, a Vietnamese only two years in America, planned to apply to the Police Academy once his training ended; and Tuco, who was Puerto Rican, had been fighting since he could make a fist; but a delicate young man named Andrea, a blue sash, was an actor in the drama department at the university. His kwoon training, he said, was less for self-defense than helping him understand his movements onstage— how, for example, to convincingly explode across a room in anger. Her husband liked them, Evelyn realized in horror. And they liked him. They were separated by money, background, and religion, but something she could not identify made them seem, those nights on the porch after his class, like a single body. They called Rudolph "Older Brother" or, less politely, "Pop."

His sifu, a short, smooth-figured boy named Douglas Chan, who Evelyn figured couldn't be over eighteen, sat like the Dalai Lama in their tiny kitchen as if he owned it, sipping her tea, which Rudolph laced with Korean ginseng. Her husband lit Chan's cigarettes as if he were President Carter come to visit the common man. He recommended that Rudolph study T'ai Chi, "soft" fighting systems, ki, and something called Tao. He told him to study, as well, Newton's three laws of physics and apply them to his own body during kumite. What she remembered most about Chan were his wrist braces, ornamental weapons that had three straps and, along the black leather, highly polished studs like those worn by Steve Reeves in a movie she'd seen about Hercules. In a voice she thought girlish, he spoke of eye gouges and groin-tearing techniques, exercises called the Delayed Touch of Death and Dim Mak, with the casualness she and Shelberdine talked about bargains at Thriftway. And then they suited up, the boyish Sifu, who looked like Maharaj-ji's rougher brother, and her clumsy husband; they went out back, pushed aside the aluminum lawn furniture, and pommeled each other for half an hour. More precisely, her Rudolph was on the receiving end of hook kicks, spinning back fists faster than thought, and foot sweeps that left his body purpled for weeks. A sensible man would have known enough to drive to Swedish Hospital pronto. Rudolph, never known as a profound thinker, pushed on after Sifu Chan left, practicing his flying kicks by leaping to ground level from a four-foot hole he'd dug by their cyclone fence.

Evelyn, nibbling a Van de Kamp's pastry from Safeway—she was always nibbling, these days—watched from the kitchen window until twilight, then brought out the Ben-Gay, a cold beer, and rubbing alcohol on a tray. She figured he needed it. Instead, Rudolph, stretching under the far-reaching cedar in the backyard, politely refused, pushed the tray aside, and rubbed himself with Dit-Da-Jow, "iron-hitting wine," which smelled like the open door of an opium factory on a hot summer day. Yet this ancient potion not only instantly healed his wounds (said Rudolph) but prevented arthritis as well. She was tempted to see if it healed brain damage by pouring it into Rudolph's ears, but apparently he was doing something right. Dr. Guylee's examination had been glowing; he said Rudolph's muscle tone, whatever that was, was better. His cardiovascular system was healthier. His erections were outstanding—or upstanding—though lately he seemed to have no interest in sex. Evelyn, even she, saw in the crepuscular light changes in Rudolph's upper body as he stretched: Muscles like globes of light rippled along his shoulders; larval currents moved on his belly. The language of his new, developing body eluded her. He was not always like this. After a cold shower and sleep his muscles shrank back a little. It was only after his workouts, his weight lifting, that his body expanded like baking bread, filling out in a way that obliterated the soft Rudolph-body she knew. This new flesh had the contours of the silhouetted figures on medical charts: the body as it must be in the mind of God. Glistening with perspiration, his muscles took on the properties of the free weights he pumped relentlessly. They were profoundly tragic, too, because their beauty was earthbound. It would vanish with the world. You are ugly, his new muscles said to Evelyn; old and ugly. His self-punishment made her feel sick. She was afraid of his hard, cold weights. She hated them. Yet she wanted them, too. They had a certain monastic beauty. She thought: *He's doing this to hurt me.* She wondered: What was it like to be powerful? Was clever cynicism—even comedy—the by-product of bulging bellies, weak nerves, bad posture? Her only defense against the dumbbells that stood between them—she meant both his weights and his friends—was, as always, her acid southern tongue:

"They're all fairies, right?"

Rudolph looked dreamily her way. These post-workout periods made him feel, he said, as if there were no interval between himself and what he saw. His face was vacant, his eyes—like smoke. In this afterglow (he said) he saw without judging. Without judgment, there were no distinctions. Without distinctions, there was no desire. Without desire . . .

He smiled sideways at her. "Who?"

"The people in your kwoon." Evelyn crossed her arms. "I read somewhere that most body builders are homosexual."

He refused to answer her.

"If they're not gay, then maybe I should take lessons. It's been good for you, right?" Her voice grew sharp. "I mean, isn't that what you're saying? That you and your friends are better'n everybody else?"

Rudolph's head dropped; he drew a long breath. Lately, his responses to her took the form of quietly clearing his lungs.

"You should do what you *have* to, Evelyn. You don't have to do what anybody else does." He stood up, touched his toes, then brought his forehead straight down against his unbent knees, which was physically impossible, Evelyn would have said—and faintly obscene.

It was a nightmare to watch him each evening after dinner. He walked around the house in his Everlast leg weights, tried push-ups on his finger-tips and wrists, and, as she sat trying to watch "The Jeffersons," stood in a ready stance before the flickering screen, throwing punches each time the scene, or shot, changed to improve his timing. It took the fun out of watching TV, him doing that—she preferred him falling asleep in his chair beside her, as he used to. But what truly frightened Evelyn was his "doing nothing." Sitting in meditation, planted cross-legged in a full lotus on their front porch, with Mr. Miller blissfully curled on his lap, a Bodhisattva in the middle of houseplants she set out for the sun. Looking at him, you'd have thought he was dead. The whole thing smelled like self-hypnosis. He breathed too slowly, in Evelyn's view—only three breaths per minute, he claimed. He wore his gi, splotchy with dried blood and sweat, his calloused hands on his knees, the forefingers on each tipped against his thumbs, his eyes screwed shut.

During his eighth month at the kwoon, she stood watching him as he sat, wondering over the vivid changes in his body, the grim firmness where before there was jolly fat, the disquieting steadiness of his posture, where before Rudolph could not sit still in church for five minutes without fidgeting. Now he sat in zazen for forty-five minutes a day, fifteen when he awoke, fifteen (he said) at work in the mailroom during his lunch break, fifteen before going to bed. He called this withdrawal (how she hated his fancy language) similar to the necessary silences in music, "a stillness that prepared him for busyness and sound." He'd never breathed before, he told her. Not once. Not clear to the floor of himself. Never breathed and emptied himself as he did now, picturing himself sitting on the bottom of Lake Washington: himself, Rudolph Lee Jackson, at the center of the universe; for if the universe was infinite, any point where he stood would be at its center—it would shift and move with him. (That saying, Evelyn knew, was minted in Douglas Chan's mind. No Negro preacher worth the name would speak that way.) He told her that in zazen, at the bottom of the lake, he worked to discipline his mind and maintain one point of concentration; each thought, each feeling that overcame him he saw as a fragile bubble, which he could inspect passionlessly from all sides; then he let it float gently to the surface, and soon—as he slipped deeper into the vortices of himself, into the Void—even the image of himself on the lake floor vanished.

Evelyn stifled a scream.

Was she one of Rudolph's bubbles, something to detach himself from? On the porch, Evelyn watched him narrowly, sitting in a rain-whitened chair, her chin on her left fist. She snapped the fingers on her right hand under his nose. Nothing. She knocked her knuckles lightly on his forehead. Nothing. (Faker, she thought.) For another five minutes he sat and breathed, sat and breathed, then opened his eyes slowly as if he'd slept as long as Rip Van Winkle. "It's dark," he said, stunned. When he began, it was twilight. Evelyn realized something new: He was not living time as she was, not even that anymore. Things, she saw, were slower for him; to him she must seem like a woman stuck in fast-forward. She asked:

"What do you see when you go in there?"

Rudolph rubbed his eyes. "Nothing."

"Then *why* do you do it? The world's out here!"

He seemed unable to say, as if the question were senseless. His eyes angled up, like a child's, toward her face. "Nothing is peaceful sometimes. The emptiness is full. I'm not afraid of it now."

"You empty yourself?" she asked. "Of me, too?"

"Yes."

Evelyn's hand shot up to cover her face. She let fly with a whimper. Rudolph rose instantly—he sent Mr. Miller flying—then fell back hard on his buttocks; the lotus cut off blood to his lower body—which provided more to his brain, he claimed—and it always took him a few seconds before he could stand again. He reached up, pulled her hand down, and stroked it.

"What've I done?"

"That's it," sobbed Evelyn. "I don't know what you're doing." She lifted the end of her bathrobe, blew her nose, then looked at him through streaming, unseeing eyes. "And you don't either. I wish you'd never seen that movie. I'm sick of all your weights and workouts—sick of them, do you hear? Rudolph, I want you back the way you were: *sick.*" No sooner than she said this Evelyn was sorry. But she'd done no harm. Rudolph, she saw, didn't want anything; everything, Evelyn included, delighted him, but as far as Rudolph was concerned, it was all shadows in a phantom history. He was humbler now, more patient, but he'd lost touch with everything she knew was normal in people: weakness, fear, guilt, self-doubt, the very things that gave the world thickness and made people do things. She *did* want him to desire her. No, she didn't. Not if it meant oral sex. Evelyn didn't know, really, what she wanted anymore. She felt, suddenly, as if she might dissolve before his eyes. "Rudolph, if you're 'empty,' like you say, you don't know who—or what—is talking to you. If you said you were praying, I'd understand. It would be God talking to you. But this way . . ."

She pounded her fist four, five times on her thigh. "It could be *evil* spirits, you know! There *are* evil spirits, Rudolph. It could be the Devil."

Rudolph thought for a second. His chest lowered after another long breath. "Evelyn, this is going to sound funny, but I don't believe in the Devil."

Evelyn swallowed. It had come to that.

"Or God—unless we are gods."

She could tell he was at pains to pick his words carefully, afraid he might offend. Since joining the kwoon and studying ways to kill, he seemed particularly careful to avoid her own most effective weapon: the wry, cutting remark, the put-down, the direct, ego-deflating slash. Oh, he was becoming a real saint. At times, it made her want to hit him.

"Whatever is just *is*," he said. "That's all I know. Instead of worrying about whether it's good or bad, God or the Devil, I just want to be quiet, work on myself, and interfere with things as little as possible. Evelyn," he asked suddenly, "how can there be *two* things?" His brow wrinkled; he chewed his lip. "You think what I'm saying is evil, don't you?"

"I think it's strange! Rudolph, you didn't grow up in China," she said. "They can't breathe in China! I saw that today on the news. They burn soft coal, which gets into the air and turns into acid rain. They wear face masks over there, like the ones we bought when Mount St. Helens blew up. They all ride bicycles, for Christ's sake! They want what we have." Evelyn heard Rod Kenner step onto his screened porch, perhaps to listen from his rocker. She dropped her voice a little. "You grew up in Hodges, South Carolina, same as me, in a right and proper colored church. If you'd *been* to China, maybe I'd understand."

"I can only be what I've been?" This he asked softly, but his voice trembled. "Only what I was in Hodges?"

"You can't be Chinese."

"I don't want to be Chinese!" The thought made Rudolph smile and shake his head. Because she did not understand, and because he was tired of talking, Rudolph stepped back a few feet from her, stretching again, always stretching. "I only want to be what I *can* be, which isn't the greatest fighter in the world, only the fighter *I* can be. Lord knows, I'll probably get creamed in the tournament this Saturday." He added, before she could reply, "Doug asked me if I'd like to compete this weekend in full-contact matches with some people from the kwoon. I have to." He opened the screen door. "I will."

"You'll be killed—you know that, Rudolph." She dug her fingernails into her bathrobe, and dug this into him: "You know, you never were very strong. Six months ago you couldn't open a pickle jar for me."

He did not seem to hear her. "I bought a ticket for you." He held the screen door open, waiting for her to come inside. "I'll fight better if you're there."

She spent the better part of that week at Shelberdine's mornings and Reverend Merrill's church evenings, rinsing her mouth with prayer, sitting most often alone in the front row so she would not have to hear Rudolph talking to himself from the musty basement as he pounded out bench presses, skipped rope for thirty minutes in the backyard, or shadowboxed in preparation for a fight made inevitable by his new muscles. She had married a fool, that was clear, and if he expected her to sit on a bench at the Kingdome while some equally stupid brute spilled the rest of his brains—probably not enough left now to fill a teaspoon—then he was wrong. How could he see the world as "perfect"?—That was his claim. There was poverty, unemployment, twenty-one children dying every minute, every day, every year from hunger and malnutrition, over twenty murdered in Atlanta; there were sixty thousand nuclear weapons in the world, which was dreadful, what with Seattle so close to Boeing; there were far-right Republicans in the White House: *good* reasons, Evelyn thought, to be "negative and life-denying," as Rudolph would put it. It was almost sin to see harmony in an earthly hell, and in a fit of spleen she prayed God would dislocate his shoulder, do some minor damage to humble him, bring him home, and remind him that the body was vanity, a violation of every verse in the Bible. But Evelyn could not sustain her thoughts as long as he could. Not for more than a few seconds. Her mind never settled, never rested, and finally on Saturday morning, when she awoke on Shelberdine's sofa, it would not stay away from the image of her Rudolph dead before hundreds of indifferent spectators, paramedics pounding on his chest, bursting his rib cage in an effort to keep him alive.

From Shelberdine's house she called a taxi and, in the steady rain that northwesterners love, arrived at the Kingdome by noon. It's over already, Evelyn thought, walking the circular stairs to her seat, clamping shut her wet umbrella. She heard cheers, booing, an Asian voice with an accent over a microphone. The tournament began at ten, which was enough time for her white belt husband to be in the emergency ward at Harborview Hospital by now, but she had to see. At first, as she stepped down to her seat through the crowd, she could only hear—her mind grappled for the word, then remembered—kiais, or "spirit shouts," from the great floor of the stadium, many shouts, for contests were progressing in three rings simultaneously. It felt like a circus. It smelled like a locker room. Here two children stood toe to toe until one landed a front kick that sent the other child flying fifteen feet. There two lean-muscled female black belts were interlocked in a delicate ballet, like dance or a chess game, of continual motion. They had a kind of sense, these women—she noticed it immediately—a feel for space and their place in it. (Evelyn hated them immediately.) And in the farthest circle she saw, or rather felt, Rudolph, the oldest thing on the deck, who, sparring in the adult division, was squared off with another white belt, not a boy who might hurt him—the other man was middle-aged, graying, maybe only a few years younger than Rudolph—but they were sparring just the same.

Yet it was not truly him that Evelyn, sitting down, saw. Acoustics in the Kingdome whirlpooled the noise of the crowd, a rivering of voices that affected her, suddenly, like the pitch and roll of voices during service. It affected the way she watched Rudolph. She wondered: Who are these people? She caught her breath when, miscalculating his distance from his opponent, her husband stepped sideways into a roundhouse kick with lots of snap—she heard the cloth of his opponent's gi crack like a gunshot when he threw the technique. She leaned forward, gripping the huge purse on her lap when Rudolph recovered and retreated from the killing to the neutral zone, and then, in a wide stance, rethought strategy. This was not the man she'd slept with for twenty years. Not her hypochondriac Rudolph who had to rest and run cold water on his wrists after walking from the front stairs to the fence to pick up the *Seattle Times*. She did not know him, perhaps had never known him, and now she never would, for the man on the floor, the man splashed with sweat, rising on the ball of his rear foot for a flying kick—was he so foolish he still thought he could fly?—would outlive her; he'd stand healthy and strong and think of her in a bubble, one hand on her headstone, and it was all right, she thought, weeping uncontrollably, it was all right that Rudolph would return home after visiting her wet grave, clean out her bedroom, the pillboxes and paperback books, and throw open her windows to let her sour, rotting smell escape, then move a younger woman's things onto the floor space darkened by her color television, her porcelain chamber pot, her antique sewing machine. And then Evelyn was on her feet, unsure why, but the crowd had stood suddenly to clap, and Evelyn clapped, too, though for an instant she pounded her gloved hands together instinctively until her vision cleared, the momentary flash of retinal blindness giving way to a frame of her husband, the postman, twenty feet off the ground in a perfect flying kick that floored his opponent and made a Japanese judge who looked like Oddjob shout "ippon"—one point—and the fighting in the farthest ring, in herself, perhaps in all the world, was over.

§

Johnson presents us with two characters who conquer their fears and continue to grow as human beings. Though the story is almost evenly balanced between the two characters, it is the wife, Evelyn, who is most resistant in terms of transforming herself and accepting her husband's new self-identity.

Third person limited can encompass an unidentified narrator who can provide history and commentary as well as the viewpoints of characters.

In your journal, answer the following:

- Who speaks in the story's first sentence? Why does the story begin with a formal introduction of Evelyn and Rudolph? How does this prepare a reader for the "he" and "she" which follows?

- In the first paragraph, the unidentified narrator's presence is very subtle. Why do you think this is so? Underline the phrases or sentences you believe belong to the narrator. Next highlight those which seem to be coming more directly from the characters.

- Scanning the story, can you find any other examples of the unidentified narrator guiding the readers' focus and understanding? For example, on page 143, the fourth paragraph begins with "Evelyn knew—or thought she knew—his trouble." Whose voice is this? If it's the narrator, why is it important for the narrator to point out that Evelyn *thought* she knew what was wrong with Rudolph. How does the narrator undermine Evelyn's authority? Why is it important that readers be reminded that Evelyn's views aren't entirely trustworthy?

- Reread the last sentence of the story. What does this sentence add? Would such a sentence be possible if the story was written in first person or third person objective?

- How much of the story is written from Evelyn's point of view? How much is actually written from inside Rudolph's mind? Actions and direct dialogue teach us a great deal about both characters, but whose mind and heart do readers have the most access to? Why?

In your journal, write a paragraph about what Charles Johnson has taught you about the third person limited point of view.

POINT OF VIEW STUDY

TERRY MCMILLAN'S "MA'DEAR"

Terry McMillan's short story "Ma'Dear" presents a strong, first person narrator. It's a vibrant story about an old woman brimming with happy and romantic memories, who is surviving economic hard times and still embracing life.

Given an interesting character, an appealing voice, and, at minimum, a basic plot, McMillan proves there is nothing more satisfying than having a character speak directly to the reader and tell us a story.

⸙

For Estelle Ragsdale

LAST YEAR THE cost of living crunched me and I got tired of begging from Peter to pay Paul, so I took in three roomers. Two of 'em is live-in nurses and only come around here on weekends. Even then they don't talk to me much, except when they hand me their money orders. One is from Trinidad and the other is from Jamaica. Every winter they quit their jobs, fill up two and three barrels with I don't know what, ship 'em home, and follow behind on an airplane. They come back in the spring and start all over. Then there's the little college girl, Juanita, who claims she's going for architecture. Seem like to me that was always men's work, but I don't say nothing. She grown.

I'm seventy-two. Been a widow for the past thirty-two years. Weren't like I asked for all this solitude, just that couldn't nobody else take Jessie's place is all. He knew it. And I knew it. He fell and hit his head real bad on the tracks going to fetch us some fresh picked corn and okra for me to make us some succotash, and never come to. I couldn't picture myself with no other man, even though I looked after a few years of being alone in this big old house, walking from room to room with nobody to talk to, cook or clean for, and not much company either.

I missed him for the longest time and thought I could find a man just like him, sincerely like him, but I couldn't. Went out for a spell with Esther Davis's ex-husband, Whimpy, but he was crazy. Drank too much bootleg and then started memorizing on World War I and how hard he fought and didn't get no respect and not a ounce of recognition for his heroic deeds. The only war Whimpy been in is with me for not keeping him around. He bragged something fearless about how he coulda been the heavyweight champion of the world. Didn't weigh but 160 pounds and shorter than me.

Chester Rutledge almost worked 'ceptin' he was boring, never had nothing on his mind worth talking about; claimed he didn't think about nothing besides me. Said his mind was always clear and visible. He just moved around like a zombie and worked hard at the cement foundry. Insisted on giving me his paychecks, which I kindly took for a while, but when I didn't want to be bothered no more, I stopped taking his money. He got on my nerves too bad, so I had to tell him I'd rather have a man with no money and a busy mind, least I'd know he's active somewheres. His feelings was hurt bad and he cussed me out, but we still friends to this very day. He in the home, you know, and I visits him regular. Takes him magazines and cuts out his horoscope and the comic strips from the newspaper and lets him read 'em in correct order.

Big Bill Ronsonville tried to convince me that I shoulda married him instead of Jessie, but he couldn't make me a believer of it. All he wanted to do was put his big rusty hands all on me without asking and smile at me with that big gold tooth sparkling and glittering in my face and tell me how lavish I was, lavish being a new word he just learnt. He kept wanting to take me for night rides way out in the country, out there by Smith Creek where ain't nothing but deep black ditches, giant mosquitoes, loud crickets, lightning bugs, and loose pigs, and turn off his motor. His breath stank like whiskey though he claimed and swore on the Bible he didn't drank no liquor. Aside from that his hands were way too heavy and hard, hurt me, sometimes left red marks on me like I been sucked on. I told him finally that I was too light for him, that I needed a smaller, more gentle man, and he said he knew exactly what I meant.

If you want to know the truth, after him I didn't think much about men the way I used too. Lost track of the ones who upped and died or the ones who couldn't do nothing if they was alive nohow. So, since nobody else seemed to be able to wear Jessie's shoes, I just stuck to myself all these years.

My life ain't so bad now 'cause I'm used to being alone and takes good care of myself. Occasionally I still has a good time. I goes to the park and sits for hours in good weather, watch folks move and listen in on confidential conversations. I add up numbers on license plates to keep my mind alert unless they pass too fast. This gives me a clear idea of how many folks is visiting from out of town. I can about guess the color of every state now, too. Once or twice a month I go to the matinee on Wednesdays, providing ain't no long line of senior citizens 'cause they can be so slow; miss half the picture show waiting for them to count their change and get their popcorn.

Sometimes, when I'm sitting in the park, I feed the pigeons old cornbread crumbs, and I wonders what it'll be like not looking at the snow falling from the sky, not seeing the leaves form on the trees, not hearing no car engines, no sirens, no babies crying, not brushing my hair at night, drinking my Lipton tea, and not being able to go to bed early.

But right now, to tell you the truth, it don't bother me all *that* much. What is bothering me is my case worker. She supposed to pay me a visit tomorrow because my nosy neighbor, Clarabelle, saw two big trucks outside, one come right after the other, and she wondered what I was getting so new and so big that I needed trucks. My mama used to tell me that sometimes you can't see for looking. Clarabelle's had it out to do me in ever since last spring when I had the siding put on the house. I used the last of Jessie's insurance money 'cause the roof had been leaking so bad and the wood rotted and the paint chipped so much that it looked like a wicked old witch lived here. The house looked brand-new, and she couldn't stand to see an old woman's house looking better than hers. She know I been had roomers, and now all of a sudden my case worker claim she just want to visit to see how I'm doing, when really what she want to know is what I'm up to. Clarabelle work in her office.

The truth is my boiler broke and they was here to put in a new one. We liked to froze to death in here for two days. Yeah, I had a little chump change in the bank, but when they told me it was gonna cost $2,000 to get some heat, I cried. I had $862 in the bank; $300 of it I had just spent on this couch I got on sale; it was in the other truck. After twenty years the springs finally broke, and I figured it was time to buy a new one 'cause I ain't one for living in poverty, even at my age. I figured $200 was for my church's cross-country bus trip this summer.

Jessie's sister, Willamae, took out a loan for me to get the boiler, and I don't know how long it's gonna take me to pay her back. She only charge me fifteen or twenty dollars a month, depending. I probably be dead by the time it get down to zero.

My bank wouldn't give me the loan for the boiler, but then they keep sending me letters almost every week trying to get me to refinance my house. They must think I'm senile or something. On they best stationery, they write me. They say I'm up in age and wouldn't I like to take that trip I've been putting off because of no extra money. What trip? They tell me if I refinance my house for more than what I owe, which is about $3,000, that I could have enough money left over to go anywhere. Why would I want to refinance my house at fourteen and a half percent when I'm paying four and a half now? I ain't that stupid. They say dream about clear blue water, palm trees, and orange suns. Last night I dreamt I was doing a backstroke between big blue waves and tipped my straw hat down over my forehead and fell asleep under an umbrella. They made me think about it. And they asked me what would I do if I was to die today? They're what got me to thinking about all this dying mess in the first place. It never would've layed in my mind so heavy if they hadn't kept reminding me of it. Who would pay off your house? Wouldn't I feel bad leaving this kind of a burden on my family? What family they talking about? I don't even know where my people is no more.

I ain't gonna lie. It ain't easy being old. But I ain't complaining neither, 'cause I learned how to stretch my social security check. My roomers pay the house note and I pay the taxes. Oil is sky-high. Medicaid pays my doctor bills. I got a letter what told me to apply for food stamps. That case worker come here and checked to see if I had a real kitchen. When she saw I had a stove and sink and refrigerator, she didn't like the idea that my house was almost paid for, and just knew I was lying about having roomers. "Are you certain that you reside here alone?" she asked me. "I'm certain," I said. She searched every inch of my cabinets to make sure I didn't have two of the same kinds of food, which would've been a dead giveaway. I hid it all in the basement inside the washing machine and dryer. Luckily, both of the nurses was in the islands at the time, and Juanita was visiting some boy what live in D.C.

After she come here and caused me so much eruptions, I had to make trip after trip down to that office. They had me filling out all kinds of forms and still held up my stamps. I got tired of answering the same questions over and over and finally told 'em to keep their old food stamps. I ain't got to beg nobody to eat. I know how to keep myself comfortable and clean and well fed. I manage to buy my staples and toiletries and once in a while a few extras, like potato chips, ice cream, and maybe a pork chop.

My mama taught me when I was young that, no matter how poor you are, always eat nourishing food and your body will last. Learn to conserve, she said. So I keeps all my empty margarine containers and stores white rice, peas and carrots (my favorites), or my turnips from the garden in there. I can manage a garden when my arthritis ain't acting up. And water is the key. I drinks plenty of it like the doctor told me, and I cheats, eats Oreo cookies and saltines. They fills me right up, too. And when I feels like it, rolls, homemade biscuits, eats them with Alga syrup if I can find it at the store, and that sticks with me most of the day.

Long time ago, used to be I'd worry like crazy about gaining weight and my face breaking out from too many sweets, and about cellulite forming all over my hips and thighs. Of course, I was trying to catch Jessie then, though I didn't know it at the time. I was really just being cute, flirting, trying to see if I could get attention. Just so happens I lucked up and got all of his. Caught him like he was a spider and I was the web.

Lord, I'd be trying to look all sassy and prim. Have my hair all did, it be curled tight in rows that I wouldn't comb out for hours till they cooled off after Connie Curtis did it for a dollar and a Budweiser. Would take that dollar out my special savings, which I kept hid under the record player in the front room. My hair used to be fine, too: long and thick and black, past my shoulders, and mens used to say, "Girl, you sure got a head of hair on them shoulders there, don't it make your neck sweat?" But I didn't never bother answering, just blushed and smiled and kept on walking, trying hard not to switch 'cause mama told me my behind was too big for my age and to watch out or I'd be luring grown mens toward me. Humph! I loved it, though, made me feel pretty, special, like I had attraction.

Ain't quite the same no more, though. I looks in the mirror at myself and I sees wrinkles, lots of them, and my skin look like it all be trying to run down toward my toes but then it changed its mind and just stayed there, sagging and lagging, laying limp against my thick bones. Shoot, mens used to say how sexy I was with these high cheeks, tell me I looked swollen, like I was pregnant, but it was just me, being all healthy and everything. My teeth was even bright white and straight in a row then. They ain't so bad now, 'cause ain't none of 'em mine. But I only been to the dentist twice in my whole life and that was 'cause on Easter Sunday I was in so much pain he didn't have time to take no X-ray and yanked it right out 'cause my mama told him to do anything he had to to shut me up. Second time was the last time, and that was 'cause the whole top row and the fat ones way in the back on the bottom ached me so bad the dentist yanked 'em all out so I wouldn't have to be bothered no more.

Don't get me wrong, I don't miss being young. I did everything I wanted to do and then some. I loved hard. But you take Jessie's niece, Thelma. She pitiful. Only twenty-six, don't think she made it past the tenth grade, got three children by different men, no husband and on welfare. Let her tell it, ain't nothing out here but dogs. I know some of these men out here ain't worth a pot to piss in, but all of 'em ain't dogs. There's gotta be some young Jessies floating somewhere in this world. My mama always told me you gotta have something to give if you want to get something in return. Thelma got long fingernails.

Me, myself, I didn't have no kids. Not 'cause I didn't want none or couldn't have none, just that Jessie wasn't full and couldn't give me the juices I needed to make no babies. I accepted it 'cause I really wanted him all to myself, even if he couldn't give me no new bloodlines. He was satisfying enough for me, quite satisfying if you don't mind me repeating myself.

I don't understand Thelma, like a lot of these young peoples. I be watching 'em on the streets and on TV. I be hearing things they be doing to themselves when I'm under the dryer at the beauty shop. (I go to the beauty shop once a month 'cause it make me feel like thangs ain't over yet. She give me a henna so the silver have a gold tint to it.) I can't afford it, but there ain't too many luxuries I can. I let her put makeup on me, too, if it's a Saturday and I feel like doing some window shopping. I still know how to flirt and sometimes I get stares, too. It feel good to be looked at and admired at my age. I try hard to keep myself up. Every weekday morning at five-thirty I do exercises with the TV set, when it don't hurt to stretch.

But like I was saying, Thelma and these young people don't look healthy, and they spirits is always so low. I watch 'em on the streets, on the train, when I'm going to the doctor. I looks in their eyes and they be red or brown where they supposed to be milky white and got bags deeper and heavier than mine, and I been through some thangs. I hear they be using these drugs of variety, and I can't understand why they need to use all these thangs to get from day to day. From what I do hear, it's supposed to give 'em much pleasure and make their minds disappear or make 'em not feel the thangs they supposed to be feeling anyway.

Heck, when I was young, we drank sarsaparilla and couldn't even buy no wine or any kind of liquor in no store. These youngsters ain't but eighteen and twenty and buys anything with a bite to it. I've seen 'em sit in front of the store and drank a whole bottle in one sitting. Girls, too.

We didn't have no dreams of carrying on like that, and specially on no corner. We was young ladies and young men with respect for ourselfs. And we didn't smoke none of them funny cigarettes all twisted up with no filters that smell like burning dirt. I ask myself, I say Ma'Dear, what's wrong with these kids? They can read and write and do arithmetic, finish high school, go to college and get letters behind their names, but every day I hear the neighbors complain that one of they youngsters done dropped out.

Lord, what I wouldn'ta done to finish high school and been able to write a full sentence or even went to college. I reckon I'da been a room decorator. I know they calls it be that fancy name now, interior designer, but it boil down to the same thang. I guess it's 'cause I loves so to make my surroundings pleasant, even right pretty, so I feels like a invited guest in my own house. And I always did have a flair for color. Folks used to say, "Hazel, for somebody as poor as a church mouse, you got better taste in thangs than them Rockefellers!" Used to sew up a storm, too. Covered my mama's raggedy duffold and chairs. Made her a bedspread with matching pillowcases. Didn't mix more than two different patterns either. Make you dizzy.

Wouldn't that be just fine, being an interior designer? Learning the proper names of thangs and recognizing labels in catalogs, giving peoples my business cards and wearing a two-piece with white gloves. "Yes, I decorated the Hartleys' and Cunninghams' home. It was such a pleasant experience. And they're such lovely people, simply lovely," I'da said. Coulda told those rich folks just what they needed in their bedrooms, front rooms, and specially in the kitchen. So many of 'em still don't know what to do in there.

But like I was saying before I got all off the track, some of these young people don't appreciate what they got. And they don't know thangs like we used to. We knew about eating fresh vegetables from the garden, growing and picking 'em ourselves. What going to church was, being honest and faithful. Trusting each other. Leaving our front door open. We knew what it was like to starve and get cheated yearly when our crops didn't add up the way we figured. We suffered together, not separately. These youngsters don't know about suffering for any stretch of time. I hear 'em on the train complaining 'cause they can't afford no Club Med, no new record playing albums, cowboy boots, or those Brooke Shields–Calvin Klein blue jeans I see on TV. They be complaining about nonsense. Do they ever read books since they been taught is what I want to know? Do they be learning things and trying to figure out what to do with it?

And these young girls with all this thick makeup caked on their faces, wearing these high heels they can't hardly walk in. Trying to be cute. I used to wear high heels, mind you, with silk stockings, but at least I could walk in 'em. Jessie had a car then. Would pick me up, and I'd walk real careful down the front steps like I just won the Miss America pageant, one step at a time, and slide into his shiny black Ford. All the neighbors peeked through the curtains 'cause I was sure enough riding in a real automobile with my legitimate boyfriend.

If Jessie was here now I'd have somebody to talk to. Somebody to touch my skin. He'd probably take his fingers and run 'em through my hair like he used to; kiss me on my nose and tickle me where it made me laugh. I just loved it when he kissed me. My mind be so light, and I felt tickled and precious. Have to sit down sometime just to get hold of myself.

If he was here, I probably woulda beat him in three games of checkers by now and he'd be trying to get even. But since today is Thursday, I'd be standing in that window over there waiting for him to get home from work, and when I got tired or the sun be in my eyes, I'd hear the taps on his wing tips coming up the front porch. Sometime, even now, I watch for him, but I know he ain't coming back. Not that he wouldn't if he could, mind you, 'cause he always told me I made him feel lightning lighting up his heart.

Don't get me wrong, I got friends, though a heap of 'em is dead or got tubes coming out of their noses or going all through their bodies every which-a-way. Some in the old folks' home. I thank the Lord I ain't stuck in one of them places. I ain't never gonna get that old. They might as well just bury me standing up if I do. I don't want to be no nuisance to nobody, and I can't stand being around a lot of sick people for too long.

I visits Gunther and Chester when I can, and Vivian who I grew up with, but no soon as I walk through them long hallways, I get depressed. They lay there all limp and helpless, staring at the ceiling like they're really looking at something, or sitting stiff in their rocking chairs, pitiful, watching TV and don't be knowing what they watching half the time. They laugh when ain't nothing funny. They wait for it to get dark so they know it's time to go to sleep. They relatives don't hardly come visit 'em, just folks like me. Whimpy don't understand a word I say, and it makes me grateful I ain't lost no more than I have.

Sometime we sits on the sun porch rocking like fools; don't say one word to each other for hours. But last time Gunther told me about his grandson what got accepted to Stanford University, and another one at a university in Michigan. I asked him where was Stanford and he said he didn't know. "What difference do it make?" he asked. "It's one of those uppity schools for rich smart white people," he said. "The important thang is that my black grandson won a scholarship there, which mean he don't have to pay a dime to go." I told him I know what a scholarship is. I ain't stupid. Gunther said he was gonna be there for at least four years or so, and by that time he would be a professional. "Professional what?" I asked. "Who cares, Ma'Dear, he gonna be a professional at whatever it is he learnt." Vivian started mumbling when she heard us talking, 'cause she still like to be the center of attention. When she was nineteen she was Miss Springfield Gardens. Now she can't stand the thought that she old and wrinkled. She started yakking about all the places she'd been to, even described the landscape like she was looking at a photograph. She ain't been but twenty-two miles north of here in her entire life, and that's right there in that home.

Like I said, and this is the last time I'm gonna mention it. I don't mind being old, it's just that sometime I don't need all this solitude. You can't do everything by yourself and expect to have as much fun if somebody was there doing it with you. That's why when I'm feeling jittery or melancholy for long stretches, I read the Bible, and it soothes me. I water my morning glories and amaryllis. I baby-sit for Thelma every now and then, 'cause she don't trust me with the kids for too long. She mainly call on holidays and my birthday. And she the only one who don't forget my birthday: August 19th. She tell me I'm a Leo, that I got fire in my blood. She may be right, 'cause once in a while I gets a churning desire to be smothered in Jessie's arms again.

Anyway, it's getting late, but I ain't tired. I feel pretty good. That old case worker think she gonna get the truth out of me. She don't scare me. It ain't none of her business that I got money coming in here besides my social security check. How they 'spect a human being to live off $369 a month in this day and age is what I wanna know. Every time I walk out my front door it cost me at least two dollars. I bet she making thousands and got credit cards galore. Probably got a summer house on the Island and goes to Florida every January. If she found out how much I was getting from my roomers, the government would make me pay back a dollar for every two I made. I best to get my tail on upstairs and clear everything off their bureaus. I can hide all the nurses's stuff in the attic; they won't be back till next month. Juanita been living out of trunks since she got here, so if the woman ask what's in 'em, I'll tell her, old sheets and pillowcases and memories.

On second thought, I think I'm gonna take me a bubble bath first, and dust my chest with talcum powder, then I'll make myself a hot cup of Lipton's and paint my fingernails clear 'cause my hands feel pretty steady. I can get up at five and do all that other mess; case worker is always late anyway. After she leave, if it ain't snowing too bad, I'll go to the museum and look at the new paintings in the left wing. By the time she get here, I'ma make out like I'm a lonely old widow stuck in a big old house just sitting here waiting to die.

McMillan puts readers right on the porch steps with Ma'Dear. As in traditional first person narratives, Ma'Dear is the main protagonist of her story. Unquestioningly, readers feel that the forthright Ma'Dear is telling the truth and sharing wisdom. There is also the delightful sense of Ma'Dear's uniqueness, a belief that no other "I" could have the same insights, reflections, memories, and responses to the world.

The first person point of view is limited to a single character's perceptions. There is no unidentified narrator. The "I" speaks directly to readers, bridging the emotional distance between storyteller and reader.

In your journal, answer the following:

  ≷ McMillan uses her story title to introduce the "I." Why would it be awkward for the narrator to introduce herself? How does the title allow for the story to begin immediately focused on the character?

  ≷ Ma'Dear begins her story with conflict: "Last year the cost of living crunched me . . ." Why didn't McMillan begin with the first lines of the second paragraph: "I'm seventy-two. Been a widow for the past thirty-two years"? How does the first sentence more quickly pull readers into her story? How does it help to establish emotional intimacy and a possible common bond between readers and Ma'Dear?

  ≷ The first paragraph emphasizes Ma'Dear's daily life and the second paragraph emphasizes her past life. How does the "I's" concern for both past and present enrich her characterization? It would be remarkable if a seventy-two-year-old didn't have memories. Nonetheless, notice how Ma'Dear weaves a balance between being alive and being attentive to the dead. How does this pattern throughout her story serve to make it more interesting?

  ≷ The first person narrator supplies the senses (sight, sound, taste, and smell) which readers need to experience her world. How well does Ma'Dear describe her world? How well does she help us "see" her other characters?

≷ Would the story have been as effective told in third person limited?

In your journal, write a paragraph about what Terry McMillan has taught you about the first person point of view.

POINT OF VIEW STUDY

J. CALIFORNIA COOPER'S "THE MAGIC STRENGTH OF NEED"

J. California Cooper uses a first person griot, an unidentified story-teller, to tell her tale. The storyteller's informal exuberance makes readers feel as though she's gathered them on the front porch or around a campfire to teach them a lesson about life. Like an omniscient author, the storyteller knows everything about Burlee and weaves Burlee's history to convey the "magic of need" to her listeners/readers.

≷

THERE'S MAGIC IN every life, I do believe! You just got to find it! I don't know how to explain it, but I do know it's not the kind of magic you read about that changes everything like for Cinderella. The real magic is something you got to think on, work on! It's a job! But it's the thing that brings your life through and you have some happiness. It's a hard job cause you don't never know which way the magic is going. You got to have some kind of good sense. Common sense!

Sometime, the magic fools you! It be setting there like a big unlucky, ugly . . . unwanted something! A person will walk over it,

step on it, throw it out, beat it up, hide it! Drown it in alcohol! Send it
into a coma with dope! Mildew it with tears or just kick it to the side
as they go out to dance! Some folks never find it!

Now, I'ma show you what I mean!

There was a girl named Burlee was born the seventh child to a
big, poor family. Burlee was what is called ugly! Even very ugly! The
world got a lot to pay for messing up a lotta people's minds with all
that division stuff! Now, rich and poor and North and South divides
things up and that's okay with things like that that can't feel nothing.
But when they made ugly and pretty, they was messing with people's
minds! Their lives!

I'ma tell you something! God didn't make no ugly people! Man
did! Talking about what was pretty and what was ugly. If it's somebody for everybody, then everybody is pretty to somebody! And it
wasn't none of them people's business who started this ugly-pretty
business to get in everybody's business like they did! You ever notice
that somebody the world says is ugly, you might even agree, but when
you get to know that person, you don't see ugly no more?! That goes
to show you! God didn't make ugly people! Man did!

Burlee's life started off wrong cause her mama meant to name her
"Berylee." A nurse who just passed right on through her life and out,
looked down at Burlee and decided she had just the right look for
"Burlee" and put that down. Some people are like that. Run in your
life and run out, leaving you something you got to deal with the rest of
your life!

Anyway, Burlee . . . was ugly. I mean ugly! Even her mama
knew that. Look like Burlee knew it too, cause she looked mad right
from the minute they put her in her mother's arms! Her mama said,
"Hm! Hmmm! Well, things will get better." But they didn't. Burlee
stayed ugly.

She was a quiet baby, just lay around looking mean. She had
plenty to cry about too! Wasn't much food (well, seven kids, you
know) and her diapers always wet making little sores on her baby-soft
behind. She grown now and still got some of the marks! Little eyes be
matted sometimes with something and nose all runny cause not
enough heat for the house. They paid rent but nobody ever fixed that

little house up! Paint rotted away, peeling walls, mildew even grew on the walls, and it was almost too cold for rats in there. Anyway, Burlee suffered all what being one of seven kids will make you suffer when your family is poor. The mama can try all she want too, she can't be everywhere doing everything at the same time! And sometime the dear sweet man be laying in your bed waiting for you to get through doing your work so you can come to bed and he can give you the start of something big that will wear you out some more in another nine months! He may not mean to, but, see, he may think you his magic! Thats a real funny valentine, ain't it?

However which way it was . . . Burlee was the last one cause her mama said she must be the bottom of the barrel!

Naturally, she went through the whooping cough and measles, mumps, and some of them things left little marks on Burlee's face to make that matter worse.

As she grew up, she wore all the hand-me-downs that made it down to her, went barefoot and without everything else when she had to.

As she got older, she made a secret place somewhere and would go off to that place and sit all day and think. I don't know all she was thinking of but I do know she was like a lot of people who want things. Things they see other people have. She was sick and tired and shamed of being laughed at and called "U-ga-ly!" She didn't have nothin . . . but her mama, who held her lots of times cause she knew Burlee needed it! They would talk.

"Burlee, don't cry. Don't pay no tention to what them kids say."

Burlee would cry back, "Mama, I can't help it!"

Mama would say, "You can help anything, Burlee."

Burlee would sniffle, "I try, Mama."

Mama would pet and rub. "You not ugly to me. And pretty ain't everything! Pretty is as pretty do!"

Through the warmth of her mother's love, Burlee would whisper, "What does pretty do, Mama?"

Mama would hold her closer. "Pretty go to school, study harrrrd, and learn how not to need nobody but herself!"

Burlee would smile a little. "I do that Mama. That don't make me pretty!"

Mama would smile back. "Yes it do! A little more every day! You watch and see. It adds up! You learn all you can! When you gets through learning, you gon see something!" Then another child would need Mama, cause children are jealous of each other sometimes! Mama would give Burlee a quick squeeze and turn to the next one. She was a thin, wiry woman, but she had strength she got from somewhere. She said it was from God. She had told her husband the Lord said to her, "Stop makin love" (cause she was tired). He said, "Then what I'm sposed to do?" She answered, "I don't know. You got to ask the Lord that!"

Anyway, Burlee did study hard. She was smart too! Quick to learn but always stayed in the background of things. Silent. All during high school she still went to sit in her quiet secret place, thinking. She knew what she wanted now.

Mama was bending from the weight of life . . . and was tired, very tired. When Burlee hugged her now, she would tell her, "Just hold on, Mama. I'll take care of you! I may not be getting pretty, but I am getting smart! I'm gonna find me a *rich man* and he gon marry me! I will sit you down! We'll both sit down!" Being sat down is a lotta people's dream.

Mama would smile, nod, and pat Burlee as she looked at her uncomely daughter with the shoulders and bust wider than any other part of her body. She looked like an exclamation point! Wasn't any curves and her head sat down in her shoulders with hardly no neck!

"Just be a good girl, Burlee," Mama would sigh.

"I'm too smart to be bad, Mama!" Burlee would smile and hug her one more time before some other child took over. Off she would go to her secret place and sit and dream, cause she was serious about marrying up with a Rich Man. Didn't know where they were or who they were, but they were out there! Didn't care was he black or white, just rich!

Now, it's somebody for everybody, I don't care who you are nor what you look like! At least one! Burlee had one who liked her by name of Winston. Winston wasn't too good-looking either, but he was better lookin than Burlee. The girls didn't pay him no mind. He was always leaning against some wall or tree, looking at things going on round him. He liked sports but had to work to help his mama and wasn't even in school too much, just enough to get by. He would walk home with Burlee sometime, telling her he liked her. Catching up to her he would say, "I'm going your way, Burlee." She'd fling over her shoulder, "Not far!" He'd reach for her books, she'd snatch her arm away. He'd be hurt.

"How come you don't like me, Burlee? I ain't done nothin to you! I'm always tryin to help you!" He use to fight the other kids bout callin her names. He never did 'low nobody to hurt her if he could help it. He got whipped hisself sometime but that never did stop him!

She would ease up. "I like you, Winston, you alright. I just ain't got no time for you!"

Reaching for crumbs again, he would say, "I know you get lonely sometime, Burlee. I even know you goes off by yourself."

Burlee would snap, "Ain't cause I'm lonely! And I told you to stop watching me! Leave me alone!"

Winston smiled. "Can't help it cause I'm lonely. I ain't got nobody, you don't go with nobody, why can't we keep company?"

Just before she ran off Burlee would snap, "Cause you too poor! I don't want nothin to do with no poor man! You just ain't rich enough!"

Winston hollered after her, "Money, ain't everything! And where you gon find a rich man?!"

Which is the question Burlee thought about in her secret place that day. Which question made her come up with the idea that rich men go shopping in department stores and own em to! She was going to get a job in one and find her man! She got a part-time job fore she graduated.

She started to wearing all that makeup she got on discount to cover her pimply skin. She looked a mess! Thick pancake makeup, blue or green eye shadow, bright red lipstick and rouge, black pencil round her eyes and false eyelashes so thick and stiff with that stuff that goes on them. If she'd fallen down and hit her face it would have

cracked cause it was that stiff! She looked worser . . . ugly plus ridiculous! Winston told her so and she took to hating him for it. Then her
boss at the store told her if she kept wearing makeup like that, she
could only clean up in the stockrooms instead of all over the store. She
changed.

Now, she hung out, or rather I should say, the cleanest place in
the store was round the offices where she could watch the men going
in all dressed up in their suits. She was learning things too, cause she
now knew the ones who owned the store were not dressed up or flashy
like the ones who only worked there! After she cut down on the
makeup, she decided to work more over by the beauty shop so she
could maybe learn how to work on her face. Besides all the hair stuff,
she saw people doing fingernails and toenails, facials and stuff like that!

Burlee didn't make much money, ain't hardly no need to say it,
but she saved. From the money she insisted on giving her mama she
saved 50¢ a week for four weeks to get one of them man-u-cures! The
lady who gives em, a regular poor woman, thought Burlee was crazy,
but took her money anyway and gave her a quick, lousy man-u-cure
for her four weeks of saving and dreaming! Ain't it funny how most
people, poor people, will cheat people just like themselves? And kiss
the yes-yes-yes of somebody with money who wouldn't give them the
time of day in return? Well, they do it all the time!

Anyway, them painted nails of Burlee's was scratched up and
gone in two days! The first day she just looked at em and waved her
hands in everybody's face! The second day her boss told her her work
was suffering. Burlee got to work and the nails got wiped out,
scratched up! Now, she didn't want to save four weeks for two days, so
she decided to learn how to do it herself! That was the magic working,
don't you see?! She asked the nail lady and the nail lady begrudged
telling her, thinking Black folks always trying to take over things they
didn't belong in. But she knew it was in the phone book, so she told
her. Burlee signed up for the hand course. They didn't want her, but
what the hell! Money is money!

Burlee really saved then! Her mama helped her cause she
wanted her daughter to want something, to do something for herself! Sit in a chair and do white folks' nails, stead of in the kitchen

or somewhere with a mop and broom! Burlee went! She practiced on her mama, which made them both happy! Little happinesses are awful good too!

Naturally, she was looking round her at school and learned about the hair. They didn't teach nothing bout no Black hair and Burlee wondered why and where she could go to learn it. There was nowhere, she was told. No school for Black hair! The magic again! Burlee talked to the only Black beautician she knew, who drank beer and smoked as she straightened and curled. She had been doing hair thirty years or so, and Burlee asked the woman to teach her. The woman thought of the competition mongst the already small clientele til Burlee said she would pay her. So, on to saving again! She learned, but she only wanted to do her own hair. She also learned she would like to own a Black hairdresser school. She talked to her mama again. Her mama offered to try to make a small loan if Burlee would pay it. She also talked to Winston, who still came around. He was working and saving his money so he could be rich someday, plus still helping his mother! That man really loved Burlee. She didn't want him from nothing!

Winston offered to give her his savings. Burlee said no to that, but would give him 25 percent of the business. That happened.

She found a small, tired-out office where a doctor used to be and rented it, getting the first three months free in exchange for cleaning, painting, and fixing it up. The landlord planned to put her out when all the work was done, so when she asked for the contract in writing, he and his wife refused! That sent Burlee to her secret place to sit and think!

When Burlee came out of that secret place, she went to the landlord and told them the bank (there was none) wanted the written agreement to give her the loan for a year's rent. Well, money and loans was part of their world so they gave her a written agreement, which Burlee put away.

She had already offered the hairdresser who had taught her, 25 percent to teach in the "Beauty College," as she now called it. You know, that hairdresser, who had long ago given up dreams and hopes except for some good man to come along, looked up at Burlee and saw a little light in her life! She accepted and took some of her little savings and got a teaching license. Before they knew it the ads was in the paper and the school was open! And doing alright!

Burlee, with 50 percent, took over the books. Winston, with 25 percent, kept it clean after leaving his regular job. Watching Burlee with his love in his eyes! The teacher, with 25 percent, taught! Plenty people came and brought their $5.00 cause it cost $8.00 at a regular shop and didn't always look any better! The students paid too, that was the main idea, so all in all Burlee was doing all right! She was saving steady and in a year or so, added a small supply shop that was 100 percent hers.

She hadn't got married yet but she was a good saver, so in a few years she bought a better home for her mama and daddy and told those sisters and brothers still at home to get out in the world and make their own way. Now!

Burlee was still looking for a rich man, but the magic was working through her!

Burlee, also, got out more and visited beauty shops and learned about that makeup stuff! Her nails were pretty all the time now, free, and she didn't have to do them herself! Pretty was still on her mind, along with that rich man. She asked one of the white ladies she met about teaching makeup at her college. The woman frowned, but Burlee said, "Just one day a week. I'll pay you good!" The woman smiled and soon was teaching. Burlee learned. Her makeup improved and the college did too. The customers were mixed colors now and she had some Latin students, so she got a Latin teacher. Just going on, chile!

Winston wanted to get married, still, but he always got the same old answer. He wasn't rich! But I'll tell you this! He was saving!!

Now, Burlee had done come in contact with all kinds of women and was always talking bout a rich man. One old one, who hustled the hard way for her living, told Burlee she couldn't get no rich man living in no house like the one she shared with her mama! Said Burlee didn't have nothing but a room! How a rich man gonna look at somebody living in a room in a house with they mama and think they deserve *him,* a rich man?! "And where your furs?" (the woman went on) "Your diamonds?" (she laughed) "And look at your clothes! Look at you! What a rich man gon see to want you for?"

Now, Burlee got mad! The magic always come when Burlee start thinking! She knew bout her clothes, but she was kinda tight with her money and, remember, she had responsibilities, her mama and all, you know! That's a long word, ain't it? Anyway, she had looked at clothes and the prices of what she liked was too high! Sides, she didn't have nowhere to go noway! She looked all over and found a lady who could sew to beat the band and wasn't doing nothing but sitting round the house getting fat. She ordered a couple outfits out of a book and paid well, but less!

Burlee also started looking round for another house, found one, a nice one, and paid down on it and was almost moving in when her father got sick. The magic worked again and she decided to stay with her mama and help her daddy and she rented the new house out. Got good rent for it! In a short time she took the basement, had Winston fix it up, and she opened a seamstress shop and school called "Fix-its." Winston got 25 percent of the business for his help. Burlee hated to give him money! Her bank accounts was getting on, chile!

She was still planning on that rich man tho. Burlee was doing all this for HIM!

Burlee's body started giving her problems round bout midnight on most nights, and all day and night on the rainy ones! She looked around her, carefully, cause she wanted to wait for her rich man, give him something special, you know? Most men want that something *special!*

I know a woman had five husbands and told every one of them but the first one that the last one had raped her first and she had married him because she couldn't bear to be had by a man she was not married to! *And* that *he* was the first man she had ever given herself to! They *all* had loved her!

Anyway, Burlee was having these messages from her body bout some attention! Now, Winston, being in her face a lot and she trusted him, believed he loved her and thinking she could handle him, she told him he could be her lover. That magic is somethin!

She was thinking of satisfaction and he was thinking of love, so she got more out of it than he did! But, again, because he loved her, he was one happy, satisfied man! He thought Burlee and marriage were getting closer. Everything they had was already tied up!?! So!

Burlee was amazed at this feeling she felt *with* Winston but her inexperience didn't know that kind of lovemaking came with love, so she still didn't feel she felt anything *for* Winston! But a big chunk of her heart was moving over, following that big chunk of her body, into a warm, secret place inside her. The magic working again! She didn't treat him no better outside the bed tho, and she saw him only when she wanted to!

"Are you busy tonight, Mr. Winston?" She called him that in front of other people.

"What time are you thinking of, Burlee?" He just wasn't phony at all!

"I'll let you know as soon as I can, *Mr.* Winston!"

"Alright, Burlee! I blieve I'm free!" He went home to get the house he had bought ready.

But one day she said, "Are you busy tonight, Mr. Winston?"

He being a little tired of her wanting, but not wanting, him, said, "Yes, Miz Burlee. Yes, I am!"

Burlee like to broke her neck when she turned it so fast she fell off that stool she was perched on! She left the college early that day and didn't even go by the other shops! Just went home and locked up in her secret place in her mind, worried! Thinking bout Winston, not wanting to. Hating him . . . she thought!

Burlee thought she would never ask him again! For the next two months or so, she didn't! Then winter came . . . and the rains. She made sure he asked her . . . and she went . . . for a while.

Thinking she was getting way off her plans for her life, she took a trip East to look over the rich men. She let a travel agency set up her schedule and she stayed at the best hotel, ate at the best places, saw theater. Always dressed . . . and always lonely. Happy, pleased, but lonely anyway. She didn't meet anyone who paid her special attention so she went home and opened up a Bar-B-Q place and served it with cloth napkins, tablecloths and real plated silver and champagne!

Everyone came! 25 percent was Winston's again and he helped her. They still made love sometime but she urged him to love someone else. He used to look down at her, when she got through moaning and groaning and hollering under him, while she told him he should find someone to love him. He thought she was crazy!

Winston became more thoughtful, giving the matter of someone else serious thought. He started taking someone he already knew out. A stash of his, I guess. The stash was a good-looking woman and she showed she liked Winston . . . a lot! She's the one who gave him birthday presents, valentine cards and Easter eggs. Cooked him break-fast sometimes, when he let her. Left pretty little notes under his pillow, if she was inside. Pretty little notes under his door, if she was outside. He wouldn't give her a key.

Burlee noticed he was pretty busy.

"Well!! I guess I lost my loving buddy?!" She smiled.

"No. You don't have to lose me!" came the reply.

"Yes I do!" she snapped back. 'I don't want no disease! Who knows who else that sorry-looking woman is screwing!" She walked away.

It must have made Winston mad, cause a month or so later when Burlee said, "Are you busy this evening, Mr. Winston?" with that special light in her eyes, Winston answered, "Yes! I got a date with that beautiful woman who screws!" Then he walked away.

Couple weeks later, Burlee went to the West Coast to check on her rich man. She had plenty money now. She looked real good. She was dressed! That woman surely dressed! She moved in some fairly nice circles now and everyone knew she had that money, all them houses and business! She met her rich man! Extended her trip so they could get to know each other better, talk more. The talk finally moved to marriage cause Burlee was not going to sleep with him til it did! The commitments were almost made and he took her to his large, rambling house. The Mercedes and the Rolls in the garages. The swimming pool, the cabanas, the cook, the maid, the gardener, the thick carpets and plush luxurious furniture. Upstairs to his enormous seven-by-seven bed with the fur spread and the soft lights! Burlee was in seventh heaven! Picturing herself walking up and down these stairs, days and nights, surveying all that was hers! My, my!

She unpacked her beautiful nightgown, bought just for this occasion. Slipped as best she could between satin sheets and waited for him to come to her. A little frightened, but smiling.

Soon he came with glasses of champagne. He talked gently and softly, as he turned on the overhead lights and got into the bed and . . . grabbed her with fingers and arms that felt more like steel than flesh! He pinched and twisted the nipples of her soft human breast, then grabbed a handful of the same soft breast and squeezed hard, very hard! A thought arrived just before the small scream came. "Does he think this feels good?" He let go, so she didn't hit him, just threw her arm out, knocking over the glass of champagne she had placed on the bedside table when she was smiling. It spilled into the bed on the fine satin sheets! She was looking to see what she had done when his steel-trap hand trapped her in that warm, soft little space that is very special to us ladies. It was painful! He then pressed his hard, dry lips against hers and the hard, wet tongue through them, and proceeded to roll over on her in what I would personally call stupid jerky movements! Trying to tear the beautiful gown out the way! Did he think that was sexy? Burlee almost screamed again as it flashed through her mind all the days and nights of this there would be if she married the rich man! He was struggling around on top of her now and the only soft thing on his body wouldn't work! His face had a strange leer on it just before he raised from biting her breast, hard, and dove under the covers to sink his teeth into her leg! Burlee was confused a moment and overwhelmed by a totally new experience with what she called love! Only for a moment tho, because before even she knew it, she had thrown the cover back and slapped the living shit out of the man! Now, you can slap someone pretty hard, but to get the living shit slapped out of you . . . is to really be hit! He screamed and grabbed his rich head that the toupee had flown off of, at the same time Burlee got up! His teeth fell from her thigh as she hit the floor and grabbed her things, rushing her exclamation point body down them beautiful stairs onto the plush carpet, where she dressed and called a cab!

The rich man came rushing down the stairs screaming, "What's the matter with you? Are you crazy?"

Burlee answered with conviction, "Nothing now! I'm alright!"

He gasped, *"You're* alright?! Look at my face! Look at what you've done!"

As she went out the door, she said, "You look at it! I surely do not want to see it again!"

Slam! went the door!

She went straight to the airport from the hotel, waited for her plane and flew home . . . wanting *something* with all her mighty heart!

Burlee rested, had to, the first day she got home. She thought all night practically. Didn't once think of them businesses! She took herself out to dinner the next night . . . alone! She thought about the years that were passing while she fooled around with a dream that was getting raggedy!

She had plenty money! Houses! Everything but . . . *something!* She was living good, but . . . she wasn't LIVING!

Her little heart under that fine soft breast and them expensive materials, yearned and yearned.

The lobster was like cotton, tasteless. The champagne was expensive dishwater. She had ordered what she loved most but it didn't taste like nothing! She put the silver fork down and thought some more.

"What have I done with my life? What am I doing with it?" The magic was working! Her eyes filled with tears. To stop them she took a deep breath and looked around the room to see who could see she was crying. That's when she saw Winston sitting there with his good-looking girlfriend! Without knowing why, she got mad! She'd been sitting there wanting SOMETHING. Wasn't he SOMETHING?

She got up and, looking like a mad exclamation point, she pointed herself toward Winston and walked over to him and said, "I want to see you! I want to talk to you!"

Calmly Winston replied, "I'm busy now, Miz Burlee!"

Burlee looked at the woman. "No, you ain't busy! I said I want to *see* you!"

Winston stood up. "I said I was busy, so I am busy! Can't you see us sitting here?! What's wrong with you!?"

Burlee was almost crying. "You ain't busy! You ain't never been busy when I want to talk to you, Winston! I want to talk to you, now!" She grabbed his shoulders and shook him.

He firmly grabbed her hands and removed them and, looking into her eyes, said, "If you are through eating your dinner all by yourself, go home! Go somewhere! I'm not stopping my life anymore for you to get on or get off whenever it pleases you!!"

Burlee bent her head, standing all alone, sniffling. "I got to talk to you . . . about you . . . about me. About . . . about life!"

Winston waited a few seconds, looking at her and at his girlfriend, who didn't know how to look. He said, "Go home, Burlee. I'll be by there when I am finished!"

Burlee looked at the astonished woman. "Take her home first!"

Winston sighed, "Go home, Burlee." He walked her to her car. She grabbed him and pleaded. "Come now! Pleassssssse come now!" (We all know how that is.)

Winston remained silent, looking at her. "What did you find out there in the West that got you so ready for me?"

Burlee screamed at him. "Do you still love me?"

Winston opened her car door. "Get in, go home. I'll be there soon."

She got in, but as he walked back to the club she screamed, "You promised you would love me forever! Don't you lie to me!"

He turned. "I didn't say I'd *wait* forever tho!"

"Forever ain't over!" she screamed!

"No, you told me to find somebody else!" he threw back.

She looked tired. "I didn't know I was lyin. Oh hell! Winston, can't you see I love you . . . now. I want you to love me . . . now."

He looked at her for a long time, turning his head to the side.

She looked up at him, feeling the very air against her perspiring, hot skin, felt the very sweat in her armpits, the very real need in her soul.

He smiled. "I'll be over in a little while."

She left thinking, "He's almost rich!"

Later, he did go by. Yes, they talked a long time. Yes, he still loved her. Seems some people is just for some people! Yes, he made love to her, the kind she understood. Yes, they soon got married.

Burlee lately gave Winston a little son and named it Winston Burl. I'm glad they got that over with and out the way before they had a daughter!

I see her sometimes. She is happy. Winston takes care more of the business cause she takes care more of the house. She wants to! Says she done worked enough in her life for three people. Says all these white women tryin to get out in the workplace, don't understand that that's where her people been all the time! Say she tryin to get out of it! She still takes care the money and the books tho! She also got her pet projects. She holds free classes every week for poor young girls and boys she gets from schools, to teach them how not to feel left out of life. Burlee always looks carefully over them youngsters for the ones the world might call "Ugly." She asks them to do *her* a favor, and sends them through all her beauty stuff for a week, free. So they will know how to do something for themselves to make themself feel better! When they smile at their new selves in a mirror, Burlee laughs a deep, happy laugh and sends them on their new way.

There is magic in life, if you can find it. It's a job tho! Oh yes, you got to think . . . and work on it! And don't forget love . . . there is magic in love too! Work on it!

≶

In your journal, answer the following:

≶ How does Cooper's story make you feel as though you're listening to rather than reading a story? How do phrases like "I'ma tell you something! God didn't make no ugly people!" encourage intimacy and bonding between the storyteller and the readers?

§ Would this story be as effective told from Burlee's third person limited point of view? What would the story gain (if anything) or what would the story lose (if anything) if the narrator's voice were dropped?

§ In the next-to-last paragraph, the storyteller says: "I see her sometimes. She is happy." How do these lines make the teller seem almost like a character? Do you think the narrator lives in the same community as Burlee? Is she a griot holding the community together by telling stories? Does it matter? Does the storyteller's omniscience seem less credible if she's a character?

§ Throughout the story, Burlee gains insight and wisdom about her needs as a woman. In what final dramatic scene is Burlee the most vocal about her realization that life is about love, not money? Why is the narrator silent during this scene?

§ Why does the story conclude with the narrator? What does she mean by "Work on it!"?

§ If you were to revise this story, would you change the point of view?

In your journal, write a paragraph about what J. California Cooper has taught you about using first person as omniscient story-teller.

Writers struggle to find their voices and to give themselves per-mission to speak. For me, selecting the proper point of view has always been a similar kind of empowerment. As a writer you must dig deep within your own soul to find the multitude of voices you need to give to identified or unidentified narrators. Answering "Who tells the story?" is still fundamentally about self-discovery. In how many tongues, in how many voices can I, as a writer, speak? Likewise, given the differing lenses, writers discover through their narrators how many ways they can perceive.

Celebrate each time you successfully create a point of view to tell a story. With each discovery of a narrator's voice, you are expanding your own voice. With each shift in point of view, you are expanding your own perception. Point of view, in fiction and in life, is essential to *being*.

8

DESCRIPTION, SETTING, AND ATMOSPHERE

Truth is in the details. Show me and I'll believe. Tell me and I won't imagine.

Since beginning the exercises in this book, you have been engaged in reaching for the right descriptors, the right words to say what you mean. To *show* what you mean.

You can tell a reader: "Each summer morning, before my brother and I awoke, my mother was up for hours cooking our breakfast, readying our house for the day."

Not a bad sentence. But the sentence is a "telling" one—and, ironically, its biggest fault is that it tells *too little*. Readers want their hearts to come alive to a story. They want to experience it through their senses. Just as a baby learns from taste, touch, sight, smell, sound—so too readers want to learn about fictional worlds through sensory details.

Andrea Lee, in an excerpt from her novel *Sarah Phillips,* renders the meaning of my sentence more brilliantly:

> In the summer my mother got up just after sunrise, so that when she called Matthew and me for breakfast, the house was filled with sounds and smells of her industrious mornings. Odors of frying scrapple or codfish cakes drifted up the back stairs, mingling sometimes with the sharp scent of mustard greens she was cooking for dinner that night. Up the laundry chute from the cellar floated whiffs of steamy air and the churning sound of the washing machine. From the dining room, where she liked to sit ironing and chatting on the telephone, came the fragrance of hot clean clothes and the sound of her voice: cheerful, resonant, reverberating a little weirdly through the high-ceilinged rooms, as if she were sitting happily at the bottom of a well.

Andrea Lee "shows" a world. She gives sensory details: *smells and tastes:* "whiffs of steamy air"; "codfish cakes . . . mingling with the sharp scent of mustard greens"; *sounds:* a voice "cheerful, resonant, reverberating"; a "churning . . . washing machine"; *sights:* the mother "ironing and chatting on the telephone"; "sitting happily at the bottom of a well"; "high-ceilinged rooms"; *touch:* "hot clean clothes"; "steamy air."

While sensory details are essential for creating good concrete description, Lee also proves that *specificity* adds authority and makes her world even more believable. "Summer morning" becomes "just after sunrise;" "my brother" becomes "Matthew." Mother's "cooking . . . readying our house" becomes detailed pictures of cooking, washing, folding and ironing laundry.

Lee also uses *comparisons* in her description. "As if she were

sitting happily at the bottom of a well" forces us to "see" and understand the mother's happiness in a new way. It suggests her industrious-
ness is sufficiently soul-satisfying and joy-inspiring and that she would
be happy even if she were at the bottom of a well. The comparison also
helps us "hear" her call, the echoing resonance from downstairs to the
children upstairs.

Reread Lee's paragraph. Feel how *alive* it is—how energized. Active verbs such as "mingling," "floated," "sitting," "ironing," "chatting," bring a liveliness and intensity to the description. She also uses
the *active voice* which means the mother acts rather than is acted upon.
"Mother cooked the food!" not "The food was cooked by Mother."

Most importantly, Lee proves that *good description serves multiple
ends.* By making her world visual and active, she improves:

> *Characterization—Those Who Live in the
> Story*
> Can you not hear and see the mother bustling about?
> Can you not feel her love of domestic pleasures?

> *Setting—Where the Story Takes Place*
> Can you not see the two-story, high-ceilinged house?
> The dining room with the ironing board and tele-
> phone? Imagine the basement with its laundry chute?
> "Home" is clearly central for the plot and the devel-
> opment of the mother's character.

> *Atmosphere—The Attitude and Place
> That Shape the Story's Emotional Quality*
> Can you not sense that this is a happy environment?
> The mother is happy, the children are happy, and
> summer adds more daylight for these busy, cheerful
> people. Can you not infer that this is a family not
> struggling with economic pressures but instead thriv-
> ing in a fine home, well fed, and wrapped in their
> mother's cleanliness and cheer?

As a beginning writing student, I used to skip descriptive paragraphs. I thought they were boring! I only wanted to know plot, what happened next. I wrote lean, tight stories with lots of action and dialogue. *Voodoo Dreams* humbled me, taught me that a story is a complex, integrated whole. How could I separate voodoo from the bayou setting and New Orleans? How could I show Marie developing into a Voodoo Queen without detailing ritual? Without concretely describing her miracles? How could readers "see" Marie without seeing her relationship to her African gods? If readers couldn't "see" and, therefore, *feel* Marie's world, then I knew I would never engage them enough for them to understand voodoo as a powerful religion. Rewriting paragraph by paragraph, I would ask: What have I failed to describe? What do readers need to "see" to understand my story?

Plot can never be separated from descriptive language. Sensory details provide the filter to enhance the meaning and nuances of a story. Characters can't come alive without proper descriptions. Neither can the setting or the tone and attitudes of the world your characters live in be shown or suggested without descriptive language. Avoiding description means wasting a valuable resource. Your story will lack depth, literally lack its lifeblood without finely tuned description.

On the other hand, description for the sake of description is meaningless. Most beginning writers "overdescribe," inserting clumps of language which slow the plot and seem insignificant to the reader. *The key is to make details significant—to add only those details which are "functional" to the whole.* "Function" implies usefulness—what's useful in conveying your story's character, plot, and ideas. For example, if you're writing a story about a young man's foolish pride, then descriptions should "show" this. You might write about Harvey's vanities of dress—his designer shoes, thin silk ties; his vanities of possession—a sleek red Porsche, a Rolex watch; his vanities of place—a condo in Beverly Hills, a high-rise office with a beach view. You might write how when given a choice between two paintings, he buys the one he doesn't like, simply because it's more expensive. It wouldn't be functional to describe *all* of Harvey's likes and dislikes. A writer selects only those details which best serve the story.

MY BEST ADVICE

Quality not quantity governs good description. A few well-selected
sensory details encourage greater imaginative involvement from
readers than numerous insignificant details.

Stories never unfold in a vacuum. Description creates setting—the
place, the world for your story to reside. For the most part, setting
complements the action. A horror story takes place in a haunted
house. Crime dramas explode in cities. Love flourishes on an island
paradise. A family drama resonates in a brownstone row house in
Baltimore. While these settings may seem obvious and unoriginal,
their uniqueness lies in the details, how well they're described.

Setting has always been a major influence for many writers. In
Gloria Naylor's fiction, settings have "lives" which reflect their resi-
dents' lives, their dreams and desires:

> No one cries when a street dies . . . It dies when the
> odors of hope, despair, lust, and caring are wiped out by
> seasonal winds; when dust has settled into the cracks and
> scars, leveling their depths and discolorations—their rea-
> sons for being; when the spirit is trapped and fading in
> someone's memory. So when Brewster dies, it will die
> alone.
>
> It watched its last generation of children torn away
> from it by court orders and eviction notices, and it had
> become too tired and sick to help them. Those who had
> spawned Brewster Place, countless twilights ago, now
> mandated that it was to be condemned. With no heat or
> electricity, the water pipes froze in the winter and well
> into the spring. Hallways were blind holes, and the plas-
> ter crumbled into snaggled gaps. Vermin bred in uncol-
> lected garbage and spread through the walls. Brewster had
> given what it could—all it could—to its "Afric" children,

and there was just no more. So it had to watch, dying but not dead, as they packed up the remnants of their dreams and left . . .

Brewster Place, from *The Women of Brewster Place,* is, perhaps, Naylor's most famous setting. It contains "four double housing units" and a wall which made it a dead-end street, shut off from the business district and economic health of the town. This street provides the *atmosphere* where "colored daughters . . . milled like determined spirits among the decay, trying to make it a home." Atmosphere is created by combining setting and the narrator's attitude. The narrative voice states directly and indirectly with descriptive details that Brewster Place is a place of thwarted desires like its "Afric" people.

Setting usually complements your story's action. April Sinclair's jubilant *Coffee Will Make You Black* uses the exuberant South Side of Chicago to show a young girl coming of age in a loving extended family. The time period of 1965–70 is just as essential as the descriptions about the community. Chants of "Power to the people," references to LSD, Smokey Robinson's new album, and Yoga's life-enhancing potential create the social and historical atmosphere during Stevie's critical transition to young womanhood.

Sometimes setting contrasts with story action. Arna Bontemps' "A Summer Tragedy" uses a lovely summer day as setting for the double suicide of an old married couple. Their children dead, too worn to make a living sharecropping—they take a last ride down country roads and through fields before overturning their car in the river. This contrast of setting and action makes the story more poignant. It also reminds us that horrible events do happen on bright, sunshine-filled days. Conversely, beauty can be found in seemingly desolate landscapes.

Churches, the pastoral South, the unpastoral South with images of oppression and lynching, northern cities such as Detroit, Philadelphia, and Chicago which received waves of hopeful African Americans migrating North for greater civil liberties and economic opportunities, have all served as important settings and atmosphere in the history of

African American literature. Harlem is considered to be the quintessential African American setting of black creativity and at times, conversely, black urban despair. Some authors, by virtue of their own histories and interests, have made other settings resonate as rich, complex sites of black life: John Edgar Wideman's *Homewood Trilogy* is a testament to the struggles of the Homewood community in Pittsburgh, Pennsylvania; Dorothy West in *The Wedding* renders visible the privileged "talented tenth" in Massachusetts' Martha's Vineyard; Anita Richmond Bunkley explores Texas in *Black Gold;* and Randall Kenan mythologizes Tims Creek, North Carolina, in *Let the Dead Bury Their Dead.* All of these settings come alive because of specific, descriptive details.

Description which can embody aspects of characterization, setting, and atmosphere adds a fine sheen, making stories an "experience" for readers. "Showing" with sensory details versus "telling" celebrates and encourages the imaginative bond between readers and writers. Becoming more attuned to your own senses will help you create more powerful, effective descriptions.

EXERCISE 1

SENSORY MOMENTS

Select a book or story you've recently read, and for an hour study its use of description. Does the author "show" rather than "tell"? Are the descriptions appealing to your senses—can you taste, smell, touch, see, and hear their characters and fictional world? Do they rely on varying senses or mainly on one or two such as sight and sound? Are the descriptions active—moving and energetic rather than statically told?

What would you do to improve the description you've read? Anything? Some minor tinkering or a major overhaul? In your journal, write what the author has taught you about description's power.

. . .

Now review several pages of your own writing. Using a high-lighter, underline any general statements which "tell" rather than "show" your characters and their world. For example:

Carolyn always thought her eyes were her best feature. Can you show this? What is Carolyn doing? Is Carolyn applying mascara in a mirror or sitting across from a date? What is the color, texture, and shape of her eyes and brows? Is she speaking or thinking? Comparing her eyes to her mouth? Her nose? Can you draw sensory comparisons which might help readers see Carolyn's eyes and her attitude about them even more clearly?

Select a "telling" sentence from your own writing. Spend twenty minutes revising your work to show what you want to say more descriptively.

EXERCISE 2

SETTINGS WE KNOW, REMEMBER, AND IMAGINE

Creating a setting can require observation, recall, and imagination.

Observation
Visit a cafe, a ballpark, a nightclub, a classroom—anything you choose. Like a sketch artist, practice re-creating the setting with word pictures. Write as many details of touch, taste, sight, smell, and sound as possible.

After writing for twenty minutes, read your "setting." Is it as alive as the setting before your eyes? Spend another twenty minutes revising, adding details you left out.

Memory
Re-create a setting you remember. It can be a child's playroom, a Sunday school classroom, your grandfather's garage, your family

backyard, or a cruise ship in St. Thomas. Write as many details of touch, taste, sight, smell, and sound as possible.

After writing for twenty minutes, read your "setting." Is it as alive as the landscape you remember? Spend another twenty minutes revising, adding details you left out.

Imagination

Create a setting of a place you've never been: Paris, Cannery Row in Monterey, a village in Nigeria, or a barge trip down the Nile River. Visit the library in search of photo-essays and travel guides about the place you selected. Different historical eras too require a leap of imagination. Photos of Texas in 1892 or Atlanta in 1972 can provide concrete details; your imagination, though, can fill in smells, sounds, tastes. Science fiction and fantasy settings also require imagination—but many such settings are exaggerations of existing worlds. To make sure your setting doesn't become abstract, begin with reality and known facts and then extrapolate. For example, a fantasy forest may be based on Yosemite with its geysers and ancient redwoods. Death Valley's flat, bleak landscape might suggest a postnuclear world. Whatever landscape you choose to imagine, write as many details of touch, taste, sight, smell, and sound as possible.

After writing for twenty minutes, read your "setting." Do you think you've added enough details to make it believable to a reader? What would improve it? Spend another twenty minutes revising, adding new sensory details.

EXERCISE 3

BREATHING ATMOSPHERE

Setting and narrative attitude create atmosphere—an emotional quality for your characters' lives and world.

Nella Larsen, in her Harlem Renaissance novel *Quicksand,* writes about a confused biracial woman caught between cultures, trying to determine the best course for her life:

> The night was far from quiet, the streets far from empty. Clanging trolley bells, quarreling cats, cackling phonographs, raucous laughter, complaining motor horns, low singing, mingled in the familiar melody that was Harlem. Black figures, white figures, little forms, big forms, small groups, large groups, sauntered or hurried by. It was gay, grotesque, and a little weird. Helga Crane felt singularly apart from it all. Entering the waiting doorway, they descended through a furtive, narrow passage, into a vast subterranean room. Helga smiled, thinking that this was one of those places characterized by the righteous as hell.
>
> A glare of light struck her eyes, a blare of jazz split her ears. For a moment, everything seemed to be spinning around; even she felt she was circling aimlessly, as she followed with the others the black giant who led them to a small table, where, when they were seated, their knees and elbows touched.

The novel concludes with Helga in despair, married to a church revivalist she does not love, living in a community which values respectability and conformity, and her body broken by continuous childbearing.

Look at the above example again. Larsen has created an atmosphere of contrasts and alienation. What descriptive clues suggests unhappiness? Confusion? Why does no one have a name except Helga? Why are people "giants" or "figures"? Do these words suggest Helga's lack of connection with people? Do you think Larsen intended for the nightclub setting to contrast with the provincial home life Helga chooses at the novel's conclusion?

Think of a highly emotional plot event: a wedding, a death; a shipwreck, a riot, a drug addict needing a fix, a young man finding his true love, a girl undergoing abortion, an adventurer sailing from Barbados to Africa. What emotions dominate?

For twenty minutes, write a paragraph which suggests through setting and descriptive detail the overriding emotions, the atmosphere your fictional characters might live in.

DESCRIPTION STUDY

RANDALL KENAN'S "A VISITATION OF SPIRITS"

Kenan is a master of sensory detail which illuminates character, setting, atmosphere, and plot. Like a musical score, his description heightens the emotional pull of his fictional world. His details are specific, significant. Each detail is carefully layered to help readers understand the disorder of a sixteen-year-old driven mad by the limitations of his society and the curse of being "the Chosen Nigger." Kenan's descriptions are functional, never extraneous. He describes what readers need to know, see, feel, touch, hear, and smell—to respond empathically to an unsettling and unsettled character who yearns for spiritual and physical transformation. With details, Kenan encourages us to believe spirits can and do walk the earth.

≷

April 29, 1984
11:30 A.M.

WHAT TO BECOME?
. . . At first Horace was sure he would turn himself into a rabbit. But then, no. Though they were swift as pebbles skipping across a pond, they were vulnerable, liable to be snatched up in a fox's jaws or a hawk's talons. Squirrels fell too easily into traps. And though mice and wood rats had a magical smallness, in the end they were

much smaller than he wished to be. Snakes' heads were too easily crushed, and he didn't like the idea of his entire body slithering across all those twigs and feces and spit. Dogs lacked the physical grace he needed. More than anything else, he wanted to have grace. If he was going to the trouble of transforming himself, he might as well get exactly that. Butterflies were too frail, victims to wind. Cats had a physical freedom he loved to watch, the svelte, smooth, sliding motion of the great cats of Africa, but he could not see transforming himself into anything that would not fit the swampy woodlands of southeastern North Carolina. He had to stay here.

No, truth to tell, what he wanted more than anything else, he now realized, was to fly. A bird. He had known before, but he felt the need to sit down and ponder the possibilities. A ritual of choice, to make it real. A bird.

With that thought he rose, his stomach churning with excitement. A bird. Now to select the type. The species. The genus. He knew the very book to use in the school library; he knew the shelf, and could see the book there in its exact placement, now, slightly askew between a volume on birdfeeders no one ever moved and a treatise on egg collecting; he could see the exact angle at which it would be resting. Hadn't the librarian, Mrs. Stokes, always teased him that he knew the library better than she ever would? And wasn't she right?

He was sitting on the wall at the far end of the school campus, on the other side of the football field, beyond the gymnasium, beyond the main school building. He had wanted to be alone, to think undistracted. But now he was buoyed by the realization that he knew how he would spend the rest of his appointed time on this earth. Not as a tortured human, but as a bird free to swoop and dive, to dip and swerve over the cornfields and tobacco patches he had slaved in for what already seemed decades to his sixteen years. No longer would he be bound by human laws and human rules that he had constantly tripped over and frowned at. Now was his chance, for he had stumbled upon a passage by an ancient mystic, a monk, a man of God, and had found his salvation. It was so simple he wondered why no one had discovered it before. Yet how would anyone know? Suddenly poor old Jeremiah or poor old Julia disappears. Everybody's distraught; everybody worries. They search. They wait. Finally the missing person is declared dead. And the silly folk go on about their business and don't realize that old Julia turned herself into an eel and went to the bottom of the deep blue sea to see what she could see. There are no moral laws that say: You must remain human. And he would not.

His morning break was over. The other students were hustling back to third period. But he decided to skip. What did it matter? In a few days he would be transformed into a creature of the air. He could soar by his physics class and listen to Mrs. Hedgeson deliver her monotone lecture about electrons; he could perch on the ledge and watch the biology students dissect pickled frogs; hear the Spanish class tripping over their tongues; glide over the school band as they practiced their awkward maneuvers on the football field, squawking their gleaming instruments. All unfettered, unbound, and free.

As he walked down the hall, he suddenly realized he had no hall pass and that the vice-principal might walk by and demand it. But no. He was Horace Thomas Cross, the Great Black Hope, as his friend John Anthony had called him. The Straight-A Kid. Or once, at least. Where most students would be pulled aside and severely reprimanded, he could walk unquestioned. In his mind he could see his Cousin Ann smiling her cinnamon smile and hear her say in her small, raspy voice: But don't you know it yet, Horace? You the Chosen Nigger.

The library was empty except for old Mrs. Stokes, who stood by the card catalogue and smiled at him, nodding knowingly. If she only realized—her gray hair would turn white. He walked straight to the exact aisle, the exact shelf, selected the exact book, and took it to a table in the back of the library, even though he was the only other person in that large room. He sat by a window overlooking the long, sloping lawn, spring green, that dipped into the pine-filled woods.

It was a huge book. White cloth with elegant gold lettering: *Encyclopedia of North American Birds,* a book he had known since elementary school, with its crisp photographs and neat diagrams and its definitions upon definitions upon definitions. Because it was a reference book he couldn't check it out, so for long hours he would sit and read about migratory paths, the use of tail feathers, the gestation periods of eggs. . . .

As he opened the book he felt the blood rush to his head, and the first color plates cranked up his imagination like a locomotive: gulls, cranes, owls, storks, turkeys, eagles. He flipped through the book, faster and faster. Which bird? Sparrow, wren, jay. No, *larger*. Mallard, grouse, pheasant. *Larger*. Goose, swan, cormorant. *Larger*. Egret, heron, condor. Pages flipped; his heart beat faster; his mind grew fuzzy with possibilities. Raven, rook, blackbird. Crow . . .

He slammed the book shut, realizing that he had been riffling through the pages like a madman. Mrs. Stokes looked up quickly, startled, then gave him that brief, knowing smile.

He closed his eyes and thought of the only way he could make his decision. He thought about the land: the soybean fields surrounding his grandfather's house, the woods that surrounded the fields, the tall, massive long-leaf pines. He thought of the miles and miles of highways, asphalt poured over mule trails that etched themselves into the North Carolina landscape, onto the beach, sandy white, the sea, a murky churning, the foam, spray, white, the smell of fish and rotting wood. He thought of winters, the floor of the woods a carpet of dry leaves, brown-and-black patchwork carpet. He thought of the sky, not a blue picture-book sky with a few thin clouds, but a storm sky, black and mean, full of wind and hate, God's wrath, thunder, pelting rain. He thought of houses, new and old, brick and wood, high and low, roofs mildewed and black, chimneys, lightning rods, TV antennas. He was trying to think like a bird, *the* bird, the only bird he could become. And when he saw a rabbit, dashing, darting through a field of brown rye grass, and when he saw talons sink into the soft brown fur, he knew.

But he had known before, had realized when he stumbled across the pact the old monk had made with the demon in the book, that if he were to transform himself, irrevocably, unconditionally, he would choose a red-tailed hawk. He opened the book to the hawk family— pausing at the eagle, but knowing that was too corny, too noticeable, not indigenous to North Carolina—and flipped to the picture of his future self. He could not help but smile. The creature sat perched on a fence post, its wings brought up about its neck, its eyes murderous. Many times he had admired the strong flight of the bird, the way it would circle the field like a buzzard, but not like a buzzard, since the rat or the rabbit or the coon it was after was not dead—yet. Talons would clutch the thrashing critter tighter than a vise, its little heart would beat in sixteenth notes, excited even more by the flapping wings that beat the air like hammers and blocked the sun like Armageddon. Then the piercing of the neck, the rush of hot, sticky blood. The taste of red flesh. He felt a touch of empathy for the small mammal, its tail caught in the violent twitching of death thralls, but he was still thrilled.

He turned and looked to the woods and sighed, the sigh of an old man, of resigned resolve and inevitable conclusion. A sigh too old for a sixteen-year-old boy. He rose and replaced the book. The bell rang, signaling the end of third period. He thought of never walking down this aisle and past that shelf again; he would read none of these volumes again. He allowed himself to swell up. Not with sadness, but with pride. He had found the escape route, of which they were all ignorant. Mrs. Stokes once again gave her knowing nod. He winked at her and did not look back.

He sat through the rest of his classes, taking no notes, not listening, more as a matter of form, a fare-thee-well. No one bothered him. He had noticed that for the last few weeks people had been staying away from him, whispering behind his back that he was acting strange. But it was no matter. Soon it would all be over.

He rode the bus home in peace. Track practice was over. There were only two weeks left before summer vacation, but he would have skipped practice anyway. He sat back and watched the other students in their horseplay and shenanigans, the girls lost in their gossip, the boys bragging and arm-wrestling, playing cards. From the window he watched the land, the land over which he would soon rise. Soon and very soon.

Looking out the window, he felt a brief wave of doubt flicker within. Had he gone mad? Somehow slipped beyond the veil of right reasoning and gone off into some deep, unsettled land of fantasy? The very thought made him cringe. Of course he was not crazy, he told himself; his was a very rational mind, acquainted with science and mathematics. But he was also a believer in an unseen world full of archangels and prophets and folk rising from the dead, a world preached to him from the cradle on, and a world he was powerless not to believe in as firmly as he believed in gravity and the times table. The two contradicting worlds were not contradictions in his mind. At the moment it was not the world of digits and decimal points he required, but the world of messiahs and miracles. It was faith, not facts he needed; magic, not math; salvation, not science. Belief would save him, not only belief, but belief in belief. Like Daniel, like Isaac, like the woman at the well. I am sane, he thought, smoothing over any kinks in his reasoning and clutching fear by the neck. He had no alternative, he kept saying to himself. No other way out.

When he got home, he went straight to his room and closed the door. His grandfather was out, but he didn't want to risk tipping his hand. His room, the entire house, smelled of hard pine and the lingering smell of paint and floor varnish, of cypress window frames and heavily oiled oak furniture and dust trapped in the curtains, the farmhouse dust from the dirt road and the fields—but more than anything else there was the ever-present smell of pine. Heart pine, the old folks called it. The hardest there is. Better than oak. A seventy-one-year-old smell he had smelled all his life, through the many coats of antique white paint, through the well-coated floors, through the dust. In his mind it was the smell of prayer, the smell of childbirth, the smell of laughter, the smell of tears, dancing, sweat, the smell of work, sex, death.

On the white walls of his room hung his many friends. Over the bed was the Sorcerer—the Conjurer, the Supreme Magician. His eyes were a mysterious blue, piercing and all-knowing. Over his eyes hung a great shock of black hair, showing his virility; the hair at his temples was snowy white, showing his wisdom. His great red cape was caught in a wind, making it billow as dramatically as a thunderclap. His stance—you could tell he was commencing to cast a spell because his hands were surrounded by an electric-blue glow—resembled a pouncing tiger's. His body was well muscled and lean, covered in skintight blue leggings and a blue tunic with an Egyptian ankh on its chest. A huge amulet was suspended from a chain about his neck, a half-open eye peering through.

On the other walls hung a huge green monster-man so muscled he appeared to be a green lump, with huge bare feet, clad only in tattered purple pants, giving an animal leer; a woman whirling a golden lasso, wearing a brassiere shaped like an eagle and zooming through the air atop an airplane made of glass; a Viking with long yellow hair and bulging muscles, swinging a hammer as large as he, his icy blue eyes flashing a solemn warning; a man dressed in a midnight-blue cowl with pointy ears like a cat and a midnight-blue cape to match, which billowed even more than the sorcerer's, the emblem of a bat planted across his chest. There were posters of little creatures with hair on their feet as thick as rugs, who possessed round bellies and smoked huge pipes. There were designs for starships, and diagrams of battlestars, star maps and star charts, a list of names of demons and pictures of gryphons and krakens and gorgons. . . .

Papers were scattered about the room; on the bed, on the floor, on the desk and the dresser and the nightstand. And the books. Books piled high, opened and marked. Old books, new books. Colorful and drab. Books half-read standing on their parted pages, the spines pointing toward the ceiling. Boy, his grandfather would say, cross and vexed, can't you keep your room no neater than this? What you gone do when they puts you in the army? They don't have no such foolishness there. But the A's and A-pluses on his report card would quiet his grandfather's commands—Clean up that room, boy—to mere grumbles, mild reproaches, disapproving shakes of his head.

The school library allowed Horace, or any other student, to check out only three books at a time. So he also belonged to both the county library in Crosstown and the local library in Sutton. Then there were the book clubs: the Book-of-the-Month Club, the History Book Club, the Science Fiction Book Club. . . . He borrowed books from his teachers, from his friends. When he went to larger cities— Wilmington, Kinston, Goldsboro—he would buy even more books, usually paperbacks. Most of them he had read, some more than once; in others, mostly the nonfiction, he read the parts that interested him most, from ancient Chinese history to shipbuilding to biographies of famous businessmen and great scientists. But that had been before; now he concentrated on the occult.

Littered about the room were books with titles like *Black Magic/ White Magic, The Arcane Art, Witches, Voodoo, Essays on the Dark Arts, Third World Religions, A History of Magic, Magicians of the Bible, Gray's Index to the Bizarre and the Unusual, Demon Lore.* It was in one of these volumes that he found the key, and he had spent weeks checking and double-checking, cross-referencing, correlating, compiling his facts and perfecting the perfect spell. To him this room was not a high school lad's bedroom in an old farmhouse on a dirt road in the backwoods, but the secluded and mysterious lair of an apprentice sorcerer about to step into the realm of a true mystic. The walls were not wood; they were ancient and chipped stone. The books were not paperbacks and library loans; they were parched scrolls and musty tomes.

Simplicity. The simplicity alone swept him away. The very notion that the entire ordeal was no ordeal at all—not for those who read and thought and were unafraid. He looked at the list before him. On the surface it looked like a grocery list, but as you read it the oddity struck. What kind of cake could be baked from cat's urine and the whole head of a hummingbird? The list was long and complicated, each ingredient demanding its own special care and sometimes an ingenious method of collection. It had taken well over a month to compile this list. How do you capture the stale breath of a hag threescore and ten? Where could he possibly find the ground tooth of a leviathan? But after painfully checking and rechecking with similar recipes and rites, he was sure it was okay to substitute nail clippings for the breath. And a shark's tooth instead of a real sea monster's. He was confident the substitutions would work, except for one: the most powerful ingredient was the body of a babe, no older than three years. He could not decide if the "babe" had to be human or whether it could be any species of infant. The worry had caused him many a sleepless night and many dark dreams of sneaking into a house after midnight and stealthily snatching an infant who would look dolefully into his eyes, innocent and quiet, sucking its thumb in sweet contentment. In the dream he would sing to the child, singing: *Hush, little baby, don't you cry,* as he smothered it to its white death beneath a goose-stuffed pillow and when he raised the pillow in the dim starlight the silent child would still be staring at him, this time the eyes a little puzzled, unfocused, slobber rolling fresh from its still-smiling, slightly parted lips. He would wake from these dreams with a moan at the back of his throat, chill sweat beading his forehead, the fear of the wrath of the one true God beating in his breast, frantic to escape. But it would be madness to commit such a horrible sin to obtain his freedom. For was not this dipping, this dunking, this drowning in magic an attempt to escape from that sin he would surely commit if he remained human?

So, confident that his spells would work, he collected the sack-cloth bag containing all the powerful talismans of his liberation and left the room, walking down the heart-of-pine floor and out the back door. In the backyard, beyond the lawn, was an apple orchard, begun with saplings his grandfather's mother had planted even before the house was built. Most of the yard had been a chicken pen, with bare dirt from their scratching. But when his grandmother died, his grand-father decided to get shed of the chickens and let the grass grow over the earth. Here he now cut the grass once a week, beginning in May, going almost into October, grass that grew greener and tougher with each summer rain.

The apple trees bore pale-green fruit no larger than his thumb this time of the year. By August they would be a little smaller than his fist and red like roses' red. They were what people called horse apples, sour and small, only good for making tart apple pies and cobblers. Come July he would pluck one off every now and again, remembering how as a little boy he would be so sternly reprimanded: Boy, them green apples will give you a stomachache. Make you sick as a dog. But he would eat them anyway. And miraculously he never got those green-apple bellyaches. He did so love that tart and sour taste that drew his mouth up the way a lemon would, the texture of the white flesh on the inside, even the crisp crunch it made when you bit into it. While thinking this a wave of sadness washed over him, for he realized birds can't really bite into an apple; they peck. And only chickens peck at barnyard apples. But he would feast on squirrel and rabbit—he would lose green apples for a real chance at eternal life.

Twilight was falling. The days were beginning to lengthen, so he had time to prepare; he knew his grandfather would be away until very late. The day before he had set up the pyre. A slab of metal to hold the ingredients. A few pieces of old pine, dripping strong with turpentine. Oak and hickory. A little tar, because one spell called for pitch. Then he spread the sack over the pyre and checked his grim ingredients against the list. The plastic bag that held the body of the kitten he had killed was thick with moisture, the animal's hair matted, black, and lank. Then with a strike-anywhere match he set it all afire. It was slow to blaze, but after a while—he had stuck some straw between also—its flames licked and belched and farted and sparked in a way that aroused him. The black smoke from the tar wisped up through the apple trees and danced high.

He began to chant some archaic words, most of whose meaning he had no notion of, but which he suspected had to be powerful, words he had spliced together from different rites and rituals from similar conjurings and acts of high sorcery. The words sounded German and French and Latin and Greek, and because he had no true knowledge of any other language than his high school Spanish, he created a special accent for this chant, which he fancied a cross between High German and French. And in the middle of his chant the smell of the burning cat struck him full in the face—a green, vile smell of guts and hair and dried urine and feces. But he continued, as he choked on the noxious fumes, to recite in his elegant accent.

When he had finished chanting the chant, thrice—an act that would make the ashes holy and protect him from the demon he would summon—he committed the paper with the chant and the paper with the list to the fire and went behind an apple tree and retched in violent spasms that brought tears to his eyes. Weakly he walked to the water spigot by the pump house that sat on top of the very well where once his great-grandmother had hauled up water in a wooden pail. The water was still well-sweet and well-bitter and tasted thick with iron. First he washed his mouth out and then he drank deeply of the sweet and bitter water, finally washing his face in its coolness. He sat on the back stoop, watching the fire die down and down. The sky, which had been high and blue earlier, streaked with thin white clouds, was now collecting clouds the color of tar smoke. His stomach began to knot for fear of what the gathering clouds could mean or should mean to a true mystic.

About an hour later, when the fire was no more than coals crackling with heat, he went to bank the smoldering ashes so they would be ready for the hour of his transfiguration. He went into the house, into his room, and began to tidy up, the neatest it had ever been. Books stacked in straight piles, papers filed away, clothes folded and put in a drawer. He did not worry about the library loans, for it would all be part of his disappearance. Now he was excited and restless. He considered leaving his grandfather a note: Granddaddy, I have been transformed. I will see you in the rapture. But no, his grandfather would think it a queer and peculiar joke. It would confound and confuse him and then, when his grandson did indeed actually disappear without a trace, it would leave him thinking strange and bizarre thoughts, because he would have no knowledge of the dazzling, wondrous truth.

He went back out to the pile of ashes, now all white and less hot. He stoked them yet higher and went back inside to complete the last leg of his conjuring. His grandfather had returned while he had been outside and asked why he had not touched the food his aunts had left. Horace complained of not being hungry and went into his neat room and lay down in the darkness, knowing he would not fall asleep. He set his alarm clock for fifteen minutes to twelve. Then, suddenly appearing in the doorway, his grandfather asked: What you been burning, boy? Smells like you been burning tires or something. He told his grandfather: Just some old planks that kept getting in my way when I cut grass. His grandfather stood silently for a while, peering into the black, silhouetted by the light from the kitchen. Rather than ask, as Horace was sure he would, if he was feeling sick, the old man turned and went back into the kitchen. Horace heard the sounds of his grandfather washing his one dish: the water pipes clunking; the water splashing; a plate being set in the dish rack to dry; the refrigerator door opening and closing. He heard the light go out—for his eyes were closed—and the sound of the metal chain chinking like a pendulum against the hollow light bulb; then he and the house were locked in one dark velvet quiet. He listened to his grandfather shuffle out to the porch where he sat in his rocking chair and rocked, the planks of the wooden porch beneath groaning in a slow rhythm. Had the doctor not made his grandfather give up chewing tobacco, he knew he would have heard the splat of juice, flawlessly aimed, hit the azalea bush.

Crickets and frogs and cicadas chirped the beating of a thousand tiny hearts. A turtledove cooed in the woods in the distance, and he did not think of birds and soaring and freedom as he had earlier, but of his humanity, his flesh, his blood, his soon-to-be-gone, soon-to-be-changed life. He considered the deep quiet called death and how different it was from this blue solitude, here, now, on his bed surrounded by thinly made sound and soft black.

After an hour or so his grandfather stopped rocking, stood, and walked into the house. The screen door banged behind him loudly. Well, his grandfather said, good night. After a pause his grandfather asked if he was all right. Quickly, too quickly, Horace said yes, in a voice that was almost puzzled. His grandfather said nothing more, shuffling softly to his room, turning on no light. Horace heard the old man remove his clothes and get into his pajamas—he was sure they were the light-blue pajamas he wore in summer, the ones his aunts ironed with too much starch—and ease into bed. Then the light came on and he heard the rustle of paper, the onionskin pages of a book. He knew it was the Bible his grandfather kept on his nightstand, for that was the only book his grandfather ever read, save the *Lady's Birthday Almanac* (which was really a magazine). Not long after the book went back on the nightstand, the light went out, and his grandfather sighed a long sigh, almost a sound of frustration. Once again there were only the other sounds, the natural, small music of the night.

He would not look at the clock—though, in truth, he had stolen a glance earlier to see if it was working. It was. So he just lay immobile, thinking of white ashes. At one point his grandfather rose to go to the bathroom. Sounds of the house, settling, sounds he once thought—and sometimes still thought—to be ghosts drifted in and out. But soon it was time, and five minutes before the alarm was to go off he rose, retrieved the candle from his drawer, and walked quietly out the front door.

The candle was a regular white affair, but he had placed it under the pulpit that past Sunday before the services and had snuck it out afterward, so he was confident it had been sufficiently blessed. Once outside, he struck a match and lit the candle. Its light was weak, but intense enough to blind his dark-adjusted eyes. A breeze played with the flame and finally blew it out. He stuffed it into his pocket and went on about his task.

Though the moon was not full—the rituals did not call for a full moon—there was a good-sized crescent peeking through the thick clouds to light his activity. The ashes were now only warm; there was but a faint glow in the very middle. With a trowel he stirred the center of the pile, and after he had a substantial heap of what he was sure was the mixture of powder he wanted, he carried a shovelful over to what was roughly the center of the apple orchard and began to design a pattern on the ground. It was a complicated and jagged pattern, a combination of the European Circle of Power and an American Indian figure he thought to be Hopi. After eleven trips with the trowel he was sure the design was complete. The breezes were strong, but his intensity was such that he barely noticed. Finally he sat in the center of the design—careful not to step on the ashes—and once again he lit the candle, blocking the wind with his body.

It was after twelve, he was sure. The time when demons walked the earth most freely. He tried to clear his mind of all except for the name of the High Demon confronted by the good monk, in the story, who forced the demon to do his bidding—the great and fierce demon who would ordinarily crush this puny child. But he was ready, armed not with the armor of righteousness and the shield of truth, but with the arcane knowledge that he firmly believed was the more powerful. It had chained the demon once, and he would be damned if he did not chain the demon again.

The breeze turned to gusts, which he took for a sign that his mojo was working. Some of the ashes blew in his face, but he was concentrating, concentrating, concentrating on the name of the name. Kneeling, he began to repeat the dread name aloud, his chest pounding as if his heart would jump out and run away. When the clouds covered what moon there was, he took it for His sinister presence. As he continued to chant the name of the demon, his eyes wide with fright, he wondered in part of his mind what the demon would look like. Tall, perhaps taller than the apple trees, the pine trees even. Red and fierce, with huge yellow teeth and foul breath. But no, this was a great demon, a member of Satan's High Court, the Inner Cabal. Maybe it would take the form of a centaur, of a gigantic fiery bird; mayhap it would come as a snake or a woolly beast. Or even in the form of a man, a devil like the one Reverend Hezekiah preached about, not with horns and a pitchfork, but in a white suit, with a handsome face and white teeth, smiling, as the devil is known to do.

He chanted. The name became a mantra, losing all meaning; it was a beautiful name with nice vowels and a foreign sound. He repeated and repeated and repeated. The intense fear that had crouched in his stomach started to fade, and for the first time he really allowed himself to think how silly this all was; how foolish and juvenile and desperate and impossible and insane; how there was no monk who saved a village by chaining a demon and releasing him only after he did his bidding; how there were, in fact, no such things as demons who walked the earth after midnight, or at any other time, for that matter; how if there were such things as demons he hadn't the slightest notion of how to force them to transform him, or even how to plead with them; how all those people who disappeared either really ran away or just died—the way he would.

Then, at first like a gentle kiss, here, there, light but unmistakable. Rain. Soon it was falling in a downpour. Water and water. The candle had long ago been doused. Now he sat with the water soaking him, streaming into his eyes and his mouth. A joke, he realized, this had been an elaborate joke he had played on himself. He was sixteen years of age and out in a rainstorm in the wee hours of the morning, calling on ancient demons to save him from—from what?—from himself? He noticed he was crying; hot tears stung his eyes. He shivered and slumped, and finally sprawled on the wet earth, cold not with the freezing cold of winter, but with a surface chill, like swimming in the ocean after dark in July.

He was not aware of the rain stopping or of the cloud drifting away from the crescent moon. He just lay there, wet and shivering; even the sobs had gone, leaving him with an empty feeling of exhaustion and confusion. His was the sudden feeling of falling down a well, knowing no one will come to the rescue for days. The dread of a horrible, inevitable, known future.

A voice. Where? In his head? In his mind? In his soul? It was the voice of a chorus, a host like the host that welcomed Jesus to the earth on that starry night in Bethlehem, and at the same time the voice of a wizened old man racked with pain, and the very voice of pain and anguish and sorrow itself, and the voice of lust and hate and war-torn plains with wind whistling and whispering through trees, the voice of wisdom, old and all-knowing, and the voice of foolishness, ignorance, and childish bliss. But a voice. One voice.

The voice said: Come.

The sky, now a classic spring sky after a quick rainstorm, seemed higher, wider, cleaner. The frogs, now happy and wet, sang joyous and raucous songs. He smiled and reached into the mud, into the soggy sod where the ashes had melted, and in one motion smeared his face with them, as though to reacquaint himself with the sensation of touch. Again he smiled, his face as vacant as his soul. The voice said rise, and he rose, stripping buck naked, as the voice told him, tearing off his clothing as though he were afire, wallowing like a hog where the ashes were, with innocent abandon. The voice told him to go into the house and get his grandfather's old rifle. He did, and turned and waited for the voice in his head, staring over the starlit fields toward the woods. The voice said merely, Walk. He did, his body mottled in clotted wood ash and mud, his skin cool but not cold, listening, listening for the voice that now seemed his only salvation. Salvation? Was that it, now? Beyond hope, beyond faith? Just to survive in some way. To live.

Did he see the low-swooping owl or the scurrying wood rat as it dashed into a gulley just by his bare foot? His mind was on spiritual things. For it was just as preachers had been preaching it all the years of his life, warning: There are wretched, wicked spirits that possess us and force us to commit unnatural acts. It was clear to him now: he had been possessed of just such a wicked spirit, and the rain was a sign to prove that he could not be purged. Why fight any longer? said his brain.

So he listened to the voice, the voice that was old and young, and mean and good. He put all his faith in that voice. The voice said march, so he marched, surrounded by hobgoblins and sprites and evil faeries and wargs—aberrations like himself, fierce and untamed, who frolicked about him with hellish glee at his acceptance of his doomed, delicious fate, and he was happy, oh, so happy, as he cradled the gun in his hand like a cool phallus, happy for the first time in so, so many months, for he knew the voice would take care of him and teach him and save him, and there was feeling, full and ribald and dangerous, and he reveled in the sensation and whatever felt good, and he marched leading his devilish crew, listening for the commands of the one voice, the only voice, which said, Go, and he went, surrounded by fiends who quaffed strong ales as they marched along through the fields, who danced about on the tree limbs and on the surfaces of streams all by the light of the crescent moon and fornicated and let blood from one another in bouts more violent than cockfights, smearing excrement on one another, jerking and touching and biting, shouting profanity and blasphemies, all with cheers and loud laughter, and he smiled and joined in, for this was his salvation, the way to final peace, and as he marched along, aware of the gun that he held tight in his hand, glad to be free, if *free* was a word to describe what he felt, he began to wonder—though it was much, much too late—as he pranced along alone down the road, somewhere in the small bit of his mind yet sane, he pondered: Perhaps I should have used, instead of a kitten, a babe.

§

Quality description always enhances, never detracts from the story. "A Visitation of Spirits" begins with: "What to become?" Answering this question opens a window into Horace's soul.

· · ·

In your journal, answer the following questions:

≷ How does Horace's comparison of animals reveal his character, his desires and psychological needs? Why do characteristics of a bird appeal to him? Why does Kenan allow his character time to consider so many possibilities?

≷ Horace finally decides on a red-tailed hawk and "flipped to the picture of his future self." Study the description of the red-tailed hawk. Does it have sensory appeal? Is the description active, engaging? How do verbs such as "thrashing," "piercing," "twitching" contribute to the hawk's image? How does the hawk's predatory behavior reflect on Horace's character? On the story's conclusion?

≷ Several settings are important to Horace—the high school and its library, the grandfather's house with its soybean fields, Horace's bedroom, and the North Carolina landscape. Consider each of these settings and what they add to the story. What do they "show" us about Horace and his world? Why is it important for Horace to have responses and attitudes to each setting?

≷ Study Horace's incantation scenes. How does the setting convey an atmosphere, an emotional quality of mystery and potential evil? How does Kenan's description make us believe a demon might be summoned? Take a highlighter and underline those descriptions which seem the most atmospheric, the most menacing to you. Do these descriptions appeal to your senses? Can you hear Horace's chant? Smell the burning kitten? See the fire dying? Taste the bittersweet, iron-tinged water? Feel the wind gusting?

How does the time of night—"It was after twelve, he was sure"—contribute to atmosphere?

≥ How does Kenan describe the "voice" which Horace hears? How does the voice influence Horace's actions? How do the descriptions of these actions and the setting make us understand the story's conclusion?

≥ If Kenan had simply "told" his story, do you think readers would come to believe in the possibility of spirits, believe in the emotional entanglements of an alienated boy searching for a place within society and self-transformation?

Write a paragraph about what Kenan has taught you about the power of setting and atmosphere.

During a lifetime, we move through thousands of settings, experience millions of sensory moments, and feel an emotional attachment to our world. Writers aim to re-create a similar but highly condensed sense of "life" in their fictional worlds. Well-executed fiction depends, in part, upon description to heighten readers emotional response. Fiction is forever fiction; but readers want to believe, if only for a few hours, that their lives and worlds have expanded. They want to respond as if fiction were real. Description is a powerful tool for encouraging belief in imagined worlds.

By observing, paying attention to your daily life, you can learn to write better description. Try pausing during your day—stop reading right now! Observe. Where are you? What do you see? What do you hear, touch, feel, and smell? What is the emotional atmosphere surrounding you? Take out your journal and write for a half hour.

Perhaps, one day, part of what you're experiencing *right now* can be used within a story (or several stories) as description, setting, or atmosphere. Maybe five years from now, you'll remember this moment with great clarity. You might be writing a story about an artist, or describing a student studying for exams, and your memory will help you recapture the moments when you were engaged in disciplining yourself to make your own dreams for the future come true.

Celebrate! Buy a new book, get a massage. Go to a museum. Take a long walk. By making art, you encourage yourself to live a more observant life.

9

DIALOGUE, DIALECT,

AND NARRATIVE VOICE

Good dialogue arises from surface and underlying tensions.

Just as tension informs character and plot, it is absolutely essential to good dialogue. In real life, we chitchat, "shoot the breeze," or get "carried away by the sound of our voices." Good dialogue is *always* more efficient. It is the diamond of fictional skills—reflecting characters' voices, sharpening their arguments, and shining light on motivations with intimacy and immediacy. Good dialogue enlivens plot, speeds action, and heightens conflict. All fictional skills are important to the whole, but contemporary fiction, in particular, seems to rely increasingly on dialogue for its success. Becoming expert at dialogue is a must.

In his first novel, *Billy*, Albert French writes strong, convincing dialogue. First and foremost, this dialogue arises from surface and underlying tensions:

"Are you afraid, Billy?"

Billy shakes his head no, squirms in the big chair, then nods his head yes.

"Come on, son, I told you there was nothing to be afraid of. Tell the people your name. You can do that."

"Billy Lee my name."

"Now, Billy, tell the people how old you are."

"Ah ten."

"Now, Billy, tell the people why you are here today."

"Ah don't knows. They say it's a trial."

"What's a trial, Billy? Tell the people what a trial is."

"Ah don't know."

"Billy, what happen to you at the pond? What happen, son?"

Billy is silent.

Red Pasko waits for an answer.

"What happen, Billy?"

"Them girls come. They beats me up. Theys bigger."

"Why did they beat you up?"

"Ah don'ts know. Me and Gumpy be in the pond. Theys come and git us."

"Did you try and run away from the girls, Billy?"

"Ah runs, but theys catch me. That girl, she bigger than me. She gits me down."

"Billy, what happen when they let you up? Did you try and run again?"

"Ah gits up. She comes and gits me agains."

"Did she hit you again?"

"Ah struck her. Ah make her leave me be."

"Billy, what happen to her?"

"Ah don't know. They say she deads."

Even though you may not know the novel's entire story, the dialogue makes clear that: Billy is afraid. Billy is only ten. He is on trial; he doesn't understand what a trial is. A girl is dead. Billy remembers the girl attacking him. The setting—Mississippi, 1937—makes the scene more ominous. The underlying tension, the *subtext,* is that many white Southerners of the era considered it inappropriate for a black male (of any age) to interact with a white girl (and if interaction did occur, it would always be an unwelcome sexual advance by the black male). Tension exists because of the underlying racial conflicts and the lawyer's knowledge versus the child's naive ignorance, that Billy may die. Tension also exists because of surface contrasts between child and adult and colloquial versus formal southern speech.

Good dialogue cannot be generated without tension. Dialogue arises from a blatant or subtle threat to a character's well-being: the wife argues with the husband, the private investigator's reputation depends upon her interrogations, the comic tries not to fail at humor. Though Billy doesn't understand the proceedings, he is trying to avoid punishment for a crime he didn't commit.

MY BEST ADVICE
Dialogue works best when it creates tension and reveals conflict.

Reread French's dialogue. The language is stark yet eloquent. Why? Because of the underlying and surface conflicts. But French is also exercising *emotional restraint.* His characters are not shouting, pleading, indulging in emotional hysterics. This restraint produces even more tension and makes the dialogue more credible. Characters do need to have emotional outbursts but these outbursts will work best after all attempts at emotional restraint fail. If after further questioning, Billy breaks down, screaming, "Ah didn't kill her," it'll be more effective because of his earlier restraint and quiet answers.

In good dialogue, characters' *actions/reactions and silences* also matter. Billy is asked two questions which he doesn't answer directly or with speech:

"Are you afraid, Billy?"

Billy shakes his head no, squirms in the big chair, then nods his head yes.

"Billy, what happen to you at the pond? What happen, son?"

Billy is silent.

In both instances, not speaking contributes powerfully to the dialogue. The actions and silence are consistent with a child's behavior and make his fear more palpable. What's left unsaid is as important as what's said. Billy can say "Ah ten" far easier than he can say "Ah scared." Likewise his hesitation in answering "What happen, son?" makes the dialogue more dramatic. It is harder to speak about what matters. After such hesitation, readers tend to pay more attention to what he ultimately says. For many readers, it is entirely credible that what is most emotionally significant for a character may be the most difficult to talk about.

French has an ear for the voice, the sound of his characters' speech. He captures their *rhythm, word choices, and pattern of sounds.* Billy's speech is clipped, direct, and emphasizes verbs: "gits," "comes," "says." Billy substitutes "Ah" for "I," adds an "s" sound to pronouns, verbs, and adverbs. He says "git" instead of "get," "agins" instead of "again." He uses contractions: "don't" instead of "do not." The lawyer depends upon questions and statements which are not accusatory or threatening but meant to elicit information and inspire confidence. His rhythm is more formal, calming, and less colloquial. Though there is still the suggestion of southern regional speech when he asks "What happen?" instead of "What happened?" Neither Billy nor his lawyer uses lengthy, grammatically correct sentences. People, in fact, do speak in short, ungrammatical bursts! By being attentive to patterns of rhythm and sound, by using *short sentences* and *sentence fragments,* and *distinct, colloquial language to suit each character,* French mimics real human speech.

Lastly, French doesn't overuse tags. Tags are identifying phrases

such as "he said," "she said," "Billy answered," "the lawyer asked."
Tags can help readers to keep abreast of who is talking when; unfortunately, they can also seem intrusive and slow the pace of good dialogue. If dialogue between characters is distinct enough, you don't
need tags. Billy sounds very much like Billy and not like the lawyer.
Also, if, in direct dialogue, the lawyer says, "Billy, tell me . . . ," we
can assume that Billy replies without saying, "Billy replied." Also, once
the pattern of alternating speech between characters is established,
readers will accept that each new indented line set off by quote marks
(" ") represents a new speaker:

> "Did she hit you again?"
> "Ah struck her. Ah make her leave me be."
> "Billy, what happen to her?"
> "Ah don't know. They say she deads."

Good dialogue relies upon:

> ≳ *Surface Tensions or Underlying Tensions*
> *(Subtext)*
> There should always be the sense that what's being
> said, how it is being said, and what's being left un-
> said is significant. Remember, dialogue isn't random
> but reflective of characters' emotional lives. The real
> causes of conflict, tensions between characters may
> also not be immediately evident but may hide as sub-
> text. For example, one character may know another is
> lying but never directly say so; nonetheless, the char-
> acter's hidden belief that the other is lying affects
> what is said and how it is said. Sometimes subtext is
> social and political—racism, gender and sexual poli-
> tics, nationalism, etc., can all potentially enhance un-
> derlying tensions in any conversation.

> ≳ *Emotional Restraint (and Release)*
> Characters, like people, attempt emotional restraint.
> (Subtext, by its nature, is a kind of emotional re-

straint.) Anger, fear, lust, loneliness bubbling beneath the surface are more interesting than full-throttle emotional outbursts. When outbursts do happen, the prior restraint will make them all the more significant. Dialogue should be written with a sense of restraint and with the promise and fulfillment of releasing emotional power.

Character Actions/Reactions and Silences
Engaged in dialogue, characters still have physical responses—facial gestures, stances, etc. These actions/reactions reinforce what's said or being left unsaid. A character can say, "I love you," but actions can prove whether the statement is truth or lie. Likewise, silences, hesitations can also convey the depth and truth of characters' emotions.

Speech and Rhythm Patterns to Suit Each Character
Characters' personalities, regional and class differences, type of educational background, and type of community they live in, all shape sounds and word selection. Abrupt, sweetly lyrical, or monosyllabic—the variety of speech is remarkable. Some characters will use simple words and be quite eloquent; others will use "fifty cent" words to impress. Contractions, too, alter rhythms and are more common, colloquial: "I can't go" is more informal than "I cannot go."

Short Sentences and Sentence Fragments
Lengthy, grammatically correct sentences make for stilted dialogue. Interruptions, sentence fragments, communication shortcuts, and dialect distinctions are more reflective of human speech:

"Where you going?"
"Church."

is better dialogue than:

"Where are you going?"
"I am going to church."

⸿ *Few Tags to Maintain Pacing*
Tags such as "he said," "she asked" are used only when absolutely necessary to avoid confusion about who is speaking when. Too many tags and readers will be reminded they are reading rather than imaginatively participating in a story.

Multiple-character dialogues (more than two persons) are difficult to write. You should attempt such scenes only after you're completely comfortable with two-person dialogues. In group scenes, each character presents a new element to balance but it's impossible to give all equal time and focus. In addition, you need tags to remind readers of the differing characters as well as reminders of where characters are located in space. It also helps if earlier in your story or novel you show clear physical and emotional differences between characters that will appear later as a group. But, remember, the focus of group exchanges should still be on tension, restraint, actions/reactions, and, as much as possible, unique speech for each character.

Most multiple-character dialogues degenerate into monologues or, at most, a two-person dialogue. To avoid this, you need to remind readers of the multiple characters present by letting them speak, however briefly, and giving them actions/reactions. While one or two characters may still verbally dominate the scene, there needs to be a sense that the events unfolding are significant to all of them. If five characters are present in the scene, you can't have three "disappear" while two continue to talk. Likewise, you can't "show" a mob, jury, or classroom if your scene becomes a narrowly focused monologue. For multiple-character scenes, it is essential to remember that *all* the characters are engaged in the dialogue. While speech makes any character seem more present, you still have the responsibility, as a writer, to make the minor characters visible and known (in varying degrees) within the scene via actions/reactions/silences and emotional attitudes. If you can write a successful scene which ignores the minor and supporting characters, then you might question the necessity of a group scene; however, if you truly need all the characters present to make the scene work (e.g., a battle, a concert, a marathon, etc.), then as a writer you must work hard to create the group, emotionally, visually, and orally, in your readers' imaginations.

For example, in *Magic City*, a group of Greenwood men in a church defend themselves against a Klan attack. All of the characters have been previously presented. Joe is the protagonist. Lying Man, a barber, and Nate and Gabe, two ex-veterans, are all strong supporting characters:

"Here! They're here," yelled Mr. Jackson. "They're here!"
He broke the stained glass with the butt of his rifle.
Others followed suit. Chunks of colored glass fell onto the floor.
"Hold up. Don't shoot," shouted Gabe. "Don't shoot."
"Damn," whispered Bill Johnson, awed.
Joe gripped the window ledge. Behind him stood Gabe, Nate, and Lying Man.
Gabe whispered, "War's here."
Nate sighed, "They surely hate us."
Lying Man said, "Stand."
Sandy replied sarcastic: "Nothing like good odds. Don't you think, Gabe? Nothing beats good odds."
Gabe ignored him, ordering, "Wait 'til I give the signal, men. Wait for the signal."
Joe's mouth was dry. Three truckloads of men with guns. *Ambrose Oil* was written on the cabs' sides.
"Damn that's a lot of 'em," said Chalmers.
"Just more ducks for me," called Nate, slinging

his rifle over his shoulder. "I'm going to the roof,
Gabe."

"Don't shoot 'til they're past the barricade," Gabe
hollered as Nate scrambled out the back door.

Joe held his breath as the flatbed trucks began lumbering up the hill.

"Come on, come on. A little further," Gabe urged
the drivers. "Come on." When the trucks halted in front
of the barricade, Gabe lit the fuse. Crackling smoke
snaked out of the church.

"Get down." Lying Man tugged Joe.

"Heads up," shouted Gabe, before diving, covering
his head.

The church windows shattered. "God damn, eighty
dollars," cursed Bill.

The blast had lifted the two overturned cars and the
first truck clear off the ground. The Greenwood men
cheered. Joe heard Nate banging on the roof, screaming,
"Go on, Gabe. Go on!"

"That showed them. God damn."

If this group scene worked properly, you should have a sense of
the initial Klan assault and the men's varying responses to it. This
dialogue allows the reader to shift focus with the shifting emotions of
the men. The strategy of such a multiple-voice scene is that you can
illustrate emotional complexity more fluently.

Lines such as "The Greenwood men cheered" and "Others followed suit" are intended to suggest the larger crowd. The last line—
"That showed them. God damn"—is intentionally left untagged because it could've been said by anyone. In fact, I want readers to imagine who said it.

With so many characters in the scene, tags are unavoidable. But
repeating over again "He said" or "Joe said" or "Nate replied" can get
pretty dull. By pairing tags with more interesting action verbs and
actions, the tags become less intrusive:

"Just more ducks for me," *called* Nate, *slinging his rifle* over his shoulder.

"Heads up," *shouted* Gabe, before *diving, covering* his head.

You can sometimes avoid a tag entirely by directly highlighting actions. For example:

"Get down." Lying Man *tugged* Joe.
instead of:
"Get down," *said* Lying Man, who tugged Joe.

Joe *heard* Nate banging on the roof, screaming,
"Go on, Gabe. Go on!"
instead of:
Joe heard Nate banging on the roof.
"Go on, Gabe," Nate *screamed.* "Go on!"

You can't always avoid tags but you can be more creative in suggesting who is speaking when. Likewise you can locate characters within the scene more creatively if you emphasize actions paired with dialogue.

DIALECT

Black speech patterns are richly varied and expressive. All people shift language—shift dialect usage, according to the social context; African Americans often shift between standard and Black English. Dialects have complex grammars and dictions and the variety within each language form is remarkable. Dialect is a study of contrasts: southern black dialect contrasts with hip urban speech; New Englanders' broad vowels contrast with Midwesterners' twang. Language lives, fluidly changing, adapting to the changing nature and character of American society. Slaves were forced to learn standard English, but they, in turn, influenced English with their African dialects. Many words such as tote, banjo, nitty-gritty, and banana were African contributions to southern English.

Nonetheless, during slavery, white Americans used speech differences as a marker for black inferiority. Black people were stereotypically presented as speaking gibberish, and when they did make attempts at standard English, the results were stylized as both ridiculous and humorous. Many nineteenth-century African American writers concentrated on demonstrating their command of standard English as a political defense against equating black speech with intellectual inferiority. But others such as Paul Laurence Dunbar and Charles Chesnutt used dialect to express the authenticity of expressive black vernacular.

During the 1920s Harlem Renaissance (with a striking resurgence during the 1960s Black Arts Movement), African American writers became more intent on celebrating and capturing the nuances of black speech. Experimentation ranged from phonetic representation to using blues patterns as metaphors for urban dialect to emphasizing rhymes and exaggeration as hallmarks of black storytelling tradition. Langston Hughes, Sterling Brown, Richard Wright, Zora Neale Hurston, using differing approaches, explored the variety and range of black speech. The twentieth century proudly continues to reflect black culture, via speech, from the inside out, defying stereotypical conceptions of how blacks across gender and class lines speak. Many black writers have laid claim to standard English as an equally authentic representation of black life. While nineteenth-century writers might have consciously adopted standard English to disprove inferiority, contemporary black writers lay claim to a far wider spectrum of linguistic choices as *reflective of their reality*. Standard English is no longer a code for asserting one's civil rights worthiness!

Clearly, African American writers should use any and all speech variants which best express their characters. The range is enormous in terms of tenor, rhythm, tone, and the pattern of words. Here are but two examples:

"Missie May, take yo' hand out mah pocket!" Joe
shouted out between laughs.
    "Ah ain't, Joe, not lessen you gwine gimme whateve'

it is good you got in yo' pocket. Turn it go, Joe, do Ah'll tear yo' clothes."

"Go on tear 'em. You de one dat pushes de needles round heah. Move yo' hand, Missie May."

"Lemme git dat paper sack out yo' pocket. Ah bet it's candy kisses."

"Tain't. Move yo' hand. Woman ain't got no business in a man's clothes nohow. Go way."

. . .

"Unhhunh! Ah got it. It 'tis so candy kisses. Ah knowed you had somethin' for me in yo' clothes. Now Ah got to see whut's in every pocket you got."

—Joe and Missie May
in Zora Neale Hurston's "The Gilded Six Bits"

"You've got a pretty room, a real pretty room, Miss Peace."

"You eat something funny today?"

"Ma'am?"

"Some chop suey? Think back."

"No, ma'am."

"No? Well, you gone be sick later on."

"But I didn't have no chop suey."

"You think I come all the way over here for you to tell me that? I can't make visits too often. You should have some respect for old people."

"But, Miss Peace, I'm visiting *you*. This is *your* room." Nel smiled.

"What you say your name was?"

"Nel Greene."

"Wiley Wright's girl?"

"Uh huh. You do remember. That makes me feel good, Miss Peace. You remember me and my father."

"Tell me how you killed that little boy."

"What? What little boy?"

"The one you threw in the water?"

"I didn't throw no little boy in the river. That was Sula."

"You. Sula. What's the difference? You were there. You watched, didn't you? Me, I never would've watched."

—Eva Peace and Nel Wright
in Toni Morrison's *Sula*

Both Zora Neale Hurston and Toni Morrison are splendid dialogue writers. Both paint complex and authentic portraits of black life and black speech. Hurston revels in southern black dialect: "I" becomes "Ah," "am not" becomes "ain't," "is not" becomes "tain't." Consonants and vowels are dropped—"whateve' " not "whatever," "yo' " not "you." "D" is substituted for "th"—so "that" becomes "dat," "the" becomes "de." "H" is substituted for "re" and "y"—"here" becomes "heah" and "my" becomes "mah." She also alters some words, making them a run-on of sounds. For example, "Let me" becomes "lemme," "going to give me" becomes "gwine gimme."

Morrison, on the other hand, rather than altering consonant and vowel sounds, uses rhythm and syntax to suggest the informal black speech of small-town Ohioans, Nel Wright and Eva Peace. "What you say your name was?" is rhythmically more even and blunt than "What did you say your name was?" Dropping the verb "did," while incorrect for standard English, sounds authentic and colloquial for Eva, who is elderly, poor, and wise in "life learning" rather than "book learning." Eva admonishes Nel: "Well, you gone be sick later on." This, too, is rhythmically blunt and substitutes another standard English word, "gone," for "going." Hurston might have rewritten the line to be: "Well, yo' gwine git sick later on." The effect would dramatically alter Eva's characterization. Rhythmically and tonally, Eva with a Hurston-like revision would sound less blunt, more musically folksy, and more southern!

Language is a dynamic, wonderful terrain for writers to explore! Historical time period, region, gender, class, age, and ethnicity all have the power to influence both the style and the content of a character's speech.

When reading, pay attention to differing representations of speech-dialogue. Also, listen to those around you. Use your journal to record snippets of interesting dialogue. In time you'll learn to trust your own ear in re-creating sounds. While writing fine dialogue is challenging, it is also satisfying and essential to good fiction.

NARRATIVE VOICE

Ordinarily, we think of playwriting, not fiction, as rich with monologues (scenes where a solo actor speaks directly or indirectly to an audience). First person point of view stories can be understood as extended monologues—the reader is the "audience." These stories' strong narrative voice depends upon a unique character captured in sound. Like the best oral storytellers, the "I," often through the monologue (the telling of the story), teaches moral and ethical lessons.

First person monologues should follow many of the same principles as two-person dialogues:

- surface and/or underlying tensions (subtext);

- distinct word selection and rhythm patterns;

- emotional restraint;

- actions/reactions;

- and as few tags as possible, to make a strong narrative.

But, unlike dialogue, first person voices also control larger issues of how the story is told and how conflict is revealed. A first person voice can summarize, provide background information and perspective, and command story structure in ways that are more explicit than two characters engaged in dialogue. Nonetheless, if you consider first person narratives to be monologues governed by the same principles of good dialogue, you're bound to write more effective voices.

For example, in "The Life You Live (May Not Be Your Own)," J. California Cooper's Molly advises:

> Love, marriage, and friendship are some of the most important things in your life . . . if you ain't sick or dyin'! And, Lord knows, you gotta be careful 'cause you sometimes don't know you been wrong 'bout one of them till after the mistake shows up! Sometimes it takes years to find out, and all them years are out of your own life! It's like you got to be careful what life you live, 'cause it may not be your own! Some love, marriage, or friend done led you to the wrong road, 'cause you trusted 'em!
>
> Of course, I'm talking 'bout myself, but I'm talkin' 'bout my friend and neighbor, Isobel, too. Maybe you, too! Anyway, if the shoe don't fit, don't put it on!

Contrast this voice with policewoman, Leigh Ann, in Chassie West's novel *Sunrise:*

> I'd counted on Sunrise being the same little hamlet it had been in my childhood and so far, thank God, I hadn't been disappointed.
>
> I was on leave with no clock to punch, no one to account to. I was free (well, unmarried anyway), black (on the toasted almond end of the spectrum), and solvent (one gas card and one credit card for emergencies). I was here on a whim, just passing through, as it were, and one sure way of attracting attention, which I wanted to avoid, would be to drive around the residential sections of town at five-fifty-five in the morning. So I told myself I might as well have breakfast at Fred's Diner.
>
> That's when the trouble started.

The two women characters have strikingly different voices. Read each voice aloud and you'll hear Molly's breathless, rapid pace and

Leigh Ann's voice filled with sassy asides and qualifying phrases. Both writers, consciously not randomly, created these voices through word selection and patterning of sentences. Narrative voice, just like dialogue, creates a vision of the character. However, dialogue is limited in scope, revealing characterization in specific scenes. Narrative voice, on the other hand, not only reveals character but structures the entire fictional world. The narrative voice **is** the storyteller; and as storyteller, the sentences tend to be less fragmented. Though narrative voice controls the story, a writer must still be conscious of how the "voice as character" develops through word choice, complexity of sentences, and rhythms.

> Some love, marriage, or friend done led you to the wrong
> road, 'cause you trusted 'em!
> Of course, I'm talking 'bout myself, but I'm talkin'
> 'bout my friend and neighbor, Isobel, too. Maybe you,
> too! Anyway, if the shoe don't fit, don't put it on!

Molly's diction is informal, exclamatory black dialect. Her speech creates a vision of a welcoming, generous, commonsense woman dispensing advice on her front porch. As in good dialogue, Molly reveals tensions (the "wrong road"), but shows remarkable restraint by not rushing headlong into what's wrong. Molly, like a good storyteller, is going to take her time weaving her tale for the best effect. Her language also gives clues about her reaction/responses to the "wrong road." Her voice is upbeat, confiding, and that of a survivor!

On the other hand, Leigh Ann's standard English is more formal, more intellectual than emotional than Molly's voice:

> I was here on a whim, just passing through, as it were,
> and one sure way of attracting attention, which I wanted
> to avoid, would be to drive around the residential sec-
> tions of town at five-fifty-five in the morning.

Despite her whim to visit Sunrise, Leigh Ann's language suggests such impulsiveness is unusual for her. Her complex sentence structure suggests thoughtful, probing intelligence. There is a policewoman's precision to her language—the exact time is "five-fifty-five"; she drives specifically through the "residential sections of town." Leigh Ann can be depended upon to tell the facts of any story.

As in good dialogue, Leigh Ann reveals tensions (she wants her presence undetected) and, like Molly, she shows emotional restraint by not rushing headlong into what's wrong. "That's when the trouble started" lures readers into the story, but Leigh Ann will tell it in her own good time. Leigh Ann's language also gives clues about her reaction/responses to the "trouble." She will try to avoid being pulled into the trouble, but when pulled into it, she'll give a good analytical and precise account of herself.

The key to capturing anyone's voice (either as narrator or as dialogue speaker) is to listen. Through practice you can capture sounds as you hear them. Consistency is essential. If you drop vowels, substitute "ain't" for "am not," or replace short "e" sounds with "i," then you need to do so consistently in your dialogue. Likewise word selection, sentence structure and rhythm shouldn't conflict with characters' backgrounds and experiences.

All dialogue should be read aloud. Following your own instincts, the dialogue should move with the natural energy of "real" speech. If dialogue seems stagnant, if you lose breath before finishing a sentence, then you need to revise.

Writing strong dialogue is a skill which will serve you well in each and every story. Characters don't truly come alive until they *speak,* and their speech exposes conflict and advances plot. Every hour spent practicing dialogue will reward you with more readable and interesting stories. As you become more sensitive to the sounds and speech about you, your characters will whisper, holler, and sigh new emotions and new stories.

EXERCISE 1

TALKING SOLO VOICE

Spend two days listening for a person whose speech interests you. It can be the FedEx driver from the Bronx, a Wall Street financier, or a Jamaican immigrant. Select a co-worker or family member, if you prefer; but their speech must intrigue you, must be fundamentally exciting. As you're searching for a voice, record in your journal *why* you think certain voices appeal to you. *What is it you like hearing?* Is it the rhythm, the word choices, the dialect lilt? What sentence pattern do you hear most often? Is the tone emphatic? Whiny? Measured? Aggressive? Blunt? Hesitant and shy?

Once you've selected a voice, ask the speaker if you can tape-record their dialogue. If this is impractical, rely on transcription and memory.

Next, select *one* of the situations below and write a monologue using your newly captured voice.

- Imagine a suspected bank robber pleading innocence and fabricating an alibi for a detective.

- Imagine an abused wife trying to explain to a social worker why she won't leave her husband.

- Imagine a clerk at the convenience store trying to explain to a fellow employee his infatuation with a customer who comes in every Monday and Friday for a quart of milk, two beers, and a carton of cigarettes.

- Imagine a youth explaining to his parents why he needs to abandon college to pursue a singing career.

- Imagine a middle-aged man or woman, desperate for a job, trying to explain to an interviewer why they're best qualified for a sales job beneath their skills.

¿ Imagine a dying parent trying to explain to their son
or daughter why they abandoned their child decades
ago, why they lived the life they did.

Spend an hour writing and revising a monologue in your journal. How well does your creative version compare with the original
voice? How well does the voice suit the situation and character you
created?

Does your monologue have tension? Emotional restraint? Are
there any actions/reactions and silences in your monologue? If not,
why not? Is the speech credible? Consistent?

Any weaknesses in your monologue? What are its strengths?

DIALOGUE AT ODDS

Building upon the previous exercise, expand your monologue into a
dialogue. For example, if you created the monologue of a bank robber
lying to a detective, you now need to expand it to create a two-person
dialogue. To do this you need to:

1. *Imagine the second character:*
Who is she (or he)? How long has she been a detective? Does she
like her job? What needs, motivations does she have? What does
her voice sound like?

2. *Add more tension and subtext:*
Does the detective suspect the robber is lying? Does she have
only circumstantial evidence? Is she trying to trick him into a
confession? Is she secretly sympathetic to him? Does she find him
attractive? Does she have money problems? Has she ever dreamed
of stealing?
Is the robber attracted to the detective? Is the robber carrying a

concealed weapon? Is the robber especially anxious because a new conviction will mean life imprisonment? Did the robber recently discover his wife is pregnant?

3. Establish setting:

Where are your characters? In the downtown police station? At the robber's home? In a probation office? Has the robber been run aground in a suspected crack house?

Once you've imagined the new character, established a setting, and increased surface and underlying tension, you're ready to imagine a good dialogue scene.

In your journal, write a dialogue between two people based upon your original monologue. (Remember, characters do not speak in a vacuum but within the context of who they are, where they are, and the purpose or goal they need to achieve.) Don't censor your words. Write quickly for at least thirty minutes, trying to create interesting and credible dialogue. (Don't worry about a resolution. The bank robber doesn't need to confess. The interviewer doesn't need to give the desperate middle-aged woman a job.)

Next, read your dialogue aloud. Are the speech patterns, word choices of the two characters distinct? Does the dialogue seem stilted or natural? What types of sentences do you use? Are they effective? Do you use any sentence fragments? One-word responses? If not, why not? Could you use more sentence rhythm variety? Did any of your lines sound awkward, stilted?

Have you added enough tension and subtext? Do you need to add more character responses, actions?

Spend another thirty minutes revising your dialogue. Read your dialogue aloud again. Is the second version better—easier to follow, alive with sound and substance?

EXERCISE 3

PRACTICING SUBTEXT

Underlying tensions rule much of human conversation. Polite society usually discourages direct expression of strong emotions: outrage, anger, love, desire. We learn to dissemble, bury our emotions as subtext within our speech. A teenager struck with romantic passion may blandly say, "She's okay," when his heart more eloquently speaks of love.

People often avoid saying what they mean or say less than what they mean, which creates subtext, conversational tension. This sense that another conversation underlies our dialogue or that meaning is found "between the lines" makes conversation interesting.

Pay attention to how you and those around you argue. How many times have you and your loved one argued over the toothpaste cap when you're really fighting about how you spend money? How many times have you criticized your children's clothing and hairstyles when you're really arguing about the suitability of their new friends? Arguments about food, home repairs, Christmas decorations, and when and where to vacation can all potentially hide arguments about insecurity, infidelity, child rearing, and marital rifts.

It is important to remember that subtext as a form of emotional restraint can't last throughout your story. Eventually, what's at the heart of the conversation has to be confronted. It is this confrontation your readers anticipate.

For the next twenty minutes, using *one* of the ideas below, write a sequence of dialogue that has subtext, underlying tensions. Ideally, you will want the reader to be able to tell that there is something lurking beneath the surface conversation. Leave clues: unfinished sentences; unexpected silences; emotional responses that don't fit the conversation; or more emotion than the surface situation would warrant.

>   Two characters argue about the unequal distribution of household chores.

The subtext: One partner believes the other is unfaithful.

§ Two characters argue about whether the Chicago Bulls are the best team.
The subtext: One friend has started to deal drugs.

§ Two characters argue about whether a diamond is an exploitation of black labor or an expression of love.
The subtext: Both partners are reconsidering the engagement.

§ Two characters argue about whether their child should go to Harvard or Howard University.
The subtext: The father remembers the sixties and worries about his child's assimilation.

Read the dialogue you produced. Have you established a sense of tension? Of something to be revealed later?

Write for another twenty minutes, adding to the scene and allowing the subtext, the hidden tension, to break through. For example, the wife finally accuses the husband of infidelity, the young man directly confronts his friend's drug abuse, the father bemoans his son's assimilation, etc.

In your dialogue, there may or may not be a resolution of conflict. Possibly tensions will subside, becoming subtext once again. One partner, still not sure if her lover is unfaithful, may conclude the conversation with "It's your turn to clean the bathroom."

The best thing about subtext, however, is that hidden tensions always rise to the surface. Just as in plot development, it is this rising and release of tension which will excite readers to continue reading more.

Read your entire scene aloud. What can you do to make it better? Is the language and diction credible and engaging? Are there enough clues about subtext? Is it emotionally dramatic when the subtext is revealed?

TONI CADE BAMBARA'S "RAYMOND'S RUN"

Toni Cade Bambara celebrates the humor, energy, and compassion of children. In this story, she splendidly writes a first person narrator whose voice, vibrantly alive, is a champion of respect not only for herself and her friends but also for her disabled brother. Relying on rhythm and colloquial speech, Bambara writes convincing dialogue attuned to the bickering as well as the wisdom among children.

I DON'T HAVE MUCH work to do around the house like some girls. My mother does that. And I don't have to earn my pocket money by hustling; George runs errands for the big boys and sells Christmas cards. And anything else that's got to get done, my father does. All I have to do in life is mind my brother Raymond, which is enough.

Sometimes I slip and say my little brother Raymond. But as any fool can see he's much bigger and he's older too. But a lot of people call him my little brother cause he needs looking after cause he's not quite right. And a lot of smart mouths got lots to say about that too, especially when George was minding him. But now, if anybody has anything to say to Raymond, anything to say about his big head, they have to come by me. And I don't play the dozens or believe in standing around with somebody in my face doing a lot of talking. I much rather just knock you down and take my chances even if I am a little girl with skinny arms and a squeaky voice, which is how I got the name Squeaky. And if things get too rough, I run. And as anybody can tell you, I'm the fastest thing on two feet.

There is no track meet that I don't win the first place medal. I use to win the twenty-yard dash when I was a little kid in kindergarten. Nowadays it's the fifty-yard dash. And tomorrow I'm subject to run the quarter-meter relay all by myself and come in first, second, and third. The big kids call me Mercury cause I'm the swiftest thing in the neighborhood. Everybody knows that—except two people who know better, my father and me.

He can beat me to Amsterdam Avenue with me having a two fire-hydrant headstart and him running with his hands in his pockets and whistling. But that's private information. Cause can you imagine some thirty-five-year-old man stuffing himself into PAL shorts to race little kids? So as far as everyone's concerned, I'm the fastest and that goes for Gretchen, too, who has put out the tale that she is going to win the first place medal this year. Ridiculous. In the second place, she's got short legs. In the third place, she's got freckles. In the first place, no one can beat me and that's all there is to it.

I'm standing on the corner admiring the weather and about to take a stroll down Broadway so I can practice my breathing exercises, and I've got Raymond walking on the inside close to the buildings cause he's subject to fits of fantasy and starts thinking he's a circus performer and that the curb is a tightrope strung high in the air. And sometimes after a rain, he likes to step down off his tightrope right into the gutter and slosh around getting his shoes and cuffs wet. Then I get hit when I get home. Or sometimes if you don't watch him, he'll dash across traffic to the island in the middle of Broadway and give the pigeons a fit. Then I have to go behind him apologizing to all the old people sitting around trying to get some sun and getting all upset with the pigeons fluttering around them, scattering their newspapers and upsetting the waxpaper lunches in their laps. So I keep Raymond on the inside of me, and he plays like he's driving a stage coach which is O.K. by me so long as he doesn't run me over or interrupt my breathing exercises, which I have to do on account of I'm serious about my running and don't care who knows it.

Now some people like to act like things come easy to them,

won't let on that they practice. Not me. I'll high prance down 134th Street like a rodeo pony to keep my knees strong even if it does get my mother uptight so that she walks ahead like she's not with me, don't know me, is all by herself on a shopping trip, and I am somebody else's crazy child.

Now you take Cynthia Procter for instance. She's just the opposite. If there's a test tomorrow, she'll say something like, "Oh I guess I'll play handball this afternoon and watch television tonight," just to let you know she ain't thinking about the test. Or like last week when she won the spelling bee for the millionth time, "A good thing you got 'receive,' Squeaky, cause I would have got it wrong. I completely forgot about the spelling bee." And she'll clutch the lace on her blouse like it was a narrow escape. Oh, brother.

But of course when I pass her house on my early morning trots around the block, she is practicing the scales on the piano over and over and over and over. Then in music class, she always lets herself get bumped around so she falls accidently on purpose onto the piano stool and is so surprised to find herself sitting there, and so decides just for fun to try out the ole keys and what do you know—Chopin's waltzes just spring out of her fingertips and she's the most surprised thing in the world. A regular prodigy. I could kill people like that.

I stay up all night studying the words for the spelling bee. And you can see me anytime of day practicing running. I never walk if I can trot and shame on Raymond if he can't keep up. But of course he does, cause if he hangs back someone's liable to walk up to him and get smart, or take his allowance from him, or ask him where he got that great big pumpkin head. People are so stupid sometimes.

So I'm strolling down Broadway breathing out and breathing in on counts of seven, which is my lucky number, and here comes Gretchen and her sidekicks—Mary Louise who used to be a friend of mine when she first moved to Harlem from Baltimore and got beat up by everybody till I took up for her on account of her mother and my mother used to sing in the same choir when they were young girls, but people ain't grateful, so now she hangs out with the new girl Gretchen and talks about me like a dog; and Rosie who is as fat as I am skinny and has a big mouth where Raymond is concerned and is too stupid to know that there is not a big deal of difference between herself and Raymond and that she can't afford to throw stones. So they are steady coming up Broadway and I see right away that it's going to be one of those Dodge City scenes cause the street ain't that big and they're close to the building just as we are. First I think I'll step into the candy store and look over the new comics and let them pass. But that's chicken and I've got a reputation to consider. So then I think I'll just walk straight on through them or over them if necessary. But as they get to me, they slow down. I'm ready to fight, cause like I said I don't feature a whole lot of chitchat, I much prefer to just knock you down right from the jump and save everybody a lotta precious time.

"You signing up for the May Day races?" smiles Mary Louise, only it's not a smile at all.

A dumb question like that doesn't deserve an answer. Besides, there's just me and Gretchen standing there really, so no use wasting my breath talking to shadows.

"I don't think you're going to win this time," says Rosie, trying to signify with her hands on her hips all salty, completely forgetting that I have whupped her behind many times for less salt than that.

"I always win cause I'm the best," I say straight at Gretchen who is, as far as I'm concerned, the only one talking in this ventriloquist-dummy routine.

Gretchen smiles but it's not a smile and I'm thinking that girls never really smile at each other because they don't know how and don't want to know how and there's probably no one to teach us how cause grown-up girls don't know either. Then they all look at Raymond who has just brought his mule team to a standstill. And they're about to see what trouble they can get into through him.

"What grade you in now, Raymond?"

"You got anything to say to my brother, you say it to me, Mary Louise Williams of Raggedy Town, Baltimore."

"What are you, his mother?" sasses Rosie.

"That's right, Fatso. And the next word out of anybody and I'll be their mother too." So they just stand there and Gretchen shifts from one leg to the other and so do they. Then Gretchen puts her hands on her hips and is about to say something with her freckle-face self but doesn't. Then she walks around me looking me up and down but keeps walking up Broadway, and her sidekicks follow her. So me and Raymond smile at each other and he says "Gidyap" to his team and I continue with my breathing exercises, strolling down Broadway toward the icey man on 145th with not a care in the world cause I am Miss Quicksilver herself.

I take my time getting to the park on May Day because the track meet is the last thing on the program. The biggest thing on the program is the May Pole dancing which I can do without, thank you, even if my mother thinks it's a shame I don't take part and act like a girl for a change. You'd think my mother'd be grateful not to have to make me a white organdy dress with a big satin sash and buy me new white baby-doll shoes that can't be taken out of the box till the big day. You'd think she'd be glad her daughter ain't out there prancing around a May Pole getting the new clothes all dirty and sweaty and trying to act like a fairy or a flower or whatever you're supposed to be when you should be trying to be yourself, whatever that is, which is, as far as I am concerned, a poor Black girl who really can't afford to buy shoes and a new dress you only wear once a lifetime cause it won't fit next year.

I was once a strawberry in a Hansel and Gretel pageant when I was in nursery school and didn't have no better sense than to dance on tiptoe with my arms in a circle over my head doing umbrella steps and being a perfect fool just so my mother and father could come dressed up and clap. You'd think they'd know better than to encourage that kind of nonsense. I am not a strawberry. I do not dance on my toes. I run. That is what I am all about. So I always come late to the May Day program, just in time to get my number pinned on and lay in the grass till they announce the fifty-yard dash.

I put Raymond in the little swings, which is a tight squeeze this year and will be impossible next year. Then I look around for Mr. Pearson who pins the numbers on. I'm really looking for Gretchen if you want to know the truth, but she's not around. The park is jam-packed. Parents in hats and corsages and breast-pocket handkerchiefs peeking up. Kids in white dresses and light blue suits. The parkees unfolding chairs and chasing the rowdy kids from Lenox as if they had no right to be there. The big guys with their caps on backwards, leaning against the fence swirling the basketballs on the tips of their fingers waiting for all these crazy people to clear out the park so they can play. Most of the kids in my class are carrying bass drums and glockenspiels and flutes. You'd think they'd put in a few bongos or something for real like that.

Then here comes Mr. Pearson with his clipboard and his cards and pencils and whistles and safety pins and fifty million other things he's always dropping all over the place with his clumsy self. He sticks out in a crowd cause he's on stilts. We used to call him Jack and the Beanstalk to get him mad. But I'm the only one that can outrun him and get away, and I'm too grown for that silliness now.

"Well, Squeaky," he says checking my name off the list and handing me number seven and two pins. And I'm thinking he's got no right to call me Squeaky, if I can't call him Beanstalk.

"Hazel Elizabeth Deborah Parker," I correct him and tell him to write it down on his board.

"Well, Hazel Elizabeth Deborah Parker, going to give someone else a break this year?" I squint at him real hard to see if he is seriously thinking I should lose the race on purpose just to give someone else a break.

"Only six girls running this time," he continues, shaking his head sadly like it's my fault all of New York didn't turn out in sneakers. "That new girl should give you a run for your money." He looks around the park for Gretchen like a periscope in a submarine movie. "Wouldn't it be a nice gesture if you were . . . to ahhh . . ."

I give him such a look he couldn't finish putting that idea into words. Grownups got a lot of nerve sometimes. I pin number seven to myself and stomp away—I'm so burnt. And I go straight for the track and stretch out on the grass while the band winds up with "Oh the Monkey Wrapped His Tail Around the Flag Pole," which my teacher calls by some other name. The man on the loudspeaker is calling everyone over to the track and I'm on my back looking at the sky trying to pretend I'm in the country, but I can't, because even grass in the city feels hard as sidewalk and there's just no pretending you are anywhere but in a "concrete jungle" as my grandfather says.

The twenty-yard dash takes all of the two minutes cause most of the little kids don't know no better than to run off the track or run the wrong way or run smack into the fence and fall down and cry. One little kid though has got the good sense to run straight for the white ribbon up ahead so he wins. Then the second graders line up for the thirty-yard dash and I don't even bother to turn my head to watch cause Raphael Perez always wins. He wins before he even begins by psyching the runners, telling them they're going to trip on their shoelaces and fall on their faces or lose their shorts or something, which he doesn't really have to do since he is very fast, almost as fast as I am. After that is the forty-yard dash which I use to run when I was in first grade. Raymond is hollering from the swings cause he knows I'm about to do my thing cause the man on the loudspeaker has just announced the fifty-yard dash, although he might just as well be giving a recipe for Angel Food cake cause you can hardly make out what he's saying for the static. I get up and slip off my sweat pants and then I see Gretchen standing at the starting line kicking her legs out like a pro. Then as I get into place I see that ole Raymond is in line on the other side of the fence, bending down with his fingers on the ground just like he knew what he was doing. I was going to yell at him but then I didn't. It burns up your energy to holler.

Every time, just before I take off in a race, I always feel like I'm in a dream, the kind of dream you have when you're sick with fever and feel all hot and weightless. I dream I'm flying over a sandy beach in the early morning sun, kissing the leaves of the trees as I fly by. And there's always the smell of apples, just like in the country when I was little and use to think I was a choo-choo train, running through the fields of corn and chugging up the hill to the orchard. And all the time I'm dreaming this, I get lighter and lighter until I'm flying over the beach again, getting blown through the sky like a feather that weighs nothing at all. But once I spread my fingers in the dirt and crouch over for the Get on Your Mark, the dream goes and I am solid again and am telling myself, Squeaky you must win, you must win, you are the fastest thing in the world, you can even beat your father up Amsterdam if you really try. And then I feel my weight coming back just behind my knees then down to my feet then into the earth and the pistol shot explodes in my blood and I am off and weightless again, flying past the other runners, my arms pumping up and down and the whole world is quiet except for the crunch as I zoom over the gravel in the track. I glance to my left and there is no one. To the right a blurred Gretchen who's got her chin jutting out as if it would win the race all by itself. And on the other side of the fence is Raymond with his arms down to his side and the palms tucked up behind him, running, in his very own style and the first time I ever saw that and I almost stop to watch my brother Raymond on his first run. But the white ribbon is bouncing toward me and I tear past it racing into the distance till my feet with a mind of their own start digging up footfuls of dirt and brake me short. Then all the kids standing on the side pile on me, banging me on the back and slapping my head with their May Day programs, for I have won again and everybody on 151st Street can walk tall for another year.

"In first place . . ." the man on the loudspeaker is clear as a bell now. But then he pauses and the loudspeaker starts to whine. Then static. And I lean down to catch my breath and here comes Gretchen walking back for she's overshot the finish line too, huffing and puffing with her hands on her hips taking it slow, breathing in steady time like a real pro and I sort of like her a little for the first time. "In first place . . ." and then three or four voices get all mixed up on the loudspeaker and I dig my sneaker into the grass and stare at Gretchen who's staring back, we both wondering just who did win. I can hear old Beanstalk arguing with the man on the loudspeaker and then a few others running their mouths about what the stop watches say.

Then I hear Raymond yanking at the fence to call me and I wave to shush him, but he keeps rattling the fence like a gorilla in a cage like in them gorilla movies, but then like a dancer or something he starts climbing up nice and easy but very fast. And it occurs to me, watching how smoothly he climbs hand over hand and remembering how he looked running with his arms down to his side and with the wind pulling his mouth back and his teeth showing and all, it occurred to me that Raymond would make a very fine runner. Doesn't he always keep up with me on my trots? And he surely knows how to breathe in counts of seven cause he's always doing it at the dinner table, which drives my brother George up the wall. And I'm smiling to beat the band cause if I've lost this race, or if me and Gretchen tied, or even if I've won, I can always retire as a runner and begin a whole new career as a coach with Raymond as my champion. After all, with a little more study I can beat Cynthia and her phony self at the spelling bee. And if I bugged my mother, I could get piano lessons and become a star. And I have a big rep as the baddest thing around. And I've got a roomful of ribbons and medals and awards. But what has Raymond got to call his own?

So I stand there with my new plan, laughing out loud by this time as Raymond jumps down from the fence and runs over with his teeth showing and his arms down to the side which no one before him has quite mastered as a running style. And by the time he comes over I'm jumping up and down so glad to see him—my brother Raymond, a great runner in the family tradition. But of course everyone thinks I'm jumping up and down because the men on the loudspeaker have finally gotten themselves together and compared notes and are announcing "In first place—Miss Hazel Elizabeth Deborah Parker." (Dig that.) "In second place—Miss Gretchen P. Lewis." And I look over at Gretchen wondering what the P stands for. And I smile. Cause she's good, no doubt about it. Maybe she'd like to help me coach Raymond; she obviously is serious about running, as any fool can see. And she nods to congratulate me and then she smiles. And I smile. We stand there with this big smile of respect between us. It's about as real a smile as girls can do for each other, considering we don't practice real smiling every day you know, cause maybe we too busy being flowers or fairies or strawberries instead of something honest and worthy of respect . . . you know . . . like being people.

In your journal, answer the following questions:

In the first paragraph, Hazel's voice seems to leap off the page. How does Bambara manipulate diction and rhythm to achieve this? Can you "picture" Hazel because of her voice?

≥ How does "All I have to do in life is mind my brother Raymond, which is enough" introduce subtext to the story? What details does Hazel use to quickly characterize her family and her family's values?

≥ Hazel often speaks in extremely long sentences without seeming to pause for breath! Highlight a few of Hazel's lengthy sentences. Are there any common features? What information is Hazel most likely to become breathless about? What makes these sentences seem so authentic?

≥ Group dialogue is difficult. How does Bambara manage the dialogue between Hazel and "Gretchen and her sidekicks," Mary Louise and Rosie? How does she remind you of who is talking? Do the children have different rhythm patterns? Different dictions?

≥ Actions, gestures, mannerisms enhance dialogue. Does Bambara make use of this technique? Where does it work best?

≥ Raymond is silent for most of the story. How does his silence add tension and subtext to the story? How does his silence resonate when compared with Hazel's vocalness? How do voice and silence serve to characterize Raymond and Hazel?

In your journal write what Toni Cade Bambara has taught you about crafting natural, colloquial dialogue.

DIALOGUE STUDY

GLORIA NAYLOR'S
"KISWANA BROWNE"

Gloria Naylor explores the sensitive terrain of a young woman trying to leave the family nest. Kiswana is self-confident, intelligent, and politically aware; yet, like many of us, feels childlike and stubborn when confronting Mama. Naylor expertly renders dialogue with a fine ear tuned to the child within the young woman and the empathic woman within the formidable Mama.

F ROM THE WINDOW of her sixth-floor studio apartment, Kiswana could see over the wall at the end of the street to the busy avenue that lay just north of Brewster Place. The late afternoon shoppers looked like brightly clad marionettes as they moved between the congested traffic, clutching their packages against their bodies to guard them from sudden bursts of the cold autumn wind. A portly mailman had abandoned his cart and was bumping into indignant window-shoppers as he puffed behind the cap that the wind had snatched from his head. Kiswana leaned over to see if he was going to be successful, but the edge of the building cut him off from her view.

A pigeon swept across her window, and she marveled at its liquid movements in the air waves. She placed her dreams on the back of the bird and fantasized that it would glide forever in transparent silver circles until it ascended to the center of the universe and was swallowed up. But the wind died down, and she watched with a sigh as the bird beat its wings in awkward, frantic movements to land on the corroded top of a fire escape on the opposite building. This brought her back to earth.

Humph, it's probably sitting over there crapping on those folks' fire escape, she thought. Now, that's a safety hazard. . . . And her mind was busy again, creating flames and smoke and frustrated tenants whose escape was being hindered because they were slipping and sliding in pigeon shit. She watched their cussing, haphazard descent on the fire escapes until they had all reached the bottom. They were milling around, oblivious to their burning apartments, angrily planning to march on the mayor's office about the pigeons. She materialized placards and banners for them, and they had just reached the corner, boldly sidestepping fire hoses and broken glass, when they all vanished.

A tall copper-skinned woman had met this phantom parade at the corner, and they had dissolved in front of her long, confident strides. She plowed through the remains of their faded mists, unconscious of the lingering wisps of their presence on her leather bag and black fur-trimmed coat. It took a few seconds for this transfer from one realm to another to reach Kiswana, but then suddenly she recognized the woman.

"Oh, God, it's Mama!" She looked down guiltily at the forgotten newspaper in her lap and hurriedly circled random job advertisements.

By this time Mrs. Browne had reached the front of Kiswana's building and was checking the house number against a piece of paper in her hand. Before she went into the building she stood at the bottom of the stoop and carefully inspected the condition of the street and the adjoining property. Kiswana watched this meticulous inventory with growing annoyance but she involuntarily followed her mother's slowly rotating head, forcing herself to see her new neighborhood through the older woman's eyes. The brightness of the unclouded sky seemed to join forces with her mother as it highlighted every broken stoop railing and missing brick. The afternoon sun glittered and cascaded across even the tiniest fragments of broken bottle, and at that very moment the wind chose to rise up again, sending unswept grime flying into the air, as a stray tin can left by careless garbage collectors went rolling noisily down the center of the street.

Kiswana noticed with relief that at least Ben wasn't sitting in his usual place on the old garbage can pushed against the far wall. He was just a harmless old wino, but Kiswana knew her mother only needed one wino or one teenager with a reefer within a twenty-block radius to decide that her daughter was living in a building seething with dope factories and hang-outs for derelicts. If she had seen Ben, nothing would have made her believe that practically every apartment contained a family, a Bible, and a dream that one day enough could be scraped from those meager Friday night paychecks to make Brewster Place a distant memory.

As she watched her mother's head disappear into the building, Kiswana gave silent thanks that the elevator was broken. That would give her at least five minutes' grace to straighten up the apartment. She rushed to the sofa bed and hastily closed it without smoothing the rumpled sheets and blanket or removing her nightgown. She felt that somehow the tangled bedcovers would give away the fact that she had not slept alone last night. She silently apologized to Abshu's memory as she heartlessly crushed his spirit between the steel springs of the couch. Lord, that man was sweet. Her toes curled involuntarily at the passing thought of his full lips moving slowly over her instep. Abshu was a foot man, and he always started his lovemaking from the bottom up. For that reason Kiswana changed the color of the polish on her toenails every week. During the course of their relationship she had gone from shades of red to brown and was now into the purples. I'm gonna have to start mixing them soon, she thought aloud as she turned from the couch and raced into the bathroom to remove any traces of Abshu from there. She took up his shaving cream and razor and threw them into the bottom drawer of her dresser beside her diaphragm. Mama wouldn't dare pry into my drawers right in front of me, she thought as she slammed the drawer shut. Well, at least not the *bottom* drawer. She may come up with some sham excuse for opening the top drawer, but never the bottom one.

When she heard the first two short raps on the door, her eyes took a final flight over the small apartment, desperately seeking out any slight misdemeanor that might have to be defended. Well, there was nothing she could do about the crack in the wall over that table. She had been after the landlord to fix it for two months now. And there had been no time to sweep the rug, and everyone knew that off-gray always looked dirtier than it really was. And it was just too damn bad about the kitchen. How was she expected to be out job-hunting every day and still have time to keep a kitchen that looked like her mother's, who didn't even work and still had someone come in twice a month for general cleaning. And besides . . .

Her imaginary argument was abruptly interrupted by a second series of knocks, accompanied by a penetrating, "Melanie, Melanie, are you there?"

Kiswana strode toward the door. She's starting before she even gets in here. She knows that's not my name anymore.

She swung the door open to face her slightly flushed mother. "Oh, hi, Mama. You know, I thought I heard a knock, but I figured it was for the people next door, since no one hardly ever calls me Melanie." Score one for me, she thought.

"Well, it's awfully strange you can forget a name you answered to for twenty-three years," Mrs. Browne said, as she moved past Kiswana into the apartment. "My, that was a long climb. How long has your elevator been out? Honey, how do you manage with your laundry and groceries up all those steps? But I guess you're young, and it wouldn't bother you as much as it does me." This long string of questions told Kiswana that her mother had no intentions of beginning her visit with another argument about her new African name.

"You know I would have called before I came, but you don't have a phone yet. I didn't want you to feel that I was snooping. As a matter of fact, I didn't expect to find you home at all. I thought you'd be out looking for a job." Mrs. Browne had mentally covered the entire apartment while she was talking and taking off her coat.

"Well, I got up late this morning. I thought I'd buy the afternoon paper and start early tomorrow."

"That sounds like a good idea." Her mother moved toward the window and picked up the discarded paper and glanced over the hurriedly circled ads. "Since when do you have experience as a forklift operator?"

Kiswana caught her breath and silently cursed herself for her stupidity. "Oh, my hand slipped—I meant to circle file clerk." She quickly took the paper before her mother could see that she had also marked cutlery salesman and chauffeur.

"You're sure you weren't sitting here moping and daydreaming again?" Amber specks of laughter flashed in the corners of Mrs. Browne's eyes.

Kiswana threw her shoulders back and unsuccessfully tried to disguise her embarrassment with indignation.

"Oh, God, Mama! I haven't done that in years—it's for kids. When are you going to realize that I'm a woman now?" She sought desperately for some womanly thing to do and settled for throwing herself on the couch and crossing her legs in what she hoped looked like a nonchalant arc.

"Please, have a seat," she said, attempting the same tones and gestures she'd seen Bette Davis use on the late movies.

Mrs. Browne, lowering her eyes to hide her amusement, accepted the invitation and sat at the window, also crossing her legs. Kiswana saw immediately how it should have been done. Her celluloid pose clashed loudly against her mother's quiet dignity, and she quickly uncrossed her legs. Mrs. Browne turned her head toward the window and pretended not to notice.

"At least you have a halfway decent view from here. I was wondering what lay beyond that dreadful wall—it's the boulevard. Honey, did you know that you can see the trees in Linden Hills from here?"

Kiswana knew that very well, because there were many lonely days that she would sit in her gray apartment and stare at those trees and think of home, but she would rather have choked than admit that to her mother.

"Oh, really, I never noticed. So how is Daddy and things at home?"

"Just fine. We're thinking of redoing one of the extra bedrooms since you children have moved out, but Wilson insists that he can manage all that work alone. I told him that he doesn't really have the proper time or energy for all that. As it is, when he gets home from the office, he's so tired he can hardly move. But you know you can't tell your father anything. Whenever he starts complaining about how stubborn you are, I tell him the child came by it honestly. Oh, and your brother was by yesterday," she added, as if it had just occurred to her.

So that's it, thought Kiswana. That's why she's here.

Kiswana's brother, Wilson, had been to visit her two days ago, and she had borrowed twenty dollars from him to get her winter coat out of layaway. That son-of-a-bitch probably ran straight to Mama— and after he swore he wouldn't say anything. I should have known, he was always a snotty-nosed sneak, she thought.

"Was he?" she said aloud. "He came by to see me, too, earlier this week. And I borrowed some money from him because my unemployment checks hadn't cleared in the bank, but now they have and everything's just fine." There, I'll beat you to that one.

"Oh, I didn't know that," Mrs. Browne lied. "He never mentioned you. He had just heard that Beverly was expecting again, and he rushed over to tell us."

Damn. Kiswana could have strangled herself.

"So she's knocked up again, huh?" she said irritably.

Her mother started. "Why do you always have to be so crude?"

"Personally, I don't see how she can sleep with Willie. He's such a dishrag."

Kiswana still resented the stance her brother had taken in college. When everyone at school was discovering their blackness and protesting on campus, Wilson never took part; he had even refused to wear an Afro. This had outraged Kiswana because, unlike her, he was dark-skinned and had the type of hair that was thick and kinky enough for a good "Fro." Kiswana had still insisted on cutting her own hair, but it was so thin and fine-textured, it refused to thicken even after she washed it. So she had to brush it up and spray it with lacquer to keep it from lying flat. She never forgave Wilson for telling her that she didn't look African, she looked like an electrocuted chicken.

"Now that's some way to talk. I don't know why you have an attitude against your brother. He never gave me a restless night's sleep, and now he's settled with a family and a good job."

"He's an assistant to an assistant junior partner in a law firm. What's the big deal about that?"

"The job has a future, Melanie. And at least he finished school and went on for his law degree."

"In other words, not like me, huh?"

"Don't put words into my mouth, young lady. I'm perfectly capable of saying what I mean."

Amen, thought Kiswana.

"And I don't know why you've been trying to start up with me from the moment I walked in. I didn't come here to fight with you. This is your first place away from home, and I just wanted to see how you were living and if you're doing all right. And I must say, you've fixed this apartment up very nicely."

"Really, Mama?" She found herself softening in the light of her mother's approval.

"Well, considering what you had to work with." This time she scanned the apartment openly.

"Look, I know it's not Linden Hills, but a lot can be done with it. As soon as they come and paint, I'm going to hang my Ashanti print over the couch. And I thought a big Boston fern would go well in that corner, what do you think?"

"That would be fine, baby. You always had a good eye for balance."

Kiswana was beginning to relax. There was little she did that attracted her mother's approval. It was like a rare bird, and she had to tread carefully around it lest it fly away.

"Are you going to leave that statue out like that?"

"Why, what's wrong with it? Would it look better somewhere else?"

There was a small wooden reproduction of a Yoruba goddess with large protruding breasts on the coffee table.

"Well," Mrs. Browne was beginning to blush, "it's just that it's a bit suggestive, don't you think? Since you live alone now, and I know you'll be having male friends stop by, you wouldn't want to be giving them any ideas. I mean, uh, you know, there's no point in putting yourself in any unpleasant situations because they may get the wrong impressions and uh, you know, I mean, well . . ." Mrs. Browne stammered on miserably.

Kiswana loved it when her mother tried to talk about sex. It was the only time she was at a loss for words.

"Don't worry, Mama." Kiswana smiled. "That wouldn't bother the type of men I date. Now maybe if it had big feet . . ." And she got hysterical, thinking of Abshu.

Her mother looked at her sharply. "What sort of gibberish is that about feet? I'm being serious, Melanie."

"I'm sorry, Mama." She sobered up. "I'll put it away in the closet," she said, knowing that she wouldn't.

"Good," Mrs. Browne said, knowing that she wouldn't either. "I guess you think I'm too picky, but we worry about you over here. And you refuse to put in a phone so we can call and see about you."

"I haven't refused, Mama. They want seventy-five dollars for a deposit, and I can't swing that right now."

"Melanie, I can give you the money."

"I don't want you to be giving me money—I've told you that before. Please, let me make it by myself."

"Well, let me lend it to you, then."

"No!"

"Oh, so you can borrow money from your brother, but not from me."

Kiswana turned her head from the hurt in her mother's eyes. "Mama, when I borrow from Willie, he makes me pay him back. You never let me pay you back," she said into her hands.

"I don't care. I still think it's downright selfish of you to be sitting over here with no phone, and sometimes we don't hear from you in two weeks—anything could happen—especially living among these people."

Kiswana snapped her head up. "What do you mean, *these people.* They're my people and yours, too, Mama—we're all black. But maybe you've forgotten that over in Linden Hills."

"That's not what I'm talking about, and you know it. These

streets—this building—it's so shabby and rundown. Honey, you don't have to live like this."

"Well, this is how poor people live."

"Melanie, you're not poor."

"No, Mama, *you're* not poor. And what you have and I have are two totally different things. I don't have a husband in real estate with a five-figure income and a home in Linden Hills—*you* do. What I have is a weekly unemployment check and an overdrawn checking account at United Federal. So this studio on Brewster is all I can afford."

"Well, you could afford a lot better," Mrs. Browne snapped, "if you hadn't dropped out of college and had to resort to these dead-end clerical jobs."

"Uh-huh, I knew you'd get around to that before long." Kiswana could feel the rings of anger begin to tighten around her lower backbone, and they sent her forward onto the couch. "You'll never understand, will you? Those bourgie schools were counterrevolutionary. My place was in the streets with my people, fighting for equality and a better community."

"Counterrevolutionary!" Mrs. Browne was raising her voice. "Where's your revolution now, Melanie? Where are all those black revolutionaries who were shouting and demonstrating and kicking up a lot of dust with you on that campus? Huh? They're sitting in wood-paneled offices with their degrees in mahogany frames, and they won't even drive their cars past this street because the city doesn't fix the potholes in this part of town."

"Mama," she said, shaking her head slowly in disbelief, "how can you—a black woman—sit there and tell me that what we fought for during the Movement wasn't important just because some people sold out?"

"Melanie, I'm not saying it wasn't important. It was damned important to stand up and say that you were proud of what you were and to get the vote and other social opportunities for every person in this country who had it due. But you kids thought you were going to turn the world upside down, and it just wasn't so. When all the smoke had cleared, you found yourself with a fistful of new federal laws and a country still full of obstacles for black people to fight their way over—just because they're black. There was no revolution, Melanie, and there will be no revolution."

"So what am I supposed to do, huh? Just throw up my hands and not care about what happens to my people? I'm not supposed to keep fighting to make things better?"

"Of course, you can. But you're going to have to fight within the system, because it and these so-called 'bourgie' schools are going to be here for a long time. And that means that you get smart like a lot of your old friends and get an important job where you can have some influence. You don't have to sell out, as you say, and work for some corporation, but you could become an assemblywoman or a civil liberties lawyer or open a freedom school in this very neighborhood. That way you could really help the community. But what help are you going to be to these people on Brewster while you're living hand-to-mouth on file-clerk jobs waiting for a revolution? You're wasting your talents, child."

"Well, I don't think they're being wasted. At least I'm here in day-to-day contact with the problems of my people. What good would I be after four or five years of a lot of white brainwashing in some phony, prestige institution, huh? I'd be like you and Daddy and those other educated blacks sitting over there in Linden Hills with a terminal case of middle-class amnesia."

"You don't have to live in a slum to be concerned about social conditions, Melanie. Your father and I have been charter members of the NAACP for the last twenty-five years."

"Oh, God!" Kiswana threw her head back in exaggerated disgust. "That's being concerned? That middle-of-the-road, Uncle Tom dumping ground for black Republicans!"

"You can sneer all you want, young lady, but that organization has been working for black people since the turn of the century, and it's still working for them. Where are all those radical groups of yours that were going to put a Cadillac in every garage and Dick Gregory in the White House? I'll tell you where."

I knew you would, Kiswana thought angrily.

"They burned themselves out because they wanted too much too fast. Their goals weren't grounded in reality. And that's always been your problem."

"What do you mean, my problem? I know exactly what I'm about."

"No, you don't. You constantly live in a fantasy world—always going to extremes—turning butterflies into eagles, and life isn't about that. It's accepting what is and working from that. Lord, I remember how worried you had me, putting all that lacquered hair spray on your head. I thought you were going to get lung cancer—trying to be what you're not."

Kiswana jumped up from the couch. "Oh, God, I can't take this anymore. Trying to be something I'm not—trying to be something I'm not, Mama! Trying to be proud of my heritage and the fact that I was of African descent. If that's being what I'm not, then I say fine. But I'd rather be dead than be like you—a white man's nigger who's ashamed of being black!"

Kiswana saw streaks of gold and ebony light follow her mother's flying body out of the chair. She was swung around by the shoulders and made to face the deadly stillness in the angry woman's eyes. She was too stunned to cry out from the pain of the long fingernails that dug into her shoulders, and she was brought so close to her mother's face that she saw her reflection, distorted and wavering, in the tears that stood in the older woman's eyes. And she listened in that stillness to a story she had heard from a child.

"My grandmother," Mrs. Browne began slowly in a whisper, "was a full-blooded Iroquois, and my grandfather a free black from a long line of journeymen who had lived in Connecticut since the establishment of the colonies. And my father was a Bajan who came to this country as a cabin boy on a merchant mariner."

"I know all that," Kiswana said, trying to keep her lips from trembling.

"Then know this." And the nails dug deeper into her flesh. "I am alive because of the blood of proud people who never scraped or begged or apologized for what they were. They lived asking only one thing of this world—to be allowed to be. And I learned through the blood of these people that black isn't beautiful and it isn't ugly—black is! It's not kinky hair and it's not straight hair—it just is.

"It broke my heart when you changed your name. I gave you my grandmother's name, a woman who bore nine children and educated them all, who held off six white men with a shotgun when they tried to drag one of her sons to jail for 'not knowing his place.' Yet you needed to reach into an African dictionary to find a name to make you proud.

"When I brought my babies home from the hospital, my ebony son and my golden daughter, I swore before whatever gods would listen—those of my mother's people or those of my father's people—that I would use everything I had and could ever get to see that my children were prepared to meet this world on its own terms, so that no one could sell them short and make them ashamed of what they were or how they looked—whatever they were or however they looked. And Melanie, that's not being white or red or black—that's being a mother."

Kiswana followed her reflection in the two single tears that moved down her mother's cheeks until it blended with them into the woman's copper skin. There was nothing and then so much that she wanted to say, but her throat kept closing up every time she tried to speak. She kept her head down and her eyes closed, and thought, O, God, just let me die. How can I face her now?

Mrs. Browne lifted Kiswana's chin gently. "And the one lesson I wanted you to learn is not to be afraid to face anyone, not even a crafty old lady like me who can outtalk you." And she smiled and winked.

"Oh, Mama, I . . ." and she hugged the woman tightly.

"Yeah, baby." Mrs. Browne patted her back. "I know."

She kissed Kiswana on the forehead and cleared her throat. "Well, now, I better be moving on. It's getting late, there's dinner to be made, and I have to get off my feet—these new shoes are killing me."

Kiswana looked down at the beige leather pumps. "Those are really classy. They're English, aren't they?"

"Yes, but, Lord, do they cut me right across the instep." She removed the shoe and sat on the couch to massage her foot.

Bright red nail polish glared at Kiswana through the stockings. "Since when do you polish your toenails?" she gasped. "You never did that before."

"Well . . ." Mrs. Browne shrugged her shoulders, "your father sort of talked me into it, and, uh, you know, he likes it and all, so I thought, uh, you know, why not, so . . ." And she gave Kiswana an embarrassed smile.

I'll be damned, the young woman thought, feeling her whole face tingle. Daddy's into feet! And she looked at the blushing woman on her couch and suddenly realized that her mother had trod through the same universe that she herself was now traveling. Kiswana was breaking no new trails and would eventually end up just two feet away on that couch. She stared at the woman she had been and was to become.

"But I'll never be a Republican," she caught herself saying aloud.

"What are you mumbling about, Melanie?" Mrs. Browne slipped on her shoe and got up from the couch.

She went to get her mother's coat. "Nothing, Mama. It's really nice of you to come by. You should do it more often."

"Well, since it's not Sunday, I guess you're allowed at least one lie."

They both laughed.

After Kiswana had closed the door and turned around, she spotted an envelope sticking between the cushions of her couch. She went over and opened it up; there was seventy-five dollars in it.

"Oh, Mama, darn it!" She rushed to the window and started to call to the woman, who had just emerged from the building, but she suddenly changed her mind and sat down in the chair with a long sigh that caught in the upward draft of the autumn wind and disappeared over the top of the building.

In your journal, answer the following questions:

≋ Naylor always knows the hearts of her characters.
How do you think this contributes to the fluid and
natural style of her dialogue?

≋ "Melanie, Melanie, are you there?" Why is this such
a provocative line of dialogue? How does Mrs.
Browne's refusal to say "Kiswana" serve as subtext for
the mother-daughter relationship? For what happens
during the rest of the scene?

≋ Kiswana's thoughts, the Bette Davis tone and
gestures, the newspaper, all underscore her rebellion
against her parents' lifestyle and politics. How do
these action/reactions/thoughts serve to intensify the
dialogue?

≋ "Kiswana loved it when her mother tried to talk
about sex." How does the discussion of the Yoruba
goddess show affection and understanding between
mother and daughter? How does the scene prepare
for the later, more intense discussion about revolution
and money?

≋ What bothers Mrs. Browne most about her
daughter's lifestyle and beliefs? Why is her dialogue
about her heritage so important? What is she trying
to teach?

≋ What techniques does Naylor use to finish the story
demonstrating the love between the two women?
Does Naylor rely upon just words, or upon actions,
mannerisms, etc.?

In your journal, write what Gloria Naylor has taught you about
crafting fine dialogue.

. . .

Dialogue, dialects, first person narrative voices all rely on strong appreciation for human communications. What people say, what they don't say, and how they say it echo their psychological, emotional, and intellectual selves. By exploring speech patterns, you sensitize yourself to how sounds can complement or, at times, contradict meaning and subtext. This sensitivity is what you need to create credible and moving dialogue. At times, your path to writing better dialogue will be frustrating. But as with all skills, you can improve with practice. The dialogue work you've done so far is a solid first step. Bravo!

Remember: Every time you create speech for a new character, you are building a repertoire of voices to speak your fictional dramas. Like an actor learning how to speak lines for a variety of characters, you too will develop greater flexibility to create speech for diverse characters with diverse needs and desires.

Celebrate. You've worked hard. You're growing splendidly as a writer.

10

THEME

What does a story mean? What does it make a reader feel? Think about?

Writers are continually answering these questions. But the answers aren't given via multiple choice or told didactically to a reader; rather, the answers are "shown" by the myriad technical decisions a writer makes. Characterization, plotting, description, dialogue, setting, and point of view reveal not only *what* a story means but *how* it is to be experienced intellectually and emotionally by the reader. This, then is *theme*—the sum of all the fictional skills used in creating an effective story.

Schools often teach that there are preset categories of fictional themes: Love, Death, Birth and Rebirth, Innocence vs. Experience, the Pursuit of Knowledge, Self-Identity and Fulfillment, Good vs. Evil, etc. While this notion of categories may serve readers, categories are less useful to writers because they emphasize abstractions rather than specifics.

More than anything, if you've come this far in your journey, you should have a clear sense that good writing is *always* about specifics—about specific images and characterizations, specific conflicts and resolutions.

You may, in fact, be writing a "love story" but, thematically, that is far too simplistic a statement about what you are accomplishing through your story choices. Alice Walker's *The Color Purple* is a love story. Toni Morrison's *Beloved* is a love story. Connie Briscoe's *Sisters and Lovers* is a love story. These three women write about love in exceptionally different ways. All three came to their love stories with personal histories and perspectives. *Who they are, how they view the world, what they feel and think* influence the choices which give their fictional world meaning. Categorizing literature is a convenience for scholars. Writers should be aware of thematic traditions which support their work; however, when writing, the focus should remain fixed on what is best for the particular story.

MY BEST ADVICE

Theme—what a story means—*is the sum of the story's parts. Don't focus on the abstraction of what you're trying to say; focus on the specifics of showing, scene by scene, piece by piece, what you* mean.

Because of slavery, certain themes have resonated historically in African American literature. Questing for literacy and liberty form the cornerstone of our literary history. Biblical themes of unjust persecution, escape, and redemption, family survival despite slavery and discrimination, and migration from Africa and, ultimately, across America have been essential to African American literature. Color politics, passing, and self-identity themes became common as Africans became African Americans. In general, our artists have sought to condemn racism, to repress racial and sexual stereotypes, and to promote ethnic pride and gender equity. Gay liberation is, for many contemporary writers, part of the continuing thematic press for civil rights.

Given the birth of our literature in America, it seems appropriate that many of our themes are political. But an equally impressive and important thematic strand is birthed from our oral and folk legacy tradition. The transformative power of music, of love, the need for spiritual rootedness in an ancestral heritage, the need for a comforting home and landscape, and the exhilarating and healing power of laughter springing from outrageous trickster tales are all essential to our literature. Like other cultures, we too have our story celebrations of heroes and heroines and the wry examination of our people's foibles. Like other cultures, we too can lay claim to all the themes which stir the human mind and heart and to those specific variations which bear witness to the uniqueness of our people as African Americans.

While you may want to echo or reinterpret themes handed down through our literary heritage, you can also lay claim to any theme you desire. It is the writer's privilege to choose subject matter, to choose the scale and scope of what is communicated.

Your task is to write whatever theme you do select as well as you possibly can.

EXERCISE 1

READING FOR THEME

Everything you've written so far has been an ongoing exercise in writing theme. Each detail you selected, each line of dialogue you revised, each character description you improved enhanced your story's intellectual and emotional message.

Select two of your favorite stories. These stories may be from *Free Within Ourselves: Fiction Lessons for Black Authors* or from a literary anthology. In your journal, write down the theme for each story. Spending a half hour on each story, put a check by any description, any character, any line or word, etc., which does *not* contribute to the author's theme. Ideally, nothing should be checked. However, upon closely studying how the parts of a story convey theme, you may disagree with another author's choices. But if the story is exceptional, then the bulk of the fictional skills which created the story should all serve to create theme.

E X E R C I S E   2

READING FOR THEME, PART II

Just as you've studied other authors, you ought to be able to study your own stories and answer:

> *Am I showing what I want my story to mean? Are my fictional skills contributing to my story's theme?*

Select one of your own stories. Reread it with a critical, observant eye. Check any part of the story which does not support your thematic message.

Reexamine those parts of the story you might have checked.

Would your story be better if you revised, deleted, or saved these passages for another story? If so, revise your story accordingly.

T H E M A T I C   S T U D Y

JESS MOWRY'S "CRUSADER RABBIT"

Jess Mowry's "Crusader Rabbit" is a strongly thematic short story about an urban youth searching for a father figure, for someone to love and who will love him, and searching for his own freedom from drugs and an alienated upbringing and environment.

"YOU COULD BE my dad."

Jeremy stood waist-deep in the Dumpster, his arms slimed up to the elbows from burrowing, and dropped three cans to the buckled asphalt. Raglan aligned them, pop-tops down, and crushed them to silver discs with his Nike, then added them to the half-full sack before turning to study the boy. It wasn't the first time.

"Anything's possible . . . 'least that's what *my* dad used to say."

Jeremy made no move to climb out, even though the stink of what he stood in seemed to surround him like bronze-green fog, wavering up like the spectral heat-ghosts from the other Dumpsters lining the alley. He was clad in only ragged jeans, the battered Cons on his dirty bare feet buried from sight in the garbage below; and his wiry body glistened with sweat. Not for the first time Raglan thought Jeremy a beautiful boy . . . thirteen, so he said, his young muscles pert beneath dusky black skin, his chest like a pair of small paving stones, with big hands and puppyish feet. His hair was an ebony dandelion puff . . . a boy any man should be proud to call son. A ring glinted gold and fierce in his ear, and a red bandanna hung loosely around his neck. His eyes were obsidian, usually bright, but closed now in pain. The bruise-like marks beneath them had faded a lot in the past few weeks, and his teeth flashed white as he panted. Raglan could have been a clone of the boy, twice his age but looking it mostly in size. The salt-scented haze of a West Oakland morning had burned away hours before, leaving the alley to swelter in oozing tar and yellow rot-smell, yet Raglan neither panted nor sweated. There was a last Dumpster to check, and the recycle yard would be closing by three, but he paused and asked, "Want a smoke?"

Jeremy watched through lowered lashes as Raglan's eyes changed . . . not really softening as seeming to travel light-years away into alternate space. Jeremy hesitated, his long fingers clenching as if for support on the Dumpster's rust-eaten rim. "Yeah . . . No . . . I think it's time."

Jeremy's movements were stiff and awkward as he tried to climb out. Wet garbage sucked at his feet. Raglan took the boy, slippery as a seal, under the arms and lifted him effortlessly over the edge. The boy's smell was strong and bitterly adolescent, but most of that came from a long day of digging. Together they walked to the truck.

It was a 1955 GMC, a one-ton model with dual rear wheels, and as rusty and bashed as the Dumpsters it hunted. There were splintery plywood side-boards on the six-foot wooden flatbed. The cab was crammed with things for survival, as self-contained as an African Land Rover. Even after two months it still surprised Jeremy sometimes what Raglan could pull out from under the seat or from the pile of stuff on the dash . . . toilet paper, comic books, or a .45-caliber pistol.

Raglan emptied the gunnysack into an almost-full garbage can in the back of the truck, then leaned on the side-board and started to roll a cigarette from Top tobacco, while Jeremy opened the driver's door and slipped a scarred *Sesame Street* Band-Aid box from underneath the floor mat. The boy's hands shook slightly. He tried not to hurry as he spread his things on the seat: a tiny glass bottle of grayish brown powder instead of crack crystals, a small puff of cotton, the stub of a candle, a flame-tarnished spoon and the needle, its point protected by a Styrofoam bead. On the floor by the shift lever was a plastic jug that had at one time held "Fresh Spring Water From Clear Mountain Streams." Raglan filled it from gas station hoses, and the water tasted like rubber.

Raglan finished his cigarette, fired it with a Bic, then handed the lighter to Jeremy and started rolling another. His eyes were still lost in alternate space.

Jeremy looked up as he worked. "Yo," he said, as if to accuse. "I know your real name. Seen it on your driver license. Why you called Raglan?"

Smoke drifted from Raglan's nostrils. He came close to smiling. "When you boosted my wallet a few nights ago?"

"I put it back, dint I? Nuthin' there anyways."

Still close to smiling, Raglan shrugged. "My dad called me that. From some ole-time cartoon when he was a kid. *Crusader Rabbit.* Jay Ward production. First cartoon series made for TV."

"Oh," said Jeremy. "Dint he do Rocky an' Bullwinkle, too?"

"That come later. But I never seen *Crusader Rabbit.* Anyway, the rabbit's homeboy was a tiger . . . Raglan T. 'Rags' for the street.

Maybe they was like the Lion King . . . traveled around havin' adventures. It was a long time ago."

"Kinda like Calvin an' Hobbes?"

"Guess so."

"Oh." Jeremy sat on the running board. He wrapped a strip of truck innertube around his upper arm. It was hard to get it right, one-handed. He looked up again. "Um . . ."

"Yeah." Raglan knelt and pulled the strip tighter. His eyes were far away again, neither watching nor denying as the boy put the needle in. "You got good veins," he said matter-of-factly. "Muscles like yours make 'em stand out."

Jeremy's eyes shifted from the needle, lowering to his sweaty torso, and his chest plates hardened a little. "I guess I do got some muscles, huh?"

"Why would I lie?"

The boy chewed his lip. "I used to miss 'em . . . my veins, I mean. A long time ago. An' sometimes I poked right through."

Raglan nodded. "I done that, too. A long time ago."

The boy's wiry body tensed for a moment, but then he relaxed with a sigh. His face looked almost peaceful. His eyes drifted shut, but a few seconds later they opened again and searched Raglan's.

"It only make me normal now."

Raglan nodded again. "Two a day, an' that's all folks." He handed Jeremy the second cigarette and fired the lighter for him. The boy pulled in smoke, holding it awhile before puffing out rings and watching them hang in the hot, dead air.

"Next week it only gonna be one." Jeremy held Raglan's eyes. "It gonna really hurt then, huh?"

"Why would I lie?"

"Soooo when you stop wantin' it, Rags?"

Raglan stood, snagging the jug and taking a few swallows of water. Trucks rumbled past the alley entrance on their way to where the ships were docked. Diesel fumes drifted in from the street. Flies swarmed over the Dumpsters in clouds, and a rat scuttled past in no special hurry. "When you want somethin' else more."

"What if you don't know what you want?"

"Guess y'all go lookin' for somethin' an' find out what it is on the way."

Jeremy began repacking his things. The tiny bottle was empty now . . . it, too, could be recycled, but to fill it would take most of the cans they'd collected today. "Yo. You gotta be my dad, Rags. Why else you be givin' a shit?"

"Maybe I like adventures."

Raglan could have added that, when he'd first found Jeremy, the kid wouldn't have lived another week. But why complicate things with motives? He dropped his cigarette on the asphalt, slipped the sack off the side-board, and walked to the final Dumpster. There really wasn't much use in checking it: this was the poorest part of town, and pawing through poor people's garbage was mostly a big waste of time . . . what little they had to throw away was already scraped to the bone, rusted or rotted way past redemption. Jeremy followed, his moves flowing smooth like a real kid's again.

A few feet ahead of the boy, Raglan flipped open a lid so it clanked against the sooty brick wall. Flies abandoned ship in swarms. For a second he only stood and looked at what lay on top of the trash. He'd seen this before . . . too many times . . . but it was one of the few things that still made him sad. His hand gripped Jeremy's shoulder, holding him back, but the boy saw the baby anyhow.

"Oh . . ." It came out a sigh. Jeremy pressed close to Raglan, and Raglan's arm went around him. "I . . . heard stories," Jeremy whispered, as if scared of waking what never would. "But, I wasn't sure if it happened for real."

The boy's eyes lifted to Raglan's, but Raglan's gaze was distant once more, seeing but not seeing the little honey-brown body, the tiny and perfect fingers and toes.

Jeremy swallowed. "What should we do?"

Raglan's eyes turned hard. He was thinking of cops and their cynical smirks, their accusing questions, their angry eyes, and their endless forms to fill out. Then he thought of a call from a pay phone. Time was running short. The truck was almost full of gas; but there was food to buy, and Jeremy's need, and the cans were the only money. Still, he asked, "What do you want to do?"

The boy seemed surprised for a moment, but then he looked back at the baby. Automatically he waved flies away. "Um, what do they do with 'em? . . . When you tell? Is there a little coffin? An' flowers?"

Raglan took his arm off the boy. "They burn 'em."

"No!"

"The ones they find. Other times they get hauled to the dump, an' the bulldozers bury 'em with the rest of the garbage an' nobody knows."

Almost, the boy clamped his hands to his ears, but then his fists clenched. "No! Goddamn you, shut up!" His lean chest heaved, his young muscles stood out stark and hard.

Raglan was quiet a moment, but finally he gripped the boy's shoulder again before walking back to the truck. Jermey watched from beside the Dumpster, waving flies away.

Raglan went around to the rear. There was a ragged canvas tarp folded behind the cab. On foggy or rainy nights he spread it over the side-boards to make a little tent. A piece of that would be good enough . . . but it was oily, and stank. He went instead to the cab and pulled his black T-shirt from under the seat.

The old GMC was an inner-city truck that measured its moves in blocks, not miles. It burned oil, the radiator leaked, and its tires were worn almost treadless. But it managed to maintain 55, rattling across the Oakland Bay Bridge, climbing the steep streets of San Francisco, then crossing over the Golden Gate, headed north on 101. Jeremy stayed silent, though he'd never left Oakland before in his life, rolling cigarettes for himself and Raglan, and looking sometimes through the grimy-glassed window at the little bundle in back. Even when they turned off the freeway and onto a narrow road leading west, Jeremy just stared through the windshield. His eyes were a lot like Raglan's now, not really seeing the open country and gentle green hills spreading out all around.

It was early evening with the sun slanting gold when Raglan slowed the truck to a city pace once more and searched the roadside ahead. The air was fresh and clean, scented with things that lived and grew, and tasting of ocean not far away. There was a rutted dirt road

that Raglan almost missed; hardly more than narrow twin tracks with a
strip of dandelions between. It led away toward more western hills,
through fields of tall grass and bright yellow wild mustard flowers.
Raglan guided the truck off the highway, and they rolled toward the
hills in third gear. Jeremy watched the flowery fields, then looked at
Raglan in new surprise.

"You been here before?"

"A long time ago."

Jeremy took a deep breath of the life-scented air. "I never knew
there was places like this. Except in movies an' on TV."

The road entered a cleft between the hills, and a clear rushing
stream ran down to meet it, splashing over rounded rocks with a liquid
musical sound. For a while the road followed the sparkling water,
twisting and turning at the whim of the stream, but then left the
ravine and climbed upward along the gentle green womanish curve of
a hill; and the truck took the grade, growling in second.

The road seemed to fade as it climbed, then finally just ended on
top of the hill. Raglan stopped and switched off the engine. A hundred
feet in front of the truck a cliff dropped sheer to the sea. Big waves
boomed and echoed unseen on massive rocks below, sending up silver
showers of spray.

Jeremy seemed to forget why they'd come. He jumped from the
truck and ran to the edge, stopping as close as he could like any boy
might. Then he stood gazing over the ocean.

Raglan leaned on a fender and watched.

Jeremy spread his arms wide, his head thrown back as the sea
spray shimmered and floated around him. Then he looked down at his
dirty jeans and garbage-slimed shoes. Raglan watched for a little while
longer as the boy stripped to stand naked before sea and sun. Then,
Raglan went to the rear of the truck. There was a square-nosed cement
shovel and an old Army-surplus trenching tool he used when cleaning
up yards. Jeremy joined him solemnly, though his eyes were bright,
and the sun seemed to glow on his ebony skin, which now shone wet
with spray. Raglan said nothing, though he came close to smiling
before taking the shovel in one hand and cradling the little black

bundle. Jeremy slipped back into his jeans and followed with the trenching tool.

The ground rose again to a final crown that looked out over the sea. They climbed to the top in the rosy sunlight. Raglan cut the sweet-smelling sod into blocks with his shovel, and then they both dug. The sun was almost gone when they finished, and though the air was cooling, Jeremy was sheened with sweat once more. But he picked wild mustard and dandelion flowers and laid them on the little mound.

Far out on the water, the sun grew big and bright ruddy-red before sinking from sight to rise somewhere else. Raglan made a fire near the truck; and Jeremy got out the blankets, surprised once more when Raglan produced two dusty cans of Campbell's soup and a pint of Jack Daniels from under the seat. A little while later when it was night and the food was warm inside them, they sat side by side near the crackling fire, smoking and sipping the whiskey, while the sea boomed softly below.

"Rags?" asked Jeremy. "Is this campin' out?"

Raglan looked around. "Guess it is."

Jeremy glanced at the truck. "We don't got enough gas to get back, huh?"

Raglan gazed into the flames. "Maybe there's a recycle place around here."

Jeremy looked toward the starlit sea. "Um . . . so you never seen that Crusader Rabbit? Don't know what he looked like?"

"I think he carried a sword. Probably fought dragons. Shit like that."

"An' Rags the tiger was watchin' his back?"

"Guess so."

Jeremy shifted his eyes to the fire. "It gonna hurt a lot, huh?"

"Yeah."

Jeremy moved close, and Raglan slipped his arm around him.

"You are my dad, huh?"

"Guess so."

⌇

Read Mowry's story again. On the second reading, pay close attention to *how* the story shapes its meaning. "Crusader Rabbit" is about a young boy growing up, probably the most common story subject. Yet the story's theme represents Mowry's individual perceptions and specific fictional choices. Mowry's character, Jeremy, takes his own unique steps toward manhood.

In your own words, write a paragraph in your journal explaining the theme of "Crusader Rabbit."

⌇   If theme is the sum of the story's parts, explain why
it was best for Mowry to begin his story with the
line of dialogue "You could be my dad."

⌇   How is the theme focused by having two main
characters—Raglan and Jeremy? How do the
descriptions of the older man and the younger boy
enhance the theme of growing into adulthood and
maturity?

⌇   Describe Mowry's plot. How does the conflict of
drug abuse enhance the story's theme? How does the
dramatic event of finding the dead baby intensify
conflict and propel the plot forward? How does the
escape from the city serve as a partial resolution to
the conflicts within the boy, between the boy and
Raglan, and between both characters' distaste for the
destructive city?

⌇   How is Raglan a Crusader Rabbit? Why is a cartoon
title best suited to a story about drug abuse and
striving for a better life?

§ Contrast the description of the inner city and the countryside of northern California. How do these two settings underscore Mowry's theme? What atmosphere is associated with each setting?

§ The story is told in third person limited. Given Mowry's intentions to tell a story about the developing love between a boy and a father figure, why is third person limited superior to first person or omniscient narrator in this thematic instance?

§ The dialogue is rich with subtext and emotional conflicts. Following the discovery of the dead baby in the Dumpster, explain how Jeremy and Raglan's dialogue further reveals character and the story's theme?

§ Is there anything in Mowry's story which doesn't contribute to theme? Any paragraph, any character, any description which is *not* useful for conveying his ideas?

Theme is the sum of a story's parts. Any aspect of a story, no matter how well written, no matter how interesting, should be deleted if it doesn't support your thematic message.

A good writer must learn to add necessary material as well to cut unnecessary story material. You may admire a minor character or a paragraph of brilliant description; you may have spent a month perfecting the rhythm and dialogue of one scene. Nonetheless, for the sake of your story's theme, you must be ruthless and edit out any distractions.

Stories are meant to have coherent intellectual and emotional power. *Stories mean.*

Stories can't be crafted without a theme to order the chaos of dialogue, setting, point of view, characterization, description, and plot.

Deep within our bones, within our memories, each of us carries themes expressive of our ancestral and familial heritages. As we live, each of us shapes new ideas, new messages as a response to our world. Ultimately, stories embody a writer's growing wisdom and experience of life.

Theme is the heart of the writer's intimate exchange with readers. Celebrate, always and forever, your gift to tell a story.

11

REVISIONS AND LETTING GO

How do I know when I'm done?

Sometimes there'll be a rush of satisfaction. Other times you'll wind down with a sense that everything's been written. Some days you may feel frustrated and hastily write "The End." Other days you may feel as though you've succeeded in surviving the most diffi-cult labor imaginable.

In truth, the first time you think your manuscript is done, fin-ished, *fini!*—you probably have, depending upon the size of the manu-script, several weeks, months, possibly a year or more, before your story is as good as you can make it.

MY BEST ADVICE

Take the time to revise. Revisions not only make your manuscript
better but make you a stronger writer.

It would be false to say revisions always come easily. While revising can be thrilling, it can also be hard "nuts and bolts" work. Revising takes precision, dedication, and sheer stubbornness. Below is a series of stages which can help focus your revisions. These four stages can be followed whether you're writing a short story or an epic novel.

STAGE ONE: CHECKING YOUR WORK

When you believe you've finished your manuscript, ask yourself the following:

Are my characters believable? Do they act/react, think, and speak
and express a variety of emotions? Are their actions consistent with
their development?

Is my plot interesting? Is there rising tension and release? Does the
tension build to a dramatic, credible resolution?

Do I have the best narrative voice, the best point of view to
structure the story?

Do I "show" rather than "tell" my story? Is my story rich with
sensory details? Does the setting and atmosphere enhance my tale?

Is the dialogue true, imbued with subtext and appropriate words,
rhythms, and sounds?

Does everything in the story contribute to theme?

Do I make the best choices I can make as a writer?

Don't hurry Stage One. Take as much time as needed to reflect on your manuscript and to explore whether you've wisely used all the fictional techniques available to you. Then rewrite and revise until the story is the best you can do.

STAGE TWO: SHARING YOUR WORK

Offer your story to one or two trusted readers. As the author, you may have "blind spots," assumptions you're making about how the reader will interpret your work. Remember, you already know the story—but what may be clear to you may not be clear to the reader. Perfect stories are rare. However, through constructive criticism and revisions, you can mend any gaps in your manuscript.

While you're waiting for comments from your trusted readers, relax: read a book, go to the theater, or write another story. It's important to take an emotional and mental vacation from your story. Not only will this break refresh you; it'll also help you revisit your story with new eyes.

Once your trusted readers begin to give you comments, you're obligated to listen to them with an open heart. Yes, it might be painful. Yes, you might be affronted because someone didn't like your baby! Or you may be suspicious because they *loved* your characters. Most writers I know (me included) tend to be self-doubtful even when they receive praise. Despite a tendency to be too defensive or to doubt sincere approval, LISTEN and remain OPEN-MINDED. A trusted reader, by definition, is someone you can trust to give an honest, thoughtful appraisal of your work.

Once you've received constructive criticism, REFLECT and CONSIDER whether your trusted readers' advice is entirely appropriate. As a writer, you have your own instincts about what works best for your story. Your instincts need to be balanced against your trusted readers' advice. Ultimately, you know best what you're trying to say and accomplish. If a reader's advice rings true, then follow it. If not, then abandon it. Many times a trusted reader may inspire you to add new elements to your story or to think of alternative ways to solve problems. Trusted readers always encourage your best efforts to fulfill your story's potential.

After you've considered readers' comments, after your emotional and mental break, it's time for more patience and persistence. Time for another round of revisions!

STAGE THREE: WORKING THE MANUSCRIPT LINE BY LINE

Read your story aloud. Line by line, word by word.

Listen for any phrases, sentences, or paragraphs which seem flat, redundant, or strained. Do your sentences ever lag? Is their pace too hurried? Do you run out of breath before finishing a sentence? Do the pauses seem unnatural? Reexamine any sentence which is difficult to read.

Revise again, paying particular attention to the rhythm and flow of your words.

STAGE FOUR: SOUL SEARCHING

Ask yourself:

- *Have I expressed what I passionately needed to say?*

- *Have I conveyed the "emotional truth" about my characters?*

- *Have I flinched from any difficult part of my manuscript?*

- *Have I paid tribute to my literary heritage and culture by telling a good story?*

- *Have I written my manuscript as best I can?*

If all your answers aren't "yes," consider: can you fix the problems in your story? Remember, not every story you write will be a grand slam home run. Some stories may have to be abandoned; some you may need to start over from scratch; some may just remain flawed. If you've been attentive to the revision process and can't seem ever to finish, then you may need to move on. Don't fall into the pitfall of forever revising. Revisions are meant to be productive, to move you closer to your goal of publishing. Once the process becomes entirely frustrating and uninspiring, it's time to move on to another story.

If, however, all your answers are "yes," then you should be justifiably proud of yourself! Through study and determination, you have achieved your goal of being a writer.

PARTING WORDS

Celebrate! You've finished the lessons in this book!

You have become part of a wondrous literary community. You are one of the links which carry our literary tradition and wisdom down through the generations. You have become a storyteller.

Of course, next comes the hard part *and* the good part:

- Live each day alive to the world and experiences about you;

- Live each day in recognition of the wonderful heritage which supports your efforts to tell truths, to tell tales; and

- Live each day committed to becoming a better—even great—writer.

My final advice to you is this: *believe in yourself.* No other writer can ever write the books you can. Celebrate the wisdom, passion, humor, and spirit inside you. Let your spirit flow through your writing. Be faithful. We are all each other's ancestors. You've got the tools you need to begin, the rest you just learn as you go. You learn by doing. By being a writer.

Get to it!

My spirit walks with yours.

Best wishes and congratulations. Keep on . . . growing strong,

Jewell

PART IV

Wisdom and Advice from Black Authors

BEST ADVICE FROM

BLACK WRITERS TO

BLACK WRITERS

I asked a wide variety of published writers to provide their "Best Advice," their best wisdom for you, the next generation of African American writers. Authors were encouraged to select their own topic and to write as little or as much as they wanted. (For those writers I have missed, I apologize. Feel free to contact me in care of Doubleday to add your wisdom to the next edition of *Free Within Ourselves.*)

The passion, depth, and insight of the responses have been truly gratifying—each author provides unique inspiration, motivation, and insight.

I've organized the advice loosely around common themes:

Read
Believe

Love
Pray
Listen/Remember/Feel
Learn
Work
Rewrite
Grow
Nurture

Interestingly enough, I think these themes follow the life of an artist, of a writer, and of a person.

One approach would be to read this section all in one sitting, but I advise saving these "bits of wisdom" for the times when writing is frustrating and difficult. Then pull this book off the shelf (or from beneath your unbalanced chair) and pick a selection or two or three to read.

I have no doubt that one of these passages will unblock your creative energy and inspire renewed faith in yourself and in your writing.

READ . . .

Read. Read. Read.

—John A. Williams, *The Man Who Cried I Am*, *!Click Song*

My most sound advice to black writers would be my best advice to any writer: read widely and broadly, and see movies regularly to learn about plotting, narrative voice, and dialogue. And always remember that you can only catch fish if you keep your pole in the water.

—Henry Louis Gates, Jr., *Colored People*; co-editor, *The Norton Anthology of African American Literature*

Read the classics, especially the black classics and the work of the writers from the Harlem Renaissance. Even read some of the so-called trashy stuff. Most of all, select a writer whose work you admire and read it to hear the voice and learn how characters and settings are created and plot lines developed.

—Grace F. Edwards, *If I Should Die, No Time to Die*

READ. It is amazing to me that people think they can write without reading. Many people think their own personal experience is sufficient, but personal experience isn't even a beginning. You have to have perspective, and reading provides that. READ. And learn a new way of looking at your life.

—Nikki Giovanni, *Love Poems, Blues: For All the Changes*

My advice for black writers is twofold: First, read everything that is great literature. Everything. Do not discriminate because the writer is white, or rich, or dead, or of a different gender or a different sexual persuasion. Do not even refuse to open a book because you've heard the author dislikes blacks, or is simply a pig in general. Such personal characteristics do not necessarily have to have an effect on the writing. If, once you've started to read, you feel that personal bias has tainted the quality of the writing, you may feel justified in not continuing. But do not rob yourselves of the opportunity to experience different cultures, worlds, even prejudices because of politics. Ezra Pound may have been a fool and an anti-Semite, but you can learn a lot about imagery and pure song from his poems. Read the masters as well as exciting newcomers. James Baldwin, for example, benefited from the great Russian novelists of the nineteenth and early twentieth centuries, as did Toni Morrison. Second: Do not mistake intent for artistic excellence. Just because your story is true does not automatically make it powerful for others. The only way to achieve that is to write honestly and (even more important) to write well. Language is your medium, just as clay is the potter's medium, and the human body that of a dancer's. If you don't know a past participle from a split infinitive, the language will twist back and choke just as sure as a dangling modifier will prompt a guffaw in the more heartbreaking of paragraphs. You are only as good as your "chops"—syllables and sentences and punctuation are what you start with. From then on, hopefully, strength of character will keep you honest, by which I mean: Do no swerve from an honest and accurate portrayal because of political considerations. Nothing will kill your poem or story faster than artistic dishonesty. We are all human beings and therefore we err, sometimes horrifically; this is why we have forgiveness. If you cover up the shameful omissions and occasional cowardice, the ambivalence or spiritual failings of any of your characters because they are black, you are not doing anybody—and certainly not the Race—a service: You are denying that black character his or her humanity.

—Rita Dove, *Mother Love: Poems, On the Bus with Rosa Parks*

BELIEVE . . .

Write with a passion . . . each sentence, each paragraph, each page. Write passionately because the story in your head must be told—and *you are the only one who can tell it.*

—E. Lynn Harris, *Abide With Me, Just as I Am, Invisible Life*

Deem your writing worthy!

—Linnie Frank Bailey, co-author,
This Far by Faith: How to Put God First in Everyday Living

At times some writers feel that their lives aren't interesting enough to form background material for their work. Nothing could be farther from the truth. Every writer since the beginning of time has begun with the specifics of their culture: Homer, James Joyce, Alice Walker—all of them. And it is by concentrating on the specifics that a work can become universal.

—Gloria Naylor, *Mama Day, The Men of Brewster Place*

Don't be afraid of not knowing. Don't be embarrassed by what you believe to be a hole in your scholarship or life experience. All of writing is about starting points. Curiosity is the fuel that powers the journey of writing. Having the confidence to ask many questions, dig tirelessly toward answers, and be open and responsive to the world is just as important as how to craft a lean yet powerful sentence. It's just as important as first thought, last thought.

—Lynell George, *Los Angeles Times* staff writer, author of *No Crystal Stair: African Americans in the City of Angels*

Remember that you, your culture, your experiences, and your talents are unique. Remember your dedication to craft, determination to excel, and belief in your ability to succeed. Above all, remember the three words of one of the most magnificent singer/dancer/performers of our century. Whenever your work seems too small, too thin, and too homely to follow the literary giants who came before you, say, "Yes, I can," as did the late, great, Sammy Davis, Jr.

—Evangeline Blanco, *Caribe: A Novel of Puerto Rico*

Filling a blank page can assist in closing a void, turning what can be considered a chore into a necessity. But more importantly, never be led to believe that we are fighting one another for a place. There is room for us all and all are needed.

—Brian Keith Jackson, *The View from Here, Walking Through Mirrors*

Remember you are free to embrace the spirit, to write with
embodied passion, morning by morning and day by day.
—Katie Cannon, *Katie's Canon: Womanism and the Soul of the Black
Community, Black Womanist Ethics*

Trust your gut. Understand that your voice is unique and it
will resonate soulfully. Let the words flow from your heart
shamelessly! Write about what makes you get up in the
morning, day after day, and you will undoubtedly
strike a nerve.
—Monique Jellerette deJongh, *How to Marry a Black Man: The Real Deal*

From where I stand as a Trinidadian American, not wholly
acculturated to the African American experience, I see no
true obstacles to writing if one has adequate
talent and determination.
—Kelvin Christopher James, *A Fling with a Demon Lover, Secrets, a Novel*

There's something that, despite the obstacles and
setbacks, drives us forward and causes us not to dwell on the
negatives . . . that something is the desire to weave a
luxurious tale . . . so remember this quote, the next time it
takes you two days to write one paragraph . . .
Quote by unknown author: "Man never made any material
as resilient as the human spirit."
Keep writing . . . keep dreaming.
—Anna Larence, *Love Everlasting, After Hours*

Let's face it, Black writers, like other Black professionals, are
judged by a different yardstick, held to different standards
than our White counterparts. It's not fair but it's the way it
is. Given that reality, we must spend even more time
researching our material, verifying the information,
interpreting the facts so that we connect not just with our
folks but other folks as well. But more than that we must
listen to our own heartbeats and allow our words to stand

on the shoulders of our ancestors by connecting with the
genetic memory all Blacks in the diaspora share with
continental Blacks. It's our life force. It's our voice.
It's our vision. It's our drum!

—Stan West, co-author, *Profiles of Great African Americans*

My advice is to ignore the comments of well-meaning
friends and relatives and give yourself permission to write.
No matter what your age or life path, whether you write for
the sheer joy of it (which is the only way to do it) or
because you have dreams of being a published author
(nothing wrong with that), it's not too late, too egotistical,
too selfish, or too silly to pursue your creative urges. Your
talent is a gift. Your ideas and inspiration come from the
Spirit whispering in your ear. To ignore them is to
ignore God.

—Lori Bryant Woolridge, *Read Between the Lies*

LOVE . . .

Perhaps the best advice on writing that I've encountered
came from two of the most distinguished authors in
twentieth-century American literature. It is advice that all
writers, black or white, should take to heart.
The first of these writers is Ernest Hemingway, who said,
"What we must do is write what has never been written or
beat dead men at what they have done." In terms of literary
ambition, that says it all: whatever we choose to create, it
should advance the evolution of our literature. It should
despoil possibilities. We write, if Hemingway is correct (and
I believe he is), because we have something to say (or show)
that hitherto has not been said or shown. And if we don't
have an absolutely new story, experience, idea, or perception
to communicate, then we should at least honor our

predecessors by creating literary works that build upon their
outstanding contributions, works that take their
efforts one step further.

The second item of advice that I find valuable comes from
Alex Haley. When he was asked by an interviewer what his
advice was for young authors, he replied, "Find the good
and praise it." The simplicity of this reply belies its
underlying complexity. Concealed in Haley's writing wisdom
is, I think, the belief that the artist should be a servant, that
he gives his work to others as a gift lovingly rendered. There
must be a love of the good in the work's creation, as much
love as a mother has for her only child, selfless love in its
craft. And there is yet another way to see Haley's advice:
why write about something you hate? At times the writer
must be a critic, of course, and challenge those things in the
world that he (or she) finds reprehensible; but in Haley's two
great contributions to American letters—*The Autobiography of
Malcolm X* and *Roots*—we see clearly, from one page to the
next, that Haley has chosen his subjects (Malcolm X, the
odyssey of black America) and devoted years of his life to
research and rewriting because, first and foremost, he wishes
to share the beauty, truth, and goodness he had found in his
subjects with others.

When writing my most recent novel, *Dreamer*, over the last
six years, I reminded myself time and again of the advice
from these two authors. King did not appear in our
imaginative fiction—*that* was an oversight I deeply felt
needed to be addressed (Hemingway); and the only thing
that made it possible for me to live day and night with Dr.
King, his history and legacy, was the fact that I do indeed
love his social vision and the man himself for the
sacrifices he made for all of us (Haley).

With Hemingway and Haley as one's guides, a young
writer won't go wrong.

—Charles Johnson, *Dreamer, Middle Passage*

Treat every word, every sentence, every paragraph,
and every page like gold.
—the late Len Riley,
Harlem

Love the work and not the rewards. Love conceptualizing the
story. Love sitting in the sun or in a bar and imagining the
characters, the way they look, how they speak; listen to them
inside you late at night. Love writing your story and
rewriting it. Be so enthralled with your flow of written
words that you hardly finish one book before you begin
dreaming about writing another. The work is all that is
guaranteed. Your book may not sell; the critics may trash it.
Your editor may betray you, and your friends may laugh.
But in your deepest depression the work restores you. On
the other hand, you may land at the top of the *New York
Times* best-seller list and become the darling of the literary
world. You may be lauded and feted so much that your head
expands to the size of Texas, and when it is all over—and it
will end—what remains is the work. So, in good times and
bad, you need to be passionately in love with the act of
putting words on a page before you even think
about becoming a writer.
—Bebe Moore Campbell,
Singing in the Comeback Choir,
Brothers and Sisters

Cuban revolutionary hero Che Guevera wrote that "a true
revolution is guided by great feelings of love." My best
advice to black writers is to love black people enough to
tell them the truth.
—Pearl Cleage, *What Looks Like Crazy on an Ordinary Day, Mad at*
Miles: A Blackwoman's Guide to Truth

PRAY . . .

Let the Holy Spirit guide your work. The true breakthroughs
occur when we invoke the Holy Spirit, the Divine Muse.
When we ask God for the words He would have us to write,
then we always create from a much deeper place. Say a
prayer before you sit down at your computer. Give thanks
for the opportunity to share His Light that shines from
within you. Know how blessed you are to be able to harness
the Creative Force, find the words to express that creativity,
and always be humbled by the opportunity to
share it with others.

—Andria Hall, co-author,
This Far by Faith: How to Put God First in Everyday Living

Rise an hour earlier than usual. Push yourself up and out of
the soft warm holding you in sleep. Greet the delicate
light of the rising sun.
Move to a space filled with yourself, surround yourself with
yourself. Pieces of a life and a way of living that belong to
you. These objects should be beautiful, reflecting your
own beauty back onto yourself.
Speak to the Creator before you write, in whatever way best
communicates the intent of your spirit to the Universe. Tap
the rug, light a candle, burn incense, chant, shake what your
mama gave ya, remain perfectly still: express yourself
as a part of the realm of spirit.
Now you are ready to write. And you must write.
And you will write.

—Eisa Nefertari Ulen, television, magazine, and journal writer,
has recently completed a novel,
Spirit's Returning Eye

LISTEN/REMEMBER/FEEL . . .

I believe that we write about, and out of, our obsessions, the things that haunt our souls, things we never get over. Willa Cather said something to the effect of "all you need to know in order to write, you know when you're five years old." The matters of the heart, the relation to parents and friends and lovers and institutions, are the fundamental elements of what makes a narrative. We human beings actually only have a few stories that we tell over and over again: there is the story of being an outsider, or having your world invaded; there is the story of achieving some success against great odds, or having something special and losing it; and there is the story of malice toward a brother or a mother or a father or anyone. We mix these stories up, and we turn them around and inside out—but we're all obsessed with the fundamental elements. One of my teachers said, "The great themes are given to us: Love, Death, and Pain."
—Randall Kenan, *Walking on Water, Let the Dead Bury Their Dead*

Write to be heard—get into the rhythm of words and sounds. Don't try to be a black writer, try to be an honest writer.
—Kim Brundidge, playwright, *The Workout, Sex Acts*

On a room-size dock beside a Maine lake where for thirty-some summers I've gone each morning to write, I often find myself thinking about silence. When I'm writing or, more likely, in the spaces between writing that are also writing— the spaces when words aren't being scratched on the page, either because one thought is finished or another won't come or because I'm having thoughts for which no words exist, no words I know yet anyway—when I'm pausing, looking out at water, trees, and sky, the silence of my hideaway in the

woods meets the silence inside me and forms a horizon as
tangible and razor-sharp as the shoreline across the lake,
dividing trees from their upside-down reflections on days
when water and wind are calm.

Perhaps the words lie behind this horizon, but for the
moment they are utterly inaccessible and can remain so for
what seems like minutes, hours, days . . .

The more I write, the more I realize how deeply I'm
indebted to a communal experience of time and silence, an
African American language evolving from that experience, a
language vernacular, visceral, sensuous, depending on the
entire body's expressive repertoire, subversive, liberating,
freighted with laughter, song and sigh, burdened and
energized by opposition. African-rooted, culturally descended
ways and means of speaking that emerged from the
dungeon and dance of silence.

—John Edgar Wideman, *Fatheralong, All Stories Are True*

Write from the heart as well as your head. Trust your
instincts. Keep faith in yourself and your story. Remember
that conventional wisdom exists only to be challenged.
Educate yourself about the lives and legacies of writers of all
races who have come before you. Don't *need* to be famous,
rich, or loved as a result of your writing. Remember that
reviews are only somebody's opinion, not a definitive
statement on your work or who you are. Be grateful for your
imagination. Support and cheer on other writers. Revise the
traditional definitions of success. Write the story you most
want to read. Remember that as an African American writer
you are universal, existing at the center of your own
world, reaching out to everyone else's.

—Marita Golden, *Migrations of the Heart, The Edge of Heaven*

Welcome the opportunity to work with and talk with writers
who are, perhaps, not extremely well known in the popular
market. I am always disheartened when young people who

say they want to be writers seem disdainful of working with writers who might live and work in their own communities.

—Opal Moore, author of many anthologized short stories

Like a lot of the young folk coming up in the seventies I was divided between the spirituality of Earth, Wind and Fire and the Funk of the Funkadelic. All of this diversity in black music helped me to see more clearly the complexity of the black life going on around me. I felt I didn't need to explain black life or black people to anyone. What I needed to do was write truthfully about my life. I wanted to bring to the page the wide range of black folk I knew in south central Los Angeles. My best friend in high school decided he wanted to read the Encyclopedia of Philosophy from A to Z, all six volumes. It was such a task that between chasing girls, playing chess for money, and boning up on philosophical terms he didn't have time to attend class and eventually left school. I had another friend who in the ninth grade decided he wanted to be a filmmaker right then and there and he did it. He had a film career all through high school. He made at least a dozen soundless shorts: kung fu movies, vampire movies, mad scientist movies. I was cast as an evil genius who would direct maggots to do my dirty work and of course the maggots devoured me. I had to lie motionless while Chester engaged in primitive animation, slowly moving ten pounds of rice up stairs and eventually covering me. I remember my older brother's eccentric friends who called themselves the Fellas. They'd sit for hours on the corner telling elaborate stories that to my ear sounded like an elevated kind of gossip/history. They could talk the paint off walls, and if they didn't chase me away for being too young, all I had to do was listen to develop an ear for dialogue. I knew that if I could avoid the pitfalls of sociology and just go ahead and set the landscape and let the characters come forward to inhabit it, something good would be written. My first novel, *Understand This,* was based on my

experiences teaching in south central Los Angeles. It's selling
well and I've gotten great reviews but I'm not too surprised.
I'm just following the same rules I set for myself all along;
show the life and let the characters speak. Everything
else will take care of itself.

—Jervey Tervalon, *Living for the City, Understand This*

Writing is a joy and a chore. I try to approach my craft with
an open mind, enthusiasm, and aggressiveness. Sometimes we
are tempted to toe the line, walk the walk of the norm—
instead of putting to paper the ideas that are the most
outrageous! The words that are painful for you to write will
reach the hearts of others . . . the character that reminds
you of a favorite someone will remind the reader of
a favorite somebody too! Write from a flow and edit later
and you will find your work at its freshest and at
its most real!

—Yolanda Joe, *Bebe's by Golly Wow!, He Say, She Say*

Many years ago a colleague of mine, after hearing that I
thought of myself as a creative writer, told my mother and
sister, "You know, it's very difficult having a writer in the
family." She went on to explain that the difficulty was
many-layered. We writers seldom make any money from our
labor, so we're likely to be hanging around the family
accepting whatever food, money, extra bedroom space,
shoulders to cry on that might be at home. We're asked to
explain our writing, but writing is not speech, and it is
neither easy for us to say nor for our families to hear that
we "can't talk about it." We are not at a loss for words; it is
the cadence, the color, the page that must be part of the
transaction between writer and audience.

Writers also have a tendency to use the family as a
source of inspiration. And here's where things can sometimes
become quite thorny. Writers must write the truth they

know, recognizing that the recollection of a moment witnessed, perhaps by everyone else in the family, will not carry the same meaning, density, or sense from one person to another. Whether it is painted as memoir, or used as fact or symbol in fiction or poetry, whether it flatters, condemns, or equivocates, the writer cannot censor herself or write with the anticipation of the response her writing will create in the family. It sounds so simple, yet it is so very hard: just write with truth and honesty. Whatever price the family might want to exact is nothing compared to the price of dishonesty on the page. That makes for bad writing and who needs that?

—Gayle Pemberton,
The Hottest Water in Chicago: Notes on a Native Daughter

Mama language (the first language I heard at my Black mother's breast) is central to my writing. The other day my mother's rich way with words echoed in a prayer for a young woman going off to Howard University, thousands of miles away. We, relatives, friends, and neighbors, bowed our heads and held hands in the living room, in a comforting circle of support. The grandmother prayer began: "Lord, she's got so far to go. Make her like a postage stamp. When she wants to give up, make her stick again." I'm proud to celebrate in my work what I call the mama language with all its dark earth tones, cadences, and African American nuances. When it comes to writing, may I ever be like that postage stamp and stick, and stick, and stick again."

—Joyce Carol Thomas, *Marked by Fire, I Have Heard of a Land*

I urge black writers to fill in the gaps of our collective story. Write the black story nobody has ever heard, the startling truths that emerge from your own questions. Write the story that can only come from *you.*

—Gwendolyn Parker, *These Same Long Bones,*
Trespassing: My Sojourn in the Halls of Privilege

LEARN . . .

Lesson one: Always learn the rules before you break them.
Lesson two: You've heard over and over that you must show
and not tell. Narrative worked fine before the middle of the
twentieth century. Well, it's okay to tell. Telling is
going to have its day again.
Lesson three: If it bores you while you are writing it, take
that as a signal that something is wrong. Maybe the
idea is ill-conceived. Maybe you're doing it
in the wrong voice.
Lesson four: Choosing the right point of view and voice are
crucial. Point of view determines everything else. There's
always an upside and downside based on the
choice you make.
Lesson five: If you don't love constructing sentences, maybe
you should rethink your desire to write. If you're not feeling
a sensuous pleasure (and challenge) in the process, then
your efforts may be misdirected.
Lesson six: Remember, readers like for characters to face
problems but not to solve them too quickly. Conflict
conflict conflict—is the word.
—Clarence Major, *Dirty Bird Blues, All-Night Visitors*

Try not to get discouraged. Hone your craft. Learn from
other writers. Cherish and experience life and study its
lessons so you can better share them with your readers. Take
your writing very seriously and treat it like the gift it is, and
that means giving yourself the time and space you
need to do it well.
—Valerie Wilson Wesley, *Easier to Kill: A Tamara Hayle Mystery,
Ain't Nobody's Business If I Do*

Remember that you are different. Yours is a unique vision.
God has given you a gift. You must not be afraid to use it
honestly—your biggest obstacle will not be
others, but your own fear.
Read. Read everything and read it slowly,
and then read everything again.
Write. Be regular and disciplined in your writing. Be selfish
with your time. A writer is one who writes.
Have a sense of humor. You've probably heard that writing
is sweating blood. Nonetheless, many difficult things are
enjoyable, and at some point in the process
you ought to enjoy writing. Relax.
Be kind to other writers. No one gets to the top by him- or
herself. I owe much to the encouragement of other writers,
both black and white.
Becoming a writer takes a lifetime. It is a process
of continuous self-discovery.
—Anthony Grooms, *Trouble No More*

To survive what I call the Sagging Middle, it is vital to know
where you are going. Write one sentence that represents the
beginning, another that represents the middle, and another
that represents the end of your story. Study this structure.
Flesh it out by adding more and more sentences to each part
until you have completed a mini-outline of the book, about
ten to twenty pages. This will carry you through to the end
when things get rough and out of focus.
—Anita R. Bunkley, *Steppin' Out with Attitude, Balancing Act*

Sometimes, one of the most difficult things about writing is
knowing when to stop. That book becomes your baby as
you nurture it in the cozy confines of your little writing
space for months at a time, years even, and it can be hard to
let go, even when it's time. A friend of mine has been
working on her first novel for a good three years now. She's
tinkering with the edges and freely admits that maybe it's

finished and she's just having a hard time letting it go. Some
of this is fear of the scrutiny it will face once exposed to the
outside world. But you've done your best to prepare that baby
for this moment, now give it a chance to prove itself to others.

—Connie Briscoe, *Big Girls Don't Cry, A Long Way from Home*

As a junior editor at *Essence* magazine in the mid-1980s, I
remember being hyperconscious that anything I wrote have a
certain snap, crackle, and pop. Unfortunately, my articles
would frequently get bounced back to me by the senior
editor for lacking basic information. It took a while for me
to appreciate that good-sounding fluff is worse than useless,
it wastes people's time. When I returned to *Essence* as the
senior editor in the 1990s after four years as a features editor
for a New Mexico newspaper, I came upon an article
submitted by a young popular writer. It reminded me of my
old ways. The piece had plenty of sizzle but little substance.
What was her point? What had the writer learned from the
experience that she described as if blazing the mike at a
poetry slam? Reading her work provoked me to review the
basics: Before I worry about how to communicate
something, I still have to ask myself what I'm trying to say.
Particularly for nonfiction, I ask myself what are the
elements, facts, interviews, etc.; that I need to elevate the
reader to a new place of understanding. Additionally, I may
have assumed my story was going to be about A, but the
facts lead to Z. So Z it is. As I start to work with the raw
material, I don't care if the writing is ugly, disorganized, and
unfit for human consumption. I don't have to show it to
anybody yet, so I just focus on getting it all down as best I
can. Then and only then is it time to move on to how it all
sounds. That still matters a lot to me. But substance is top
priority. Which is to say that I hope never to be accused of
hiding out in the house of style.

—Pamela Johnson, co-author, *Santa and Pete,* editor of *Tenderheaded,* an
anthology about black hair

Develop excellence. Avoid success.

—April Sinclair, *Coffee Will Make You Black, I Left My Back Door Open*

WORK . . .

It's not enough to think you can write. A real writer is
always studying the works of other writers, learning and
growing. Getting published shouldn't be the primary goal.
(If you are good, that will happen.) Becoming a good writer
is what really matters. And that takes practice and patience.

—Audrey Edwards, *Children of the Dream: The Psychology of Black Success*

I have no jewels of wisdom for anyone when it comes to
writing, other than to say, "Sit your butt down and do it."
And if you're just launching a writing career, write what you
know. If you stop to think about it, you know a heck of a
lot more than you think you do. Consider the many
different worlds black folk travel through in the course of a
day, the different "languages" we have to learn to
communicate with people of all colors, all classes—the
different roles we assume to survive. We are so versatile.
We are survivors, a dynamite subject about which
to write. So sit down and do it.

—Chassie West, *Loss of Innocence, Sunrise*

Dear Aspiring Writer:
Sit up and take notice. What I am about to tell you I will
only say once. Here are the two keys to effective writing:
(1) Writing is a discipline. Practice the habit of writing
every day. No excuses! Teachers teach; painters paint;
and writers write!
(2) Find a good editor, preferably someone who is *not*
familiar with your work(s). Why? Because everyone swears

that he or she can write, myself included. To this day, I find
myself copyediting the local newspaper. A good editor can
help polish, gloss, buff, and craft your work into a piece of art.

—Dennis Kimbro, *Think and Grow Rich: A Black Choice,*
What Makes the Great Great

If your mind, spirit, and body demand that you write, write.
But be honest, or, as we said in the flame-blooming 1960s,
be "for real." Writing that gains the world's respect is not a
spewing of disassembled feelings, nor is it a pampering of
your ego. Writing is work, a disciplined discovery of patterns
and ideas in words. You must have a sense of human history
in order to know your address in time. You must train
yourself to cope with rejection and use it as a reason to
perfect your craft. Before you begin writing, read widely and
wisely. Study your tools—words and the options for
organizing them. Study how and why your literary ancestors,
be they poets, philosophers, or historians of science, have
used the tools to communicate effectively. Chew language
slowly and reflect deeply on the ideas the flavors release.
Then write. Know for whom you are writing and why.
Above all, discipline yourself and let your writing become an
act of love, a gift of talent for now and the future. Genuine
writers do care what the world thinks of their work and how
that work gets rewarded. Nevertheless, genuine writers hold
fast to the wisdom of Langston Hughes. They are for real
and free within themselves.

—Jerry W. Ward, Jr., editor, *Trouble the Water: 250 Years of African*
American Poetry, Black Southern Voices

Write from the fire within your soul. Inside yourself and
your experiences is where you'll find the energy and passion
to create great literature. Writing is an art, but remember
that publishing is a business. A book is a product that has to
be carefully written, designed, printed, priced, distributed,
and promoted. Just as you have invested yourself into the art

of writing your book; the same time, energy, and passion
must be invested into the business of publishing.
—William July II, *Brothers, Lust and Love*,
The upcoming *Understanding the Tin Man*

Finding an agent is like getting married. It's important to
ask other writers whom the agent represents what their day-
to-day existence is like. Not just the obvious questions like
how promptly do they return phone calls or do you have to
pay for copies, but things like their disposition and
temperament with their clients. Whether they take an "all
business" approach or not. . . . I need a lot of reassurance
and cheering from my agent. It can't be all cut-and-dried.
—Evelyn Coleman, *What a Woman's Gotta Do*,
The Riches of Oseola McCarty

Write early and write often. Strap yourself to your chair if
need be. Four hours a day, every day. Let yourself get
frustrated, bored, pissed off. Inspiration will finally bubble
up out of you—in dribbles or floods—it'll come.
—Trey Ellis, *Platitudes, Home Repairs*

Many aspiring writers come to me and say, "I want to be
the next . . . (fill in the name of the current hot-ticket
author)." In reply, what I always say is that a writer would
be far better served to break new ground, to find their own
unique voice, rather than try to duplicate someone else's
style, subject matter, or structure. Those who only aspire to
the best-selling author's money without doing the hard,
lonely work that precedes it, those who are not willing to
endure the years, sometimes decades of obscurity that make
one "overnight" success, will probably share the fate of a
nova—spectacular yes, awe-inspiring surely, but ultimately
burning incredibly bright for a moment, then soon gone,
leaving only an empty space in the heavens.
—Paula Woods, *Inner City Blues*; co-author, *I, Too, Sing America:
The African American Book of Days*

Writing is like feeding the children; you have to do it
all the time.

—Bertice Berry, *Sckraight from the Ghetto*
and the upcoming *Redemption Song*

REWRITE . . .

Fall in love with your vision, not your words. Accept
constructive criticism. Writing is rewriting even after
you've attracted an agent/editor.

—Nora DeLoach, *Mama Rocks the Empty Cradle, How to Write
and Sell Genre Fiction*

The most important advice I have to offer aspiring writers is
this: Read as broadly and as deeply as possible. The second
most important kernel of advice is that the writer should
save the reader pain. Thus the writer must rewrite, revise,
rewrite, and coach the prose until it sings in perfect pitch.
Readers will appreciate what the writer does to make
his or her prose a joy to read.

—Darlene Clark Hine, *Hine Sight: Black Women and the Re-Construction
of American History*; co-author, *A Shining Thread of Hope: The History
of Black Women in America*

Learn the value of editing your work so that your voice and
message can be as clear and engaging as possible. Don't
believe the old writers' complaint that editing only dilutes
your words. Fine editing is comparable to the skill of
sculpting, or how a painter mixes colors on the palette, not
using just what's in the tube. Once we learn to trust our
truths we can all stand a little editing.
I would also urge emerging black writers not to be afraid of
rejection. Don't let anything keep you from sending your
work out into the world. Read literary magazines, identify
some that publish work in a style similar to yours and

submit to them as often as you can. Try to learn something from the rejections, ask editors their opinion, use their insights to push you to work harder.
—Jewelle Gomez, *The Gilda Stories, Don't Explain*

I have never written anything that wasn't improved by rewriting and polishing, and I don't think any "real" writer ever has. I can still read one of my "best" short stories, which has been published twenty times, and see how changing a word here and there, adding or deleting a sentence or a paragraph, can make it better.
—Jess Mowry, *Way Past Cool, Six Out Seven*

I try to write the truth, which often turns out quite funky. It's a discipline that requires me to read, research, and interview in order to get the facts my imagination couldn't dream of. Then I begin the wearying and frustrating job of writing through resistance and ignorance, past assumption and presumption. Again and again I must remind myself that I have permission to write the first draft. It is almost always disappointing. So are early rewrites: the ideas lack toughness, the characters keep their secrets, the narrative fails to move as it should. The real task of the first draft is to get honest about the parameters and the effects of the story I'm telling. I'm marking the territory I hope to explore, blocking out colors and design on the canvas—often over the objections of the internal critic, whom I keep tied and gagged while the messy work of creating and flailing around for organization goes on.

Then I let her out. I need her tough-mindedness and judgment to rewrite. Rewriting makes me think fresh: about the story, pacing, characters, ideas, tone, the phrasing of sentences, words, punctuation. If I've done my homework thoroughly, if I've become a willing student of the work, I can discover what I need while I write, "through the process." That's miraculous. Amidst the frustration, rewriting

to get honest gives me clarity. It gives the work consistency,
vigor, and coherence—without resort to ideological
rigidity or gimmicks.
This process gives me confidence that the early drafts of the
work do not justify. The process gives me moments of
stunningly pure concentration and a sense of the vastness of
the consciousness in which I participate. If I make myself a
disciple of that consciousness, if I shut up and listen, if I
move beyond my ego's illusion of separateness, then I get to
grope in the darkness where the ancestors cough up blood
and lies and hope. I rewrite, cut, reimagine,
write fresh, rewrite, until I've gotten the words as close
to what I hear, see, apprehend. What a gift to
live to tell the tale.

—Lorene Cary, *The Price of a Child*, Pride

GROW . . .

I was trained by John O. Killens. When I think what one
thing I would want to pass on, I think it would be
awareness of the divine power and responsibility of the
Word. I was taught that it is okay and fitting to aspire to
literary greatness, to aspire to be a writer of historical stature
and cultural significance. That it is, however, the
responsibility of the writer who-would-be-great to be at all
times ruthlessly serious about being a writer. To constantly
refine and purify your character, vision, and craft and to
produce artistically cutting edge/culturally significant Works.

—Arthur Flowers, *Another Good Loving Blues*,
DeMojo Blues

Write what you would want to read. Then keep working on
the literary work until it is right. Please consider my three
p's: persistence, patience, and prayer. I know that they have

aided me in my own writing along with the three *m*'s:
music, magic, and mystery.

Believe in yourself and what you have to say. The
black writer must be committed to the craft of writing and
must keep writing until the literary work is right.
Organize a writers' group to critique each other's writing
and to discuss various literary matters and concerns. You can
learn a lot from others with similar interests. And once you
find the right approach for your writing style, then you
must pass that wisdom on to the next
generation of writers.
You must work to find your own voice.

—Lenard D. Moore, *Forever Home, The Open Eye*

There is always a sense of haste when one wants to get
published. I know. I've been there. We all think that no one
has a book, an idea, or a story like ours. Don't believe any
of it. The fact is, while your story is probably special in its
own way, because we are all human and share similar
qualities, backgrounds, cultures, joys, and pain, chances are
much of what we have to offer mirrors what others have to
offer. *How* you tell it makes your story special.
Live for the moment when it feels like the story is writing
itself, when it feels like those who came before you are
speaking through you. Strive for the writer's high. When
you're one with something Higher? Strive for that.
The act of creating is a very sacred act and we must honor
it. We have to love what comes out of us so much that we
don't care if no one beyond our best friend ever reads it.
When we feel that way, we are halfway there. The
satisfaction will never come from being picked for Oprah's
Book Club, or seeing your name on the cover of a glossy
book; satisfaction really must come from within.

—Sharony Andrews Green, *Cuttin the Rug Under the Moonlit Sky: Stories
and Drawings About a Bunch of Women Named Mae*

To be young, gifted, and Black is something of a beginning
for an African American writer, and I take *young* to be
anyone starting out as a writer. Have a place where you
write on a regular basis and treat your art with respect. In
other words, don't abandon poetry to write books that make
money if you believe yourself to be a decent poet; your
writing will sustain your spirit and will to live.
—Afaa M. Weaver, *Talisman, Timber and Prayer*

My advice: start from where you are.
Many people who are interested in writing seem to think
that they have to start the process from the beginning. The
beginning of the story, the beginning of the novel, the
beginning of the tale. But that is not necessarily the best way
to start. Sometimes it is not the beginning that you see most
clearly. As a matter of fact, sometimes the beginning is the
last part of the story to become clear in your mind.
I have met many potential writers who have never started
writing because they are trying to start at the beginning.
And of course it has to be a great beginning. You do not
have to start writing a novel from the beginning. I have
found great success in starting each of my novels by writing
the scene or scenes that I see most clearly first. In my
current novel, *Serpentine's Fire* (Dutton, 1999), I actually
wrote the climax first because that was the most powerful
scene in my mind. In my first novel, *So Good* (Dutton,
1996), the scene that I thought was the beginning eventually
became a chapter in the middle.
I believe that the writing process should be allowed to
progress naturally. Once you write the clearest scene in your
mind, then write the next, and the next, and the next. If
you remain flexible the story will come to you. The key is to
write, rewrite, and write some more. Start writing from
where you are and continue writing until
your instincts tell you it's done.
—Venise Berry, *So Good, Mediated Messages and African American Culture*

Part of any writer's challenge is learning how to tune out the praise of friends, who are too willing to accept mediocrity in the interest of friendship.

—Ellis Cose, *The Rage of a Privileged Class, Color-Blind: Seeing Beyond Race in a Race-Obsessed World*

Read widely, eclectically, to learn the many ways writing can be done. Do things to help other people and thereby gain significant life experiences from which to learn about yourself, others, and the world. Write to involve readers in what you make of those experiences with concrete, sensory language. Don't give up.

—John Holman, *Luminous Mysteries, Squabble and Other Stories*

1. Go to the bookstore and see what everyone else is doing. Go home and do something different.

2. If you want to be a performer, go into show business. If you want to get rich, go to Wall Street. If you have a political agenda, go into politics. If you want to be famous, get a gun.

3. Don't engage in literary gossip. If you hear anything good, give me a call.

4. Aesthetic standards are real. If you don't like mine, make up your own. Be prepared to articulate them in an essay of no less than 3,500 words.

5. Stay home more. Read a lot. Write.

—David Haynes,
All American Dream Dolls, Right by My Side, Live at Five

Read all you can until you're twenty, live all you can till you're thirty, and write all you can after that.

—Kristen Lattany, *God Bless the Child, Kinfolks*

NURTURE . . .

It is important for black writers to acknowledge the black
literary tradition which links them to the slave narratives,
spirituals, work songs, and blues. We must write out of
memory. Black writers must also be aware of the importance
of community. Literary friendships should be strengthened
and celebrated. I place a strong emphasis on the need for
black writers to network. Open doors for others. Share
information. Never forget that it's language which holds us
together. There are still many obstacles confronting black
writers . . . there is a need for us to
become more powerful.

—E. Ethelbert Miller, *Whispers, Secrets, and Promises*; editor, *In Search of
Color Everywhere*

First, know that you ARE a writer. As writers, all of us are
continuously learning how to be truer to our craft and to
our inner voices . . . but it's not that you WANT to be a
writer—you ARE one. There are only published writers
and unpublished writers.

Believe that if you continue to work and learn to filter
out false praise (those who admire us unconditionally) and
undue criticism (those who are, perhaps, a little jealous of
our zeal?), you WILL continue to grow and improve.
Reading good books will help you be a better writer.
Turning off the TV at night to write an entry in your
journal will help you be a better writer. Getting up two
hours earlier to work on another chapter in your novel
WILL result in a finished book. A finished book will always
bring you one step closer to publication, even if that book is
never published itself. If you see your career path like a map,
with this road leading here, and this road leading there, you
will understand that there is no magic involved in being a

writer. Published writers did not simply close their eyes and
wish—they worked and they worked hard, and they know
they will have to keep on working.

Try to sell what you write. I let my first novel, *The
Between,* sit on my desk for a year before I got serious about
trying to find an agent—I had no idea I was ready to be
published. Sometimes we are not worthy judges.

And also remember that rejection does not always have
to do with quality—usually it has everything to do with
commercial viability. Not every book will have a home with
every publisher. If it isn't your natural voice to write
Waiting to Exhale, then don't try. Write what YOU have
to say, and then find your audience. Innovation is more
attractive than imitation.

—Tananarive Due, *My Soul to Keep, The Between*

My mother has an expression, "Give me my flowers while I
can smell them." Applied to black writers this means: We
need to praise each other when praise is due. It's been my
experience over the years that the good I send out
comes back to me tenfold.

As an author and as an agent, some of my best contacts have
come from what I call my "you go, girl" notes. Writers are
usually voracious readers first. What you do with the
information you read can make all the
difference in your life.

Also, I think it's important to remember that you are not in
competition with other authors, no matter how hard and
often publishers and other people will try to pit us against
each other. There's room for all of us. At white colleges and
universities, during orientation, students are asked to look to
the right and the left and then they are told, "One of these
students won't be here at graduation." At the historically
black schools, students are asked to look to the right and the
left and then are told, "It's your responsibility to see both of

these students next to you at graduation." I think that's the
attitude writers should have.

—Jackqueline Turner Banks,
Maid in the Shade,
Egg Drop Blues

Writer-friend, know your worth—your soul's worth. There
are many people who will want to lead you by the neck,
take you this way and that way, tell you what to write and
what not to write, who to write for and what to avoid.
Don't forget that what you're trying to do is make some art,
writer-friend. You are the creator and whatever you write will
ultimately carry your name and your name alone.
Writer-friend, know your literary heritage. Read for
pleasure. Read for help. Read with love.
Writer-friend, you don't have to speak for the whole race/
tribe/culture. When you speak your own personal experience,
we learn plenty too. When we visit your island, your home,
your neighborhood, when we enter your kitchen, your
bedroom, your heart, we feel privileged to partake of your
singularity. Maybe the whole race will not fit in there all at
once, but we're honored by you in the
singular as well as the plural.
And last, but not least, writer-friend, rejoice and celebrate
your victories, big and small. When that sentence you've
been struggling with for a month finally comes together, take
a moment to celebrate the process. But the bottom line,
writer-friend, is to just write. Though it never gets easier, the
more you do, the more you'll learn.

—Edwidge Danticat,
Breath, Eyes, Memory,
The Farming of Bones

PART V

TOOLS YOU MAY NEED

READING LIST

There are many fine and glorious books to read! This list is my own eclectic sampling of ninety books and a dozen anthologies which I think are historically significant to the development of African American fiction. Some of the books will enthrall, others shock and anger, and some will uplift your spirits. All of the books provide an important glimpse into our culture and illuminate the spirit of black peoples.

ORIGINALLY PUBLISHED 1800–1900

Brown, William Wells. *Clotel; or, The President's Daughter*. Dimension, 1989.

Chesnutt, Charles. *The Conjure Woman*. Dimension, 1983.

Douglass, Frederick. *Narrative of the Life of Frederick Douglass, an American Slave, Written by Himself*. Signet Books, 1997.

Harper, Frances Ellen. *Iola Leroy, or Shadows Uplifted*. Beacon Press, 1987.

Hopkins, Pauline. *Contending Forces*. Oxford University Press, 1988.

Jacobs, Harriet. *Incidents in the Life of a Slave Girl*. Oxford University Press, 1990.

Wilson, Harriet. *Our Nig, or Sketches from the Life of a Free Black in a Two-Story White House, North*. Random House, 1983.

ORIGINALLY PUBLISHED 1900–50

Attaway, William. *Blood on the Forge*. Doubleday, 1993.

Dunbar, Paul Laurence. *Sport of the Gods*. Ayer & Company, 1974.

Fauset, Jessie. *Plum Bun: A Novel Without a Moral*. Pandora Press, 1985.

———. *The Chinaberry Tree*. McGrath, 1969.

Fisher, Rudolph. *The Conjure Man Dies: A Mystery Tale of Dark Harlem*. X-Press, 1997.

Hughes, Langston. *The Ways of White Folks*. Vintage Books, 1971.

Hurston, Zora Neale. *Their Eyes Were Watching God*. HarperCollins, 1990.

———. *Jonah's Gourd Vine*. Perennial, 1990.

Johnson, James Weldon. *The Autobiography of an Ex-Coloured Man*. Doubleday, 1927.

Larsen, Nella. *Passing.* Ayer & Company, 1985.

———. *Quicksand.* Rutgers University Press, 1986.

McKay, Claude. *Home to Harlem.* Northeastern University Press, 1987.

Petry, Ann. *The Street.* Chapters Publishers Ltd., 1998.

Schuyler, George. *Black No More.* Northeastern University Press, 1989.

Thurman, Wallace. *The Blacker the Berry.* X-Press, 1997.

Toomer, Jean. *Cane.* Liveright, 1993.

Wright, Richard. *Native Son.* HarperPerennial, 1998.

ORIGINALLY PUBLISHED 1950–70

Angelou, Maya. *I Know Why the Caged Bird Sings.* Random House, 1969.

Baldwin, James. *Go Tell It on the Mountain.* Dimension, 1995.

———. *Another Country.* Vintage Books, 1993.

Brooks, Gwendolyn. *Maud Martha.* Harper & Row, 1953.

Brown, Claude. *Manchild in the Promised Land.* New American Library, 1995.

Delany, Samuel. *Babel-17.* Gollancz Publishing, 1967.

Ellison, Ralph. *Invisible Man.* Vintage Books, 1995.

Greenlee, Sam. *The Spook Who Sat by the Door.* Wayne State University Press, 1989.

Guy, Rosa. *My Love, My Love.* Holt, 1990.

Himes, Chester. *If He Hollers, Let Him Go.* Thunder's Mouth Press, 1986.

Hunter, Kristen. *God Bless the Child.* Howard University Press, 1986.

Kelly, William Melvin. *A Different Drummer.* Anchor Books, 1990.

Killens, John Oliver. *And Then We Heard the Thunder.* Knopf, 1963.

Marshall, Paule. *The Chosen Place, the Timeless People.* Vintage Books, 1992.

———. *Brown Girl, Brownstones.* Feminist Press CUNY, 1959.

Meriwether, Louise. *Daddy Was a Number Runner.* Prentice Hall, 1970.

Petry, Ann. *Tituba of Salem Village.* HarperCollins Juvenile Books, 1991.

Walker, Margaret. *Jubilee.* Bantam Books, 1984.

Williams, John A. *The Man Who Cried I Am.* Thunder's Mouth Press, 1985.

Yerby, Frank. *A Woman Called Fancy.* Dial Press, 1951.

Young, Al. *Bodies & Soul.* Berkeley Books, 1981.

ORIGINALLY PUBLISHED 1970–80

Bambara, Toni Cade. *Gorilla, My Love.* Vintage Books, 1992.

Bradley, David. *The Chaneysville Incident.* HarperCollins, 1990.

Butler, Octavia. *Kindred.* Beacon Press, 1988.

Chase-Riboud, Barbara. *Sally Hemmings.* Ballantine Books, 1994.

Childress, Alice. *A Hero Ain't Nothin' But a Sandwich.* Coward, McCann & Geoghegan, 1973.

Gaines, Ernest. *The Autobiography of Miss Jane Pittman.* Bantam Books, 1982.

———. *A Gathering of Old Men.* Knopf, 1983.

Haley, Alex. *Roots.* Dell Books, 1980.

Johnson, Charles. *Oxherding Tale.* Indiana University Press, 1982.

Jones, Gayle. *Eva's Man.* Beacon Press, 1987.

McPherson, James. *Elbow Room.* Fawcett Books, 1989.

Morrison, Toni. *Sula.* Plume/Penguin, 1973.

———. *Song of Solomon.* Plume/Penguin, 1987.

Reed, Ishmael. *Flight to Canada.* Atheneum, 1989.

———. *The Last Days of Louisiana Red.*

Taylor, Mildred. *Roll of Thunder, Hear My Cry.* Puffin Books, 1991.

Walker, Alice. *In Love and Trouble: Stories of Black Women.* Harcourt Brace, 1985.

ORIGINALLY PUBLISHED 1980–90

Ansa, Tina McElroy. *Baby of the Family.* Harcourt Brace, 1984.

Bambara, Toni Cade. *The Salt Eaters.* Vintage Books, 1992.

Cooper, J. California. *Homemade Love.* St. Martin's Press, 1988.

Delany, Samuel. *His Tales of Neveryon.* Wesleyan University Press, 1994.

Demby, William. *Love Story Black.* Dutton, 1986.

Dixon, Melvin. *Trouble the Water.* Fiction Collective, 1989.

Dove, Rita. *Fifth Sunday.* University of Kentucky Press, 1985.

Ellis, Trey. *Platitudes.* Vintage Books, 1988.

Golden, Marita. *Long Distance Life.* Doubleday, 1989.

Hamilton, Virginia. *The Magical Adventures of Pretty Pearl.* HarperCollins, 1986.

Johnson, Charles. *The Sorcerer's Apprentice.* Plume, 1994.

Kincaid, Jamaica. *Annie John.* Farrar Straus and Giroux, 1985.

Lee, Andrea. *Sarah Phillips.* Doubleday, 1984.

Major, Clarence. *Such Was the Season,* Mercury House, 1987.

Marshall, Paule. *Praisesong for the Widow.* Plume, 1992.

McElroy, Colleen. *Jesus and Fat Tuesday.* Creative Arts Book Company, 1987.

McMillan, Terry. *Disappearing Acts.* Viking, 1989.

Morrison, Toni. *Beloved.* Knopf, 1987.

Myers, Walter Dean. *Won't Know Till I Get There.* Viking Penguin, 1988.

Naylor, Gloria. *The Women of Brewster Place.* Penguin Books, 1983.

———. *Mama Day.* Vintage Penguin, 1989.

Shange, Ntozake. *Sassafras, Cypress, and Indigo.* Picador USA, 1996.

Thelwell, Michael. *The Harder They Come.* Grove Press, 1988.

Thomas, Joyce Carol. *Marked by Fire.* Avon Books, 1981.

Walker, Alice. *The Color Purple.* Pocket Books, 1995.

Wideman, John Edgar. *Hiding Place.* Houghton Mifflin, 1998.

———. *Fever.* Penguin, 1989.

Williams, Sherley Anne. *Dessa Rose.* Berkeley Publishing Group, 1996.

Since 1990 there has been a new renaissance of African American writing. Many splendid authors, too numerous to mention here, are accessible in libraries, bookstores, and through Internet venues. I would also suggest that you discover, if you haven't already, the fine books written by the authors who contributed their "Best Advice" for this book.

The anthologies below will also introduce you to old and new authors who made significant contributions to the development of African American short fiction.

Short Fiction and Folktale Anthologies

Bambara, Toni Cade, editor. *The Black Woman.* New American Library, 1970.

DeCosta-Willis, Miriam, et al., editors. *Erotique Noire, Black Erotica.* Anchor Books, 1992.

Gates, Henry Louis, and Nellie McKay. *Norton Anthology of African American Literature.* W. W. Norton, 1997.

Hurston, Zora Neale. *Mules and Men.* Perennial, 1990.

Knopf, Marcy, editor. *The Sleeper Wakes: Harlem Renaissance Stories by Women.* Rutgers University Press, 1993.

Lester, Julius. *Black Folktales.* Grove Weidenfeld, 1970.

Major, Clarence, editor. *Calling the Wind: Twentieth Century African American Short Stories.* HarperPerennial, 1993.

McMillan, Terry, editor. *Breaking Ice: An Anthology of Contemporary African American Fiction.* Viking Penguin, 1990.

Naylor, Gloria, editor. *Children of the Night: Best Short Stories by Black Writers: 1967 to the Present.* Little, Brown, 1995.

Rowell, Charles, editor. *Ancestral House: The Black Short Story in the Americas and Europe.* Westview Press, 1995.

Washington, Mary Helen, editor. *Black-Eyed Susans & Midnight Birds.* Mary Helen Washington, Doubleday, 1990.

———, editor. *Memories of Kin: Stories About Family by Black Writers.* Doubleday, 1991.

WRITING RESOURCES

General Resources

The following books are all wonderful resources for understanding the publishing business. How to find an agent, how to be your own agent, how to submit your manuscript for publication are some of the topics covered. Pay particular attention to any general information sections. Many of these books have terrific advice about paying readers' fees, entering contests, writing a good cover letter, etc.

1998 Writer's Market
F & W Publications, Inc., 1997

International Literary Marketplace, 1998
R. R. Bowker, 1997

1999 Novel & Short Story Writer's Market
editor, Barbara Kuroff
F & W Publications, Inc., 1999

1999 Children's Writers & Illustrators Market
editor, Alice Pope
Writer's Digest Books, 1999

The Insider's Guide to Getting Published: Why They Always Reject Your Manuscript and What You Can Do About It
John Boswell
Doubleday, 1998

A Writer's Guide to Book Publishing
Richard Balkin
NAL/Dutton, 1994

Writer's Guide to Book Editors, Publishers, and Literary Agents, 1999–2000
Jeff Herman
Prima Publishing, 1998

A Complete Guide to Getting Any Book Published
William July II
Khufu Books, 1998

Writing for the Ethnic Market
Meera Lester
Writer's Connection, 1991

Into Print: Guides to the Writing Life
Poets & Writers, Inc., 1998

Directory of Small Press/Magazine Editors and Publishers
Len Fulton
Dustbooks, 1997

The Association of American University Presses Directory
The Association of American University Presses, Inc., 1996

The African-American Network
Crawford Bunkley
Plume, 1996

How to Write and Sell Genre Fiction
Nora L. Frazier-DeLoach
Rotuma Publishing Company, 1999

More Specialized Resources

1. Agents serve an important role in helping an author find a publisher. While most writers have agents, I do know a few who have successfully managed the selling process on their own.

Guide to Literary Agents: 500 Agents Who Sell What You Write
editors, Don Prues and Chantelle Bentley
Writer's Digest Books, 1998

Literary Agents: The Essential Guide for Writers
Debby Mayer
Viking Penguin, 1998

How to Be Your Own Literary Agent
Richard Curtis
Houghton Mifflin, 1996

2. Protecting your authorship/ownership is discussed thoroughly in the following books:

Copyright Handbook
R. R. Bowker, 1982

A Writers Guide to Copyright
Poets & Writers, Inc., 1979

3. What to expect once your book is accepted for publication isn't widely discussed, but Appelbaum's offers thorough and practical advice:

How to Get Happily Published (5th ed.)
Judith Appelbaum
HarperCollins, 1998

4. Finding quality time and a place to write is made easier by writer's conferences, colonies, and workshop retreats. Several notable workshops are cited here, along with general resources to explore conference and workshop opportunities on your own. Also, be sure to contact your local university for any sponsored writing conferences.

Callaloo: Creative Writing Workshops for Historically Black Institutions
Callaloo
Department of English
Wilson Hall
University of Virginia
Charlottesville, VA 22903

Hurston/Wright Writers Week at Saint Mary's College
P.O. Box 4686
Moraga, CA 94575-4686

Hurston/Wright Writers Week at Virginia Commonwealth University
P.O. Box 842005
Richmond, VA 23284-20054

The Complete Guide to Writer's Conferences and Workshops
William Noble
P. S. Eriksson, 1995

Artists and Writers Colonies:
Retreats, Residencies, and Respite for the Creative Mind
Gail Hellund Bowler, 1995

The Guide to Writer's Conferences
Shaw Guides, Inc., 1992
625 Biltmore Way, Suite 1406
Coral Gables, FL 33134

Supportive Organizations

1. Nationally, there are many fine writing organizations devoted to fostering talent, informing writers about their craft and rights as authors, and publicizing publishing opportunities. In addition, most states will have their own arts commission or council which fosters literary events within the state via workshops, fellowships, and/or a reading series.

African American Resource Center
Afro-American Studies
Howard University
P.O. Box 441
Washington, DC 20059
E. Ethelbert Miller directs the center and provides information, suggestions, and advice about scholarships and creative writing. A splendid poet himself, E. Ethelbert Miller is particularly encouraging to new writers. The Center also houses a fine library which is available to the public.

The Arts Sanctuary
Church of the Advocate
1801 Diamond Street
Philadelphia, PA 19121-1590
Founded by writer Lorene Cary, this organization brings African American artists, thinkers, and activists to the heart of the Philadelphia black community. A year old, this organization has made a superb start and should continue to reflect back the rich national and international legacy of its community.

Carolina African American Writers' Collective
5625 Continental Way
Raleigh, NC 27610
Founder and executive director Lenard D. Moore inspires this wonderfully creative organization. The Collective sponsors workshops, readings, and a newsletter which provides updates about the writing craft, publishing, and community readings.

Frederick Douglass Creative Arts Center
270 West 96th Street
New York, NY 10025
This center has long been a haven for black writers. Besides an informative newsletter, it offers wonderful classes taught by expert instructors in a supportive community environment.

Gifted Voices
116 NW 13th Street, Suite 182
Gainesville, FL 32601
This is a monthly newsletter which reaches out to form a national community devoted to black literary artists. It offers book reviews and spotlight profiles of historical and contemporary artists.

Poets & Writers, Inc.
72 Spring Street
New York, NY 10012
Poets & Writers is an organization devoted to informing writers about their craft, agents, publishing, and grants and fellowships. Their newsletter is exceptional. It features updated information on contest and grant deadlines, conferences, and publishing opportunities. Write them for a complete list of their publications.

Associated Writing Programs (AWP)
Tallwood House, Mail Stop 1E3
George Mason University
Fairfax, VA 22030
This association of university-affiliated writing programs sponsors an annual conference and publishes a guide to creative writing programs. The AWP newsletter features information on grants, fellowships, awards, and publishing opportunities. It also provides in-depth articles on craft and exceptional writers.

PEN American Center
568 Broadway
New York, NY 10012
This organization is devoted to advocating writers' rights nationally and internationally. It publishes writing guides and sponsors community and national writing programs.

PEN Center USA West
672 South Lafayette Park Place #41
Los Angeles, CA 90057
Related to the PEN American Center, PEN West provides tremendous support for West-based writers. It offers readings and workshops, and its "Emerging Writers" Program pairs young writers with more experienced mentors.

YMCA, The Writer's Voice Project
5 West 63rd Street
New York, NY 10023

This is a national program that sponsors community-based writing workshops and a terrific reading series by local and national writers. Contact your local Y for information about its affiliation with the The Writer's Voice.

2. Historically, black writers across the nation have bonded to create their own organizations. Many of these organizations were founded by the vision of one person or by a community collective. While the following list is *not* exhaustive, it provides a starting point to help you link to other writers throughout the nation. But, most important, the lesson, I think, is that people with commitment can create their own community-based reading group or supporting arts organization. (If you know any other organizations which ought to be included, please don't hesitate to contact me in care of Doubleday.)

Black Writers and Artists International
P.O. Box 43576
Los Angeles, CA 90043

Black Writers Institute
1650 Bedford Avenue
Brooklyn, NY 11225

Renaissance Writers Inc.
Schomberg Library
515 Malcolm X Boulevard
New York, NY 10037

Gwendolyn Brooks Center for
Black Literature and Creative Writing
Chicago State University
LIB 210
9501 South King Drive
Chicago, IL 60628-1598

Eugene B. Redmond Writer's Club
P.O. Box 6165
East St. Louis, IL 62202
or
392 Winchester Place
Fairview Heights, IL 62208

Houston African American Writers' Society
P.O. Box 31478
Houston, TX 77231-1478

International Black Writers and Artists
2625 Piedmont Road 56–156
Atlanta, GA 30324

Sistah's: An African American Literary Group
2829 Palomor Drive
Brunswick, GA 31520

Multi-Cultural Romance Writers
405A West 13th Street
Greenville, NC 27834

Black Storytellers Association
P.O. Box 67722
Baltimore, MD 21215

Bambara Writers
Women's Center
Spelman College
350 Spelman Lane
Atlanta, GA 30314

Magazines and Journals

1. There are many fine magazines which discuss the craft of writing and professional issues for the beginning to the advanced writer. The following journals are available nationally at most newsstands:

Writers' Digest
1507 Dana Avenue
Cincinnati, OH 45207
A popular standby. The *Digest* has informative articles, many of which explore how to make a living as a writer.

The Writer
120 Boylston Street
Boston, MA 02116
A fine magazine with helpful practical articles. It also produces an excellent annual book called *The Writer's Handbook,* edited by Sylvia K. Burack.

Poets & Writers Newsletter
72 Spring Street
New York, NY 10012
A regular publication of Poets & Writers, Inc. Feature articles on great

writers and writer's issues make this an informative newsletter. Also gives details on conferences, retreats, grants, and submission information.

Writer's Chronicle
Tallwood House, Mail Stop 1E3
George Mason University
Fairfax, VA 22030
A regular publication of the Associated Writing Programs. Author interviews, grants and submission information, and excellent articles about the writing craft make the *Writer's Chronicle* very worthwhile.

2. If you're interested in book reviews and issues related to the publishing trade, *Publishers Weekly* is the guide to have. Many libraries will carry this invaluable resource in their magazine or reference section.

Publishers Weekly
245 West 17th Street
New York, NY 10011

3. Most of the following journals and magazines offer book reviews, interviews, and examples of contemporary, black fiction. Some of the journals are university-affliated; others are commercial; still others are independent efforts by caring artists. You should study copies of each of the magazines and subscribe to a few which most interest you. Some of these journals and magazines may provide avenues for publishing your fiction. Check with each for their submission policy. (This is but a partial listing of available publishing opportunities which specialize in black literature. For additions to this list, please write to me in care of Doubleday.) Don't forget, too, to search publishing guides and the Internet for additional titles—new journals are being created every day!

African American Review
Indiana State University
Department of English
Root Hall A218
Terre Haute, IN 47809
A mainstay journal in promoting black literature and art.

African American Literary Review
5381 La Paseo #105
Fort Worth, TX 76112

African Voices: The Art and Literary Publication with Class & Soul
African Voices Communications, Inc.
270 West 96th Street
New York, NY 10025
Publishes an excellent wide variety of genres.

AIM Magazine
P.O. Box 20554
7308 South Eberhardt Avenue
Chicago, IL 60619
Publishes upbeat, socially significant works on racism and multiculturalism.

Anansi: Fiction of the African Diaspora
765 Amsterdam Avenue #3C
New York, NY 10025-5707
Publishes original short fiction by talented writers.

Black Renaissance/Renaissance Noire
Journals Division, Indiana University Press
601 North Morton
Bloomington, IN 47404
Journal publishes fiction and nonfiction which addresses contemporary issues.

Black American Literature Forum
Parsons Hall 237
Indiana State University
Terre Haute, IN 47809
Articles and reviews of black literature.

Black Books Bulletin: Wordswork
Third World Press
P.O. Box 19730
Chicago, IL 60619

Blackfire
BLK Publishing Co.
P.O. Box 83912
Los Angeles, CA 90083-0912

The Black Writer
P.O. Box 1030
Chicago, IL 60690

Black Books Round-Up
c/o The Black Scholar: Journal of Black Studies
P.O. Box 2869
Oakland, CA 94609

Brilliant Corners: A Journal of Jazz and Literature
Lycoming College
Williamsport, PA 17701
Publishes jazz-related literature.

Callaloo: A Journal of African-American & African Arts and Letters
Department of English
Wilson Hall University of Virginia
Charlottesville, VA 22903
One of the premier literary journals devoted to diaspora literature.

Class
900 Broadway
8th Floor
New York, NY 10003

Contours
African American Studies Program
Duke University
Box 90719
121-S Carr Building
Durham, NC 27708
Poetry and fiction by talented writers.

Dialogue
P.O. Box 4544
Washington, DC 20017
A fine new journal devoted to promoting African American arts.

Ebony
820 South Michigan Avenue
Chicago, IL 60605
Publishes a wide variety of genres and articles related to black life.

Emerge
1700 North Moore Street, Suite 2200
Arlington, VA 22209
Hip contemporary focus on new artistic trends and issues in the black community.

Essence
1500 Broadway, 6th Floor
New York, NY 10036
Wonderful magazine devoted to black life with excellent feature writing
and fiction.

Harmony Magazine
Pratt Station
Box 050081
Brooklyn, NY 11205-0001
Devoted to racial and cultural harmony.

Jive,
Black Confessions,
Black Romance
Bronze Thrills,
Black Secrets
233 Park Avenue
New York, NY 10003
Publishes romantic stories centering on female characters.

Message Magazine
c/o Review and Herald Publishing Association
55 Oak Ridge Drive
Hagerstown, MD 21740
A Christian outreach magazine.

Mosaic Literary Magazine
Mosaic Communication
314 West 231st Street, Suite 470
Bronx, NY 10463
Devoted to black and Hispanic literature.

Obsidian II: Black Literature in Review
Department of English
North Carolina State University
Box 8105
Raleigh, NC 27695-8105
Has an on-line counterpart which also promotes black literature.

Papyrus Magazine
Papyrus Literary Enterprises
P.O. Box 270797
West Hartford, CT 06127

A quarterly devoted to ideas and stories which appeal to a black audience.

Phati'tude
Chimera Communications, Inc.
P.O. Box 214
Palisades Park, NJ 07650-0214
Multiethnic magazine devoted to writers politically, socially, and culturally aware.

Rhapsody in Black
P.O. Box 6296
Silver Spring, MD 20916
Devoted to diverse creative literary work and artwork.

Skipping Stones: A Multicultural Children's Magazine
P.O. Box 3939
Eugene, OR 97403
Stories, essays aimed at children ages 8–16.

Shooting Star Review
7123 Race Street
Pittsburgh, PA 15208-1428
An attractive magazine publishing outstanding fiction, poetry, and essays.

Warpland
Chicago State University
Gwendolyn Brooks Center for
Black Literature and Creative Writing
LIB 210
9501 South King Drive
Chicago, IL 60628-1598
Fine journal devoted to both emerging and established black writers.

Grants, Contests, and Awards

1. Grant, contest, and awards information can be found in many writing newsletters and magazines. However, if you want a basic guide to grants and award opportunities, then I highly recommend:

Grants and Awards Available to American Writers
PEN American Center
568 Broadway
New York, NY 10012

2. Following are some notable grant and award opportunities for ethnic literature:

Fannie Lou Hamer Award
A prize of $1,000 is offered to a woman "whose work combats racism and celebrates women of color."
Money for Women/Barbara Deming Memorial Fund
P.O. Box 40–1043
Brooklyn, NY 11240-1043

Grants for Minorities
The Foundation Center
79 5th Avenue
New York, NY 10003-3050

Charles H. and N. Mildred Nilon Award for Excellence in Minority Fiction
A $1,000 prize plus publication of a book-length manuscript is awarded.
Fiction Collective Two
c/o English Department Publications Center
University of Colorado
Campus Box 494
Boulder, CO 80309-0494

Papyrus Writer's Showcase Contest
P.O. Box 270797
West Hartford, CT 06127-0797

AIM Magazine Short Story Contest
P.O. Box 20554
Chicago, IL 60620

IBWA Poetry & Short Story Contests
International Black Writers & Artists
P.O. Box 43576
Los Angeles, CA 90043-0576

Audre Lorde Memorial Prose Prize in Fiction
This award offers a $250 prize and is open to feminist writers of fiction or prose.
Woman in the Moon Publications
P.O. Box 2087
Cupertino, CA 95015-2087

Charles Johnson Award for Fiction
This contest offers a $500 prize and is open to minority college students and college students whose work explores the experience of minority or marginalized culture.
Department of English
Southern Illinois University at Carbondale
Carbondale, IL 62901-4503

Zora Neale Hurston/Richard Wright Award
This contest offers a prize of $1,000 and is open to full-time graduate or undergraduate students of African descent.
Zora Neale Hurston/Richard Wright Award Director
Virginia Commonwealth University
Department of English
P.O. Box 2005
Richmond, VA 23284-2005

Coretta Scott King Awards in Fiction
This award offers $250 and is open to African American authors and illustrators.
Coretta Scott King Awards Director
American Library Association
50 East Huron Street
Chicago, IL 60611

Web Sites and the Internet

The Internet makes information readily accessible. Writers' resources are constantly changing and updating. Inquiring about information about a particular book can often lead to tie-ins ranging from an author's Web site to newspaper reviews to magazine profiles.

General Text Resources

African American Resource Guide to the Internet
c/o On Demand Press
P.O. Box 6488
Columbia, MD 21045-6488

Writers.Net: Every Writers Essential Guide
Gary Gach
Prima Publishing, 1997

The Writer's Guide to the Internet
Dawn Groves
Independent Publishing Group, 1998

Writing Resources

African-American Online Writers Guild
http://www.blackwriters.org/
This Web site was formed by Tia Shabazz to promote fellowship among the African American writing community. It provides resources for both published and unpublished writers. It has an on-line newsletter, author profiles, writer's workshop, and Web links to other important sites.

AWP: Associated Writing Programs
http://web.gmu.edu/departments/awp
This is an on-line resource for many of AWP's services, including the *AWP Chronicle* and the annual AWP conference.

Fyah.com
FICTION/POETRY@fyah.com
Fyah.com promotes black wordsmiths via articles, reviews, interviews, essays, calendars of events, etc.

Inkspot: Writing Related Resources
http://www.inkspot.com
A list of craft-related resources on and off the Web. Also has a section devoted to young (children) writers.

Official Misc.Writing WebSite
http://www.scalar.com/mw/
This is the site for the misc.writing newsgroup. Features include: writers market, writing basics, recommended reading.

Papyrus: The Writer's Craftletter Featuring the Black Experience
http://www.ReadersNdex.com/papyrus
This is an on-line craft/trade publication with an exclusive focus on African American writing. It contains articles about the craft of writing, lists contests, etc. It also has a paper magazine that one can subscribe to. Also at this site is OBSIDIAN II: Black Literature in Review, a new on-line journal.

Poets & Writers

http://www.pw.org/

Poets & Writers maintains an extensive on-line list of resources for aspiring and published authors.

WritersNet

http://www.writers.net/

This is a resource for writers, publishers, and agents. The highlight is the Internet Directory of Literary Agents.

Writers Resource Center

http://www.azstarnet.com/writer/writer.html/

This site includes articles and databases such as a list of markets and submission guidelines.

Writers Write

http://writerswrite.com/

There is a publisher directory, job listings, and a newsletter called "The Write News."

Writers Website

http://www.writerswebsite.com/

This comprehensive site includes information on contests, retreats, and markets. Also basic legal advice.

Publishing Resources

Advice and Answers About Writing and Getting Published

http://www.teleport.com/~until/faq.htm

Tara K. Harper, a professional science fiction writer, offers informative advice on query letters, agents, contacts, etc.

Bookwire: The First Place to Look for Book Info

http://www.bookwire.com

A comprehensive site about writing, books, publishing, etc.

Book Publishers Listings

http://www.arcana.com/shannon/books/publishers.html

This site lists major and minor publishers with guidelines for submissions.

Forward Motion

http://www.sff.net/people/holly.lisle/index.htp

Resource for people who want to make a living writing. There is advice from professional writers about topics ranging from quitting your day job, getting published, and dealing with editors and agents.

TimBookTu
http://www.timbooktu.com
A free Web site for African American writers to publish their work.

Obsidian II
http://www.ReadersNdex.com/papyrus
From this site you can link to OBSIDIAN II: Black Literature in Review, a new on-line journal.

Other Literary Resources

African American Literature Book Club
http://www.aalbc.com
This terrific site, founded by Troy Johnson, has an extensive listing of writing resources, book reviews, author profiles, and much more. Updating constantly, this site provides on-line guides to magazines and publishers which support black authors and also lists community-based reading groups. To purchase books, there is a link to Barnes & Noble as well as an extensive listing of African American bookstores.

African American Publications
http://www.aawc.com/aap.html
This site, created by William Richard Jones, provides links to Web sites of more than fifty publishers of magazines, journals, and newsletters that specialize in works by, about, and for African Americans. Many of these are on-line publications and many publish creative writing pieces.

Callaloo
http://muse.jhu.edu/journals/callaloo/index.html
There are some editions of this literary magazine on-line. A journal of African American and African arts and literature, Callaloo publishes original works by and critical studies of black writers worldwide. It contains a mixture of fiction, poetry, plays, critical essays, cultural studies, interviews, and visual art.

Colorado State University Libraries, African & African American Resources
http://www.colostate.edu/Depts/LTS/research/blacks.html
This is a selected list of African American novelists and other bibliographical and literary resources.

Essence On-Line
http://www.essence.com
An on-line site for *Essence* magazine.

Fourth National Black Writers Conference
http://artsnet.heinz.cmu.edu/NBWC/inet.htm
This was held in the spring of 1996. The site still has a great list of other Web resources, although it hasn't been updated since this conference. Another conference is scheduled for 2000.

HerSPHERE
http://members.aol.com/hersphere
This is a collection of links related to African American women. A special section is devoted to literature and writing and to magazines and newsletters.

The Literary Web: New Dimensions in Literature
http://avery.med.virginia.edu/~jbh/litweb.html
A site with extensive literary information, links to writing-related sites across the Web, and book club and workshop information.

Mosaic Books
http://www.mosaicbooks.com
An on-line review dedicated to black and Hispanic literature. This site features a newsletter as well as link connections to bookstores and book clubs.

QBR, The Quarterly Black Review
http://www.bookwire.com/qbr/qbr.html
This is an on-line literary journal, part of the larger Bookwire site. Features fiction and nonfiction by African American writers, as well as providing lists of black booksellers, interviews with writers, upcoming seminars, etc.

The Universal Black Pages
http://www.ubp.com/
This is a comprehensive list of African American-related topics, including publishing and magazine information (http://www.ubp.com/words).

Voices from the Gaps: Women Writers of Color
http://www-engl.cla.umn.edu/lkd/vfg/VFGHome
This site out of the University of Minnesota is devoted to women writers of color. It includes a list of sites on which one may find general resources about women writers of color.

Web Diva Infocenter: Your Tie to African Descendants Throughout the Diaspora
http://www.afrinet.net/~hallh
A comprehensive list of African and African American-related sites, with some literature/book information, and lots of historical information for research.

Writing Black: Literature and History Written by and on African Americans
http://www.keele.ac.uk/depts/as/Literature/amlit.black.html
This is a list of reading resources by author with links to those sites on the Web, plus information on oral storytelling traditions and reference books.

Writing from the Soul: Fiction of African American Women
http://www.evanston.lib.il.us/library/bibliographies/african.html
This is a short resource list of some African American novelists.

ESSENTIAL FICTIONAL TERMS

Ambiguity—an image, theme, or symbol which has two intentional mean-ings—for example, when slaves sang spirituals about "crossing the River Jordan," they were singing about an afterlife as well as a spiritual and physical release from slavery.

Antagonist—the character who creates conflicts, obstacles for the protagonist.

Atmosphere—is the tone, the emotional attitude which informs a story and/or the emotional quality associated with the story's setting.

Character—an imagined being who is the life of your story's action. The best characters are multidimensional, displaying a range of emotions and actions.

Concrete Details—description which is specific and appeals to the senses.

Conflict—specific trials, obstacles, challenges to your character's emotional, spiritual, psychological, and/or physical well-being. Conflict can be manifested by either external or internal threats.

Dialogue—words characters speak. A character can have a monologue (a speech out loud and not directed at any particular character) or a dialogue (a conversation with one or more characters). "Interior dia-logues" usually refer to a character's thoughts.

Imagery—a pattern of descriptive details which underscore the story's plot— for example, for a town engaged in mob violence, details may cluster around angry, violent images related to heat and burning.

Irony—usually a conflict or discrepancy between what is said by a character or narrator and what is known to be true by the reader. For example, "It's a wonderful day," he said—yet the reader knows the character's mother has died. Or irony can be a sense of fate, poetic justice, as when the slave trader who is afraid of water completes the Middle Passage only to die accidentally by drowning in a local creek.

Plot—the action, the sequence of events in your story.

Point of View—who tells the story, whose perception is the lens for seeing, recording, and commenting upon the plot. Choices include first person narrator ("I"), third person ("He"/"She"), who may or may not be identified as the narrator. Second person ("You") is rarely used.

Protagonist—the central character in a story.

Setting—the environment where your story's action takes place. There can be several settings necessary to your story or one major setting. Sometimes setting (such as a force of nature) can be as significant as any character.

Simile and Metaphor—a simile is a descriptive comparison using "like" or "as": "she is as cold as ice." A metaphor implies a comparison without using "like" or "as": "She is ice."

Symbol—a detail, reference, or thing which has a larger significance in the story. For example, stars may be symbolic of "lighting the way to freedom"; a remark about "strange fruit" may refer to black men lynched, hanging on trees; "blackbirds" may represent black people and liberation, may intentionally echo the folktale of African magic making black slaves capable of flying home to Africa.

Theme—what a story means, the message/emotion/belief the author is trying to develop using fictional elements of character, plot, dialogue, etc.

Tone—sometimes used interchangeably with "atmosphere." "Terrifying" or "funny" or "sad" may be the emotional quality of the story given the storyteller's attitude and/or the story's setting. Tone is also conveyed by word choices; the language may imply sarcasm, hysteria, etc.

PERMISSIONS

CHAPTER TWO
Excerpt from "Fever," from *Fever: Twelve Stories by John Edgar Wideman.* Copyright © 1989 by John Edgar Wideman. Reprinted by permission of Henry Holt and Company, Inc.

CHAPTER THREE
Ellis Cose, "How Much Is Enough When Telling People What They Want to Know?" Article originally appeared in *USA Today.* Copyright © 1997 by Ellis Cose. Reprinted by permission of the author.
Jewell Parker Rhodes, "Block Party," from *All Together,* Heath Middle Level Literature Anthology. Copyright © 1993 by Jewell Parker Rhodes. Reprinted by permission of the author.
Irving Wallace, David Wallechinsky, and Amy Wallace, "First U.S. City to Be Bombed from the Air," from *Parade Magazine.* Reprinted by permission of the authors. Reprinted by permission from Parade, copyright © 1983.

CHAPTER FIVE
Excerpt from *Your Blues Ain't Like Mine* by Bebe Moore Campbell. Copyright © 1992 by Bebe Moore Campbell. Used by permission of G.P. Putnam's Sons, a division of Penguin Putnam Inc.
Edwidge Danticat, "New York Day Women," from *Krik? Krak!* by Edwidge Danticat. Copyright © 1995 by Edwidge Danticat. Reprinted by permission of Soho Press.

CHAPTER SIX
Zora Neale Hurston, "Sweat." Copyright © 1926 by Zora Neale Hurston. Reprinted with the kind permission of the Zora Neale Hurston Estate.
Alice Walker, "Nineteen Fifty-Five," from *You Can't Keep A Good Woman Down.* Copyright © 1981 by Alice Walker. Reprinted by permission of Harcourt Brace & Company.